# Mastering the N

CW00969509

Darrell Young

James Johnson

**Darrell Young** (*DigitalDarrell*) is an information technology engineer by trade and has been an avid photographer for over 35 years. He has a rather large family, with his wife and five children, so he has a constantly interesting flow of photographic opportunities. In fact, his entire family uses Nikon cameras to pursue what has become a cohesive family hobby.

Darrell delights in using Nikon's newest digital cameras but if pressed, he will admit to being a "closet" film user too. Living next to the Great Smoky Mountains National Park has given him a real concern for, and interest in, nature photography. Darrell loves to write, as you can see in the Resources area of the Nikonians.org community. He joined the community in the year 2000, and his literary contributions led to his invitation to become a Founding Member of the Nikonians Writers Guild.

**James (Jim) Johnson.** When Jim retired from a 25-year career as a software developer for IBM, he had already been working as a contract technical editor for Microsoft. After his retirement, technical editing and technical writing became his primary source of income to cover the cost of his 'toys'—most of which were computer equipment and photographic equipment.

Jim's involvement with cameras began in the mid '50s when he needed to record the interior of caves in Kentucky. At the time, the greatest challenge was to provide adequate illumination, and in a manner that did not defile the cave, thus he purchased a Leica 3F camera (which was the norm among cavers at that time) and experimented with numerous lighting sources. In the late '60s Jim purchased a used Nikon FTn, and it's been a progression of Nikons ever since. The Nikon 990 was his introduction to digital photography, but the D100 provided the ability to use all those SLR lenses he had accumulated over the years. A D300 is his current working tool.

# Mastering the Nikon D700

**Darrell Young**

**and**

**Jim Johnson**

Darrell Young (aka Digital Darrell)
James Johnson

Editor (Rocky Nook): Gerhard Rossbach
Editor (Nikonians): Tom Boné
Production Editor: Joan Dixon
Copyeditor: Judy Flynn
Layout and type: James Johnson
Cover design: Helmut Kraus, www.exclam.de
Printer: Friesens Corporation, Altona, Canada

Cover photo: Nikon, U.S.A.
Back cover photo: James Johnson

1st Edition (2nd Printing, October 2009)
© Nikonians North America 2009
Rocky Nook Inc.
26 West Mission Street Ste 3
Santa Barbara, CA 93101-2432

Library of Congress Cataloging-in-Publication Data

Young, Darrell, 1958-
Mastering the Nikon D700 / Darrell Young, James Johnson. -- 1st ed.
    p. cm.
Includes bibliographical references.
ISBN 978-1-933952-23-9 (alk. paper)
1. Nikon digital cameras--Handbooks, manuals, etc. 2. Single-lens reflex cameras--Handbooks, manuals,
etc. 3. Photography--Digital techniques--Handbooks, manuals, etc. I. Johnson, James, 1935- II. Title.
TR263.N5Y685 2009
771.3'2--dc22
                            2009004570
Distributed by O'Reilly Media
1005 Gravenstein Highway North
Sebastopol, CA 95472

All product names and services identified throughout this book are trademarks or registered trademarks of their respec-
tive companies. They are used throughout this book in editorial fashion only and for the benefit of such companies. No such
uses, or the use of any trade name, are intended to convey endorsement or other affiliation with the book. No part of the
material protected by this copyright notice may be reproduced or utilized in any form, electronic or mechanical, including
photocopying, recording, or by any information storage and retrieval system, without written permission of the copyright
owner. While reasonable care has been exercised in the preparation of this book, the publisher and authors assume no
responsibility or errors or omissions, or for damages resulting from the use of the information contained herein.

Printed in Canada. This book is printed on acid-free paper.

# Table of Contents

x    **Foreword**

xii  **Preface**

2    **Using the Nikon D700**

3    Nikon D100 - Generation 1
3    Nikon D200 – Generation 2
4    Nikon D300 – Generation 3
6    Nikon D700 – Generation 4
7    EXPEED Image Processor
7    FX vs DX Image Sensor
8    12.1-Megapixel CMOS Sensor
8    Five or Eight Frames per Second
9    Noise Control
10   Live View
10   3-Inch Monitor
11   Fine-Tuning
11   Sensor Dust Cleaning
11   Picture Control
12   Active D-Lighting
12   51-Point Autofocus
13   12-Bit or 14-Bit Color Depth
13   Lossless Compressed NEF (RAW)
14   Exposure Delay Mode
14   Retouch Menu
14   My Menu
14   95% Viewfinder Frame
15   Rubber Covers Instead of Lost Screw-On Caps
15   HDMI Device Port
16   My Conclusions

**18   Exposure Metering, Exposure Modes, and Histogram**

19   Metering Systems
19   3D Color Matrix II Meter
20   Fine-Tuning Matrix Metering
20   Using Flash with Matrix Metering
21   Center-Weighted Meter
21   Where's the Circle?
22   What About the Averaging Meter?
22   Spot Meter
23   Exposure Modes
24   P – Programmed Auto Mode
25   Get Down, Grandpa!
25   S – Shutter Priority Auto Mode
26   A – Aperture Priority Auto Mode
26   Understanding Depth of Field
28   M – Manual Mode
29   Histogram
30   Understanding the Histogram
35   How Does the Eye React to
     Light Values?
35   Computer Adjustment of Images
38   My Conclusions

**40   Multi-CAM 3500FX Autofocus**

41   What Is the Multi-CAM 3500FX Auto-
     focus Module?
42   Understanding the Focus Modes, AF-
     Area Modes, and Release Modes
43   Focus Modes in Detail
44   AF-Area Modes in Detail
49   Release Modes in Detail
53   My Conclusions

**54    White Balance**

55    How Does White Balance (WB) Work?
55    Color Temperature
*56    Method 1* – Manual White Balance
      Using the WB Button
*61    Method 2* – Manual White Balance
      Using the Monitor LCD's Shooting
      Menu
62    White Balance Bracketing
63    AUTO White Balance
64    White Balance Tips and Tricks
65    My Conclusions

**66    Shooting Menu Banks**

67    Setting Up Shooting Menu Bank A
69    Shooting Menu's 20 Item Review
73    NEF (RAW) Format
78    TIFF Format
78    Combined NEF and JPEG Shooting
80    Notes on the Image Formats:
      RAW, TIFF, and JPEG
85    Picture Controls
100   My Conclusions

**102 Custom Setting Banks**

103 Setting Up Custom Setting Bank A
104 Configuring the Custom Settings
124 Shooting/Display
138 How to Use the Auto Bracketing System
141 Controls
155 My Conclusions – Using the Shooting Banks and Custom Banks Together

**156 Playback Menu**

157 Delete Function
158 Playback Folder
160 Hide Image
161 Display Mode
164 Image Review
165 After Delete
165 Rotate Tall
166 Slide Show
168 Print Set (DPOF)
169 My Conclusions

**170 Setup Menu, Retouch Menu, and My Menu**

171 Section 1: *Setup Menu*
199 Section 2: *Retouch Menu*
206 Section 3: *My Menu*
211 My Conclusions

**212 Nikon Creative Lighting System**

213 What Is the Nikon Creative Lighting System (CLS)?
213 How Does the D700 Fit into the CLS Scheme?
214 What Is Commander Mode and How Does it Work?
215 Using the Nikon D700 in Commander Mode
220 Nikon SB-600 Speedlight Slave Configuration
222 Using the Nikon SB-800 Speedlight as a Commander Device
227 Examining the Nikon SU-800 Wireless Speedlight Commander Unit
232 My Conclusions

235 **Nikonians Voucher**

237 **Image Credits**

239 **Index**

# Foreword

When Nikonian Jim Johnson (TechRead) retired from a 25-year career as a software developer for IBM, he had already been working as a contract technical editor for Microsoft. After his retirement, technical editing and writing became his primary source of income to cover the cost of his "toys", most of which were computer hardware and Nikon photographic equipment. Hungry for knowledge and being himself a sufferer of the dreaded Nikon Acquisition Syndrome (NAS), he fit right in at the Nikonians community.

When offered the opportunity to coauthor this D700 book, Jim found that he—and the D700—were at a crucial juncture: an age of 16-megabyte Compact Flash cards, capable of 133X (and faster!) data transfer speeds to support extensive high frame-rate shooting; terabyte hard drives for storing very large numbers of large RAW files; 20-inch, and larger, high-resolution monitors that provide outstanding color accuracy and contrast; quad-processor computers for efficient Photoshop processing of these large RAW files; Capture NX 2 and Photoshop CS4 for maximum flexibility in image enhancement; vibration-reduction (VR) lenses for optimal image stabilization; programmable, wireless Speedlights that run on AA batteries; and a camera body that provides literally hundreds of menu options, allowing the rank amateur to capture impressive images of family history, the photojournalist to document the scene at that moment, or the accomplished professional to create magnificent fine art. That represents an amazing number of combinations and permutations in the fusion of end-user objectives, computer hardware and software, lenses and camera accessories, and a magnificent camera body.

To adequately understand and manage such an aggregation requires a careful presentation of the relevant parts and processes, which Jim attempts to share in this book. The idea of sharing is therefore not strange to Jim. In fact it is a way of life; Jim also teaches classes on digital photography, Photoshop, and the various versions of Windows and Microsoft Office. A D300 is his favorite current working tool, while lusting for a D700 after using one intimately and extensively for the writing of this book.

Jim and his wife Heather live on the California coast with their home overlooking the Morro Bay estuary. The coast, the bays and the mountains all combine to host a vast array of botanical subjects, which are the focus of Jim's current photographic interest. Jim joined as a Gold member of Nikonians, having been introduced to Nikonians by Rocky Nook while working on the editing team for the Nikonians Press first volume, *Mastering the Nikon D300*, by Nikonian Darrell Young, with whom he co-authors this new book, *Mastering the Nikon D700*.

About the Nikon D700 camera Jim said: "Indeed, the D700 is quite an exquisite compilation of features, all in a reasonable size and weight. Even the price is realistic."

In this book, you will find in detail why and how to make the most out of it, as the many Nikonians owning one have discovered in awe.

We congratulate Jim and Darrell for this work, the third of the Nikonians Press books, in association with Rocky Nook.

Bo Stahlbrandt (bgs) and J. Ramón Palacios (jrp)
Nikonians Founders and Administrators
www.nikonians.org

## A note from the publisher:

Darrell Young's *Mastering the Nikon D300*, also published by Rock Nook, has received sterling reviews for its depth of content, breadth of coverage, and warmth of delivery. As the Nikon D700 is a level of technical evolution beyond the D300, the decision was made to likewise evolve the D300 book for this newer Nikon camera. To that end, coauthor James W. Johnson has used Darrell's work as the basis for describing the new features and functions of the D700 while maintaining Darrell's first-person observations and commentary.

Nikon has added some very interesting and valuable features to the D700, which have necessitated numerous changes to the technical details established for the D300 book. The intended audience is not those wishing to compare the features of the two cameras.

## We welcome your comments and concerns...

*Mastering the Nikon D700* covers the vast majority of the camera's menus, the camera's operation, and factors to consider in selecting customization options. However, if you have a question not addressed by the book, please drop a note to the publisher at this email address and we'll get you an answer: **D700@rockynook.com**

# Preface

I grew up looking at pictures.

Ever since I was a baby my mother took hundreds of photographs of our family life, capturing small pieces of time frozen in little negative squares. Today, I can still look back at those images and they awaken memories that would otherwise be forgotten.

In 1968, my dear Mom gave me my first Brownie Hawkeye camera, and that little camera ignited a fire in me for taking pictures. I remember my mother's words of instruction, "Load the film in a dark place, never open the film door until after you rewind, and keep the sun behind you when you shoot".

From that day forward I often carried a camera with me. I took the fuzzy pictures of a 13-year-old as I hiked up the Roosevelt Mountain in Rockwood, Tennessee, USA, with my brother Steven and a friend named Scott. Every major event of my life has a few frames attached.

As an adult, I began photographing my own family, and to this day I've been documenting the growth of my five children. From my earliest memories, photography has been a part of my life, and I'll keep on shooting as long as I am able.

The year 1980 was a milestone for me; that's when I got my first Nikon camera. It was a nearly new Nikon FM, and I reveled in its incredible build, and the unbelievable images it produced. Before then, I had been shooting with Kodak 110 and 126 cameras, and although those images have priceless personal value, they would win no contests. I graduated from negatives to transparencies in 1981, as I realized that even sharper and less grainy images could be created in those delightful little two-inch squares. I loved film, and shot a lot of it. I wanted to shoot even more, but the cost of raising kids took precedence over the cost of film and processing.

The year 2002 changed everything for me photographically. I had been playing around with a Kodak P&S digital camera, and I finally got a Nikon Coolpix 990. While the pictures were fun and easy to make, they did not equal the quality of my 35mm images, so I viewed digital photography only as a toy. Then Nikon released the six-MP D100, and Digital Darrell was born. Never before had I shot so many images. With the "free" use of the camera, I took thousands of photographs that I would never have considered taking with expensive film, and thus I moved to a new level of photography in the process. Digital cameras can offer an educational course in photography within themselves.

My love of digital photography grew, as did my relationship with the world's premier Nikon User Community, www.Nikonians.org. I came on board as a charter member in late 2000, and after my D100 arrived I really become involved as a member. I wrote a camera review that J. Ramón Palacios liked, (JRP is one of the co-owners of the Nikonians.org website, along with Bo Stahlbrandt) and he asked me if I'd like to write a few articles for Nikonians.org. At that time, I didn't even know I was a writer! Thank you, JRP!

I practically lived on Nikonians.org, spending hours there each day, first as a moderator, then as founding member of the Nikonian Writer's Guild. JRP asked me to write as often as I could, and he posted my articles for others to read. Wow, did my ego swell!

In 2005, I bought yet another of Nikon's excellent workhorse cameras—the D200. This camera seemed to reflect a direction toward a truly professional build in a smaller bodied camera. It has a high, 10 MP resolution, a weather-sealed frame, and a flexible feature set that includes the ability to fully use Non-CPU lenses, such as Nikkor AI and AI-S primes. I used this camera on an almost daily basis, as a "carry" camera, since the size was reasonable and the image quality outstanding. Generation Two!

Then in 2007 my photographic world was tremendously enriched. Nikon released a camera that made my eyes pop, and my Nikon Acquisition Syndrome (NAS) become overwhelming. The Nikon D300! This is third-generation 12 MP digital photography! This is the affordable, yet professional-level tool for passionate creativity!

I opened that user's manual of 421 pages and read some of it. "Wow, what a complex camera", I thought. I struggled to understand how the autofocus and other systems worked. All these modes, and banks, and custom settings! Over the next few weeks, as I learned this new and extremely powerful camera inside and out, I began writing chapters of the Mastering the Nikon D300 book, partially to teach myself how to use the complex and very flexible features of the D300, and also to help readers master their new D300. Now, we're doing it again for the Nikon D700.

Additional help is available to you at the world's premier Nikon User's Community, Nikonians.org. This truly is an International Community of over 170,000 Nikon users. Talk about a Nikon resource! As a Nikon user, you are probably already a member, but if you are not, please log on to **www.Nikonians.org** and become at least a Silver member. Nikonians.org is a gold mine of photographic knowledge for Nikon users and is unmatched by any other resource available.

This book is a joint effort to offer a resource to you that will help you understand the complexities of the important, most-used features of Nikon's latest "wonder camera". It's also designed to help you have some fun with your D700.

I feel greatly privileged to be a Nikonian, to have such knowledgeable and friendly associates, and to help provide yet another, much requested resource in the form of a printed book. I hope you enjoy this book and that you greatly benefit from it, and most of all that you find joy in using your chosen photographic tool … the Nikon D700.

Keep on capturing time …

Digital Darrell
(Darrell Young)

# Using the Nikon D700

Digital imaging changed my photography. For the last few years I've been on a technological and artistic trip that I've come to treasure: Nikon digital imaging!

I will begin by offering a background perspective introducing both the camera and my own personal viewpoint. Let me reminisce....

Since I was just a kid, I've always enjoyed photography. However, the cost of film processing kept me from shooting nearly as much as I wanted to. Raising a family through the '80s and '90s didn't leave much money for extras.

I've had all sorts of film Nikons, from my first, a Nikon FM (1980), to my last, a Nikon F5 (2004). But, one Nikon changed everything, and my photography hasn't been the same since.

## Nikon D100 - Generation 1

I bought my first digital single-lens reflex (DSLR) Nikon back in fall 2002, when I got the *Generation 1* Nikon D100. Man, was that camera cool! All my friends had digital envy when they saw it. I no longer needed film, and I was able to shoot until I was satisfied. It changed my photography forever. Experimentation was now affordable, and I learned a lot from being able to view my images immediately. I discovered that a digital camera could be a short, fast course in improving one's photography.

At the time, I still had wet darkroom equipment, but that was soon gone. I discovered Photoshop, bought a color inkjet printer, upgraded my computer with more memory and a faster video card, and set up a nice digital darkroom. My 6-megapixel D100 could make sharp medium-sized enlargements, which were pretty close to what 35mm film could do.

Soon my hard drives were overflowing with many thousands of digital images. I bought bigger hard drives and soon filled them up too. My "digital imaging" had just begun!

## Nikon D200 – Generation 2

In 2005, my NAS (Nikon Acquisition Syndrome) overcame me and I was one of the first in line for the new Nikon D200, featuring 10.2 megapixels. Nearly double the resolution of my first DSLR!

This camera was even more "professional" in build, with seals and gaskets providing protection like my pro film Nikon F5 had. The body was big and robust, with an alloy frame, robust shutter, and many internal controls.

About that time I discovered the Nikon Creative Lighting System (CLS) and loved to use the D200 as a "commander" for my SB-800 and SB-600 flash units. I also got into stock photography about that time, so I started carrying the D200 with me everywhere I went.

I was amazed at how much nicer the 2.5-inch monitor was, with its 230,000 dots of resolution. The images looked so much clearer and warmer on that larger monitor. My D100's tiny LCD screen now seemed a bit obsolete. I eventually gave the D100 to my daughter to replace her point-and-shoot digital.

The images from the D200 were more efficient too. I could make big enlargements now without too much trouble and felt that they were giving me a better look than 35mm film.

Being somewhat of a techno-geek, all this luxurious camera technology was also helping me enjoy my photography. When I wasn't out taking images, I could play with the camera, scroll through the menus, and think about taking pictures.

I wanted even more, and Nikon answered. I bought a Nikon D2X pro-level DSLR camera. Wow! This D2X is like driving a Porsche.

"I'll never need another camera," I thought to myself. I never expected what came next.

## Nikon D300 – Generation 3

When the D300 hit the market, I thought, "Well, this is a nice camera, but with my D200 and D2X, I probably don't need one". With the help of **Nikonians.org** contacts and the support of Nikon's USA press relations organization, I was given the opportunity to field-test a D300. I used this experience to write some of the detailed "menu" sections of this book. It seemed like a desirable camera, although a bit complex, as it sat there next to my computer as a reference device for chapter creation.

In fact, the D300 was so complex that I didn't have enough time with it to write a detailed book. So, I figured I'd just go ahead and buy one to complete the book. After the book was done, I could always give the D300

to my wife as a present, right? It didn't quite work out that way!

In April, I decided to take a little trip with my family to Hunting Island, South Carolina, a beautiful coastal island with a 5-mile white sand beach bathed in Atlantic Ocean sunrises. I fully intended to use my Nikon D2X to shoot a lot of great travel stock images, and maybe grab a few frames with the D300.

The first day out, I was on the beach at 6:30 a.m. with the D2X on a tripod waiting for the sunrise. I carried the D300 over my shoulder just in case I wanted to take some handheld shots. The sun came up in all its orange glory and I shot some great images with my D2X. Since it was on a tripod, and had an 80-400 mm lens on it, I couldn't use it for much more, so I started shooting with the D300.

I took a few pictures and noticed how smooth the shutter sounded. The images on that 3-inch monitor looked like actual

Figure 1 – Hunting Island Atlantic Ocean sunrise

Figure 2 – Photographer watches a Hunting Island Atlantic Ocean sunrise

pictures. I was shooting some really beautiful shots, and enjoying it. I can't explain how exactly, but the D300 "felt different" from my D200. Something about it just felt more professional, smoother, and faster. I hate to admit it, but by the end of a couple of hours of walking around with the D300, I was head over heels in love with the camera. Why? Look at the image in *figure 1*, for instance.

I was taking pictures that curled my eyelashes! I was walking around with this camera taking images that were so captivating I couldn't believe what I was seeing. I was using Nikon's latest technology and my eyes to create some of the best images of my life.

That 3-inch 920,000-dot LCD monitor was simply amazing. I could see my images in great detail by zooming all the way in past the 100% pixel-peeping level.

The sensor, at 12.3 megapixels, captures twice the resolution of the D100 I started with back in 2002. In printing, I've found that the D300 meets or exceeds anything I've done with my film-based medium-format cameras. Way better than 35mm film!

It makes me kind of sad to admit this to you, but my D2X became a backup camera body for my D300. I barely used the D2X for the rest of that trip, and I came back with over 1,500 absolutely premium images of the island. Since then, the camera has literally gone everywhere I go. People have become accustomed to "Darrell with his Nikon". I just smile, and take their picture.

The D300 is absolutely a stock shooter's dream machine. The body size is neither too small nor too large. It feels well-balanced in my hand and shoots with a smoothness that has lit a new fire in my blood for imaging.

In fact, the image in *figure 2* expresses a certain emotion that a picture can say better than words. Have you ever felt this way?

## Nikon D700 – Generation 4

In July 2008, Nikon announced the availability of the D700. Its major innovation was the full 24 × 36 mm image sensor, the same

FX-format image sensor used on the professional D3…except this one also has a dust-removal system akin to that found in the D300 (and not available in any form on the D3).

There are several other differences that set the D700 apart from the D300, and we'll look at them as we go through the book.

- One thing I'd like to mention, before I go into the details of this latest generation of near-professional Nikons, is something that might sound a little weird to some but speaks to why I now use the D700 over the D2X most of the time. The D700 is basically a miniaturized D2X, for the following reasons:
- Both provide 12+ MP resolution, but the D700 creates an FX image (24 × 36 mm).

Figure 3 – Nikon D700 top view with Nikkor 24-120 mm f/3.5-5.6 G Lens

- The D2X shoots natively at five frames per second, as does the D700 (though the D700 can shoot eight frames per second with the MB-D10 Battery Pack).
- The shutter has been tested out to the same number of actuations as the D2X (150,000).
- It has the same types of seals and gaskets protecting it from the weather.
- It has exceptional color depth with 12-bit (like the D2X) or 14-bit.
- It has virtually all the functionality of the D2X in a smaller body, similar to the professional Nikon F6 film camera.

Figure 4 – Nikon D700's EXPEED image processor

My conclusion is that the D700 is like a small D2X. In fact, it has deeper color depth, more powerful autofocus, better metering, a much better monitor, a wider ISO range, and tremendously better image-noise control. The D700 is, in many ways, better than my D2X, and become more like the Nikon D3 and the even-newer Nikon D3X. It has become my "carry" camera of choice. It truly is a near-professional camera!

Instead of simply reviewing the D700, the intent is to discuss the significant features and functions of this camera and how to make good use of them. These things are interesting for people who enjoy camera technology and who want to get the most out of their camera. *Figure 3* shows my favorite view of a D700. Now, let's look at some of my favorite features in the D700.

## EXPEED Image Processor

The EXPEED microprocessor found in the D700 is a Nikon invention for their newer DSLRs (*figure 4*). Not only does it compress and transmit the RAW image data, but it also performs noise-reduction, dynamic-range, and color-algorithm adjustments on stored JPEGs.

The EXPEED does what it implies by moving data off the sensor chip with "extra speed". The D700 needs that speed because not only can it shoot in the normal 12-bit color depth that other cameras use, it also has a 14-bit mode that captures 64 times as much color information.

Plus, the name sounds extra cool. Most of the major camera brands are creating names like this. For instance, there's Sony's Bionz, Canon's Digic, and Pentax's PRIME image processors. Being that I am a Nikon guy, I favor the name EXPEED...don't you?

## FX vs DX Image Sensor

Heretofore, digital cameras in this price range offered only "half-sized" image sensors. For Nikon, these were classed as DX cameras with an image sensor measuring approximately 24 mm × 16 mm. The Nikon D700 provides a full 35mm camera-sized image sensor (24 mm × 36 mm), known as an FX image sensor.

When a DX-class lens is mounted, it will generate the same sized image on the new sensor as it was designed to create for the DX-sized sensor. This will result in the apparent 1.5X focal-length advantage DX image sensors provide, but—with the D700 set to

DX-format or the D700 being allowed to automatically recognize when a DX lens is attached—will result in 5-megapixel images. (The image from a DX lens will always be the same size; attempting to fool the camera by forcing it to FX mode when a DX lens is attached will result in a full-frame picture that suffers serious degradation of that portion of the image that falls outside the normal DX image area.)

## 12.1-Megapixel CMOS Sensor

A major factor in the D700's excellent image quality is the 12.1-effective megapixel CMOS sensor. It captures RAW data with up to 14 bits of color for each of the red, green, and blue channels. Many other DSLRs in this class only capture at 12 bits per channel. This gives the D700 an advantage in reproducing finer color gradations, better shadow details, and a wider dynamic range. *Figure 5* shows the sensor used in the D700.

The D700's 12+ megapixels gives me an image file that is sharp and colorful enough to make enlargements in the 16 × 20-inch range and larger. This used to be the sole territory of medium-format film cameras.

With this level of resolution, the camera will not become immediately obsolete when

another camera arrives on the scene. As with 35mm film of old, this image size has enough resolution to cover the greatest majority of reasons to take a picture. Even when a newer camera comes out with higher resolution, the D700 will remain useful for many years.

## Five or Eight Frames per Second

If you are an action, sports, or wildlife shooter, you can now use a smaller body and still get the high-speed frame-rates you need to capture fast-moving subjects. If shutter speeds are high enough, the D700 shoots at five frames per second with only a single EN-EL3e battery. The MB-D10 Battery Pack adds a little extra amperage and allows the camera to jump up to eight frames per second. I just went to **YouTube.com** and searched on "Nikon D700 Shutter" and found several videos that allow one to hear the sound of a Nikon D700 firing at eight frames per second. If you don't have a D700 with an MB-D10 Battery Pack, check out the videos. It's impressive!

If you have an 8- or 16-gigabyte (or higher) compact flash (CF) memory card, you can hold hundreds or even thousands of images on one card. The D700 is plenty fast, and with a fast CF card (think "ultra direct memory access" (UDMA), capable of 40 MB/sec ), your card will hold the results. Try it out for yourself.

### More on Bits and Memory

Unlike with the D300, color bit-depth has no impact on frame rate in the D700.

Figure 5 – Nikon-designed 12.1-megapixel CMOS sensor unit

allows me more flexibility in finding just the point I want to meter, or focus on.

With so many points, it takes longer to get your AF point onto the subject with your D700's Multi Selector. If you want, you can make the D700 use 11 points instead so that it acts like your previous Nikon.

When using the D700's *Dynamic-area AF* mode, the abundance of AF points allows the D700 to more accurately track a moving subject. In fact, I've found it amazing how stubbornly the D700 will hang onto a bird flying through the air, for instance. I guess I shouldn't be amazed though, since the D700 is using the 51 AF points and the color of the subject to track it.

## 12-Bit or 14-Bit Color Depth

Until recently, our Nikon DSLRs have used a 12-bit color depth to contain the red, green, and blue (RGB) colors of the subject. Twelve bits allows us to have 4,096 levels of color for each of the three color channels in our image. That means there can be 4,096 levels of red, 4,096 levels of green, and 4,096 levels of blue.

Once you switch the camera to 14-bit mode in *NEF (RAW) recording* on the *Shooting Menu*, your D700 will now record four times more data in each color channel, or 16,384 levels for each of the red, green, and blue channels. That will necessarily make the image's file size increase, since each image has 64 times more color information.

What do you gain from shooting in 14-bit mode? Better images, mainly. You won't see a tremendous difference in normal images. However, the image can contain finer color gradations, better shadow details, and a wider dynamic range since there is significantly more color data being stored for each channel.

Even if some of today's software can't fully take advantage of the additional color levels, maybe improved software in the future will.

For my type of shooting , I'd much rather have the 14 bits of data than the 12 bits of data.

### Color Data and Frame Rates

Again, unlike with the D300, color bit-depth has no impact on frame rate in the D700.

## Lossless Compressed NEF (RAW)

NEF or RAW files can be quite large because they contain all the available information about a 12- or 14-bit image.

There has been much discussion about whether or not the previous version of NEF image file compression caused a loss of quality. Nikon called it "visually lossless," since you weren't supposed to be able to see the difference between an image shot as a compressed file and one shot as an uncompressed file. However, some have claimed that highlight detail was affected somewhat by the compression.

Nikon solved that problem completely by offering the normal *Compressed* and *Uncompressed* selections and by adding a *Lossless compressed* selection to the *Shooting Menu's NEF (RAW) recording* list of *Type* options.

The new lossless compression does not compress the image as much as normal compression, but it does so in a lossless way, similar to the way a ZIP file works in your computer. Now you can compress your images without worry about mildly damaging your image details. Here are the three types of compression, and their file size reduction percentages:

- *Lossless compressed* – Images are compressed with a "non-reversible" algorithm. The file size of the image is reduced by 20 to 40% with no effect on image quality.

- *Compressed* – Images are compressed with a "reversible" algorithm. The file size of the image is reduced by 40 to 55% with almost no effect on image quality.
- *Uncompressed* – Images are not compressed.

I leave my D700 set to *Lossless compressed* all the time. If there is no effect at all on image quality, why store larger files for no good reason?

## Exposure Delay Mode

The D700 has a Mirror Up mode *(MUP)* that allows you to raise the mirror with the first shutter release press, then take a picture with the second press. This allows you to use a tripod, raise the mirror, wait for vibrations to die down, then fire the shutter. Significantly sharper images can be the result.

The D700 also has an *Exposure delay mode* that allows you to raise your mirror between shots, like with MUP mode, but requires only a single shutter button press instead of two.

In the D200 and D2X, the mirror delay was one-half second. So you could frame your subject and press the shutter release; the mirror would raise, and one-half second later the shutter would fire. Many have felt that one-half second wasn't long enough for vibrations to die down fully, so Nikon increased the delay to one full second on the newer DSLRs, including the D700.

One second should give vibrations time to dissipate before the shutter fires. This is not adjustable and always defaults to one second. *Custom setting d9* turns *Exposure delay mode* on and off.

## Retouch Menu

*Retouch Menu* allows people who do not like working on a computer, or who find themselves in the field where a computer is not available, to "manipulate" or postprocess their images.

This is discussed in detail in chapter 8 of this book. For now, just be aware that you can do many in-camera adjustments that used to require a computer. You can "retouch" your images as soon as you take them, and the camera creates a completely new image with the results. The new image is saved to your memory card with the next available image number in the series of images on your card. Your original image is not changed in any way.

Here is a list of actions you can perform through the *Retouch Menu*:

- D-Lighting
- Red-eye correction
- Image trimming (cropping)
- Conversion to monochrome
- Applying filter effects
- Modifying the color balance
- Overlaying two images

So, if you are in the wilds of the Serengeti plains of Africa and want to do a little postprocessing, your D700, with its crisp VGA resolution monitor, will be happy to let you have at it.

## My Menu

*My Menu* allows you to take the most-used functions of your camera menus and put them in one place. You can then quickly find those menu items without having to scroll around the hundreds of menus and screens in the D700.

*My Menu* is your menu!

## 95% Viewfinder Frame

With the inclusion of the dust removal system on the FX sensor, Nikon had to revert to the 95% viewfinder frame for the D700, unlike the D300, which has a 100% viewfinder frame and a dust removal system but only a DX sensor;

or the D3, which has a 100% viewfinder and an FX sensor but no dust removal system.

## Rubber Covers Instead of Lost Screw-On Caps

I have repurchased so many of those little screw-on port caps over the years that I could buy a new camera with the amount I've paid. After a while, I just unscrewed the little caps and tossed them in a dresser drawer because within 10 seconds of taking one off in the field, it mysteriously beams up to the mother ship.

I've bought piles of them for about $4.00 on eBay, plus about $10 for shipping. But no more! Nikon has wisely given us cool rubber caps that are attached to the body. If you hate caps of any type, just snip them off. I use them because they don't get lost and are easy to open and close. I figure they may protect my camera from moisture and dirt, so I'll continue to use them. Thank you for the rubber caps, Nikon!

## HDMI Device Port

Remember back when we used to have slide shows? You'd invite your family and friends over to look at projected slides from times when everyone was still young and slim.

You've probably been shooting digitally for several years now and have hundreds of pictures. You might have wanted to do an old-fashioned slide show but didn't want to invest in an expensive digital projector. Nikon comes to the rescue!

The new HDMI port under the rubber flap on the side of your D700 allows you to connect your camera directly to your high definition (HD) TV, HDMI-capable computer monitor, or other high-definition video device. A later chapter will go into more detail about this new capability.

Now you can use your large screen HDTV to do a new-fashioned slide show, with old-fashioned style. So, buy some popcorn and pizza, then invite the friends over for some slide viewing fun. Be sure to take some more pictures!

Figure 10 – HDMI Device Port

## My Conclusions

Well, we have come to the end of the first chapter in your new *Mastering the Nikon D700* book.

I want to thank you for purchasing this book, and I invite you to contact us with any questions or comments you might have: **D700@rockynook.com**

Also, I hope that you, as a Nikon user, will join the Nikonians organization, the world's premier Nikon user community. Here you will meet over 170,000 fellow Nikon users, and will be able to join in community discussions about nearly anything Nikon. See this web page for a tour of **Nikonians.org** and information on how to become a Nikonian: **http://www.Nikonians.org/tour1.html**

The next eight chapters of this book will give you a very detailed and personal look at each menu in the Nikon D700, as well as virtually every screen in the camera. When you use this book, always have your D700 within reach so that you can immediately apply the things you are reading. If you do that, the information will stick with you longer. Also, keep your User's Manual close, since I give page numbers for extra reference points.

The Nikon D700 is a very complex camera. It is also my favorite Nikon DSLR by far. If you take the time to learn about the most needed features for your style of photography, the camera will become a tool that allows you to truly bring passion to your photography. I know it did to mine!

# Exposure Metering, Exposure Modes, and Histogram

My first Nikon was an FM back in about 1980. It used a basic center-weighted meter, and everything else was completely manual. In a way, I miss those simple days of old.

I became a proponent of digital SLRs back in August of 2002 when I bought my first serious DSLR, the Nikon D100. I left the film world in a hurry and never looked back. I rejoiced so much in Nikon digital imaging that I gained the nickname *Digital Darrell* in the **Nikonians.org** community. Later, I bought a D200 and my rejoicing became even more exuberant.

Fast-forward a few years and I now find myself with the most accurate and powerful DSLR I've ever owned. Yep, it's the same one you have, the Nikon D700. I also own a Nikon D2X, but recently it stays in the camera bag as a backup to my D700. Yes, the D700 is that good!

Figure 1 – *Metering selector*

Figure 2 – *Metering selector* set to *Matrix*

The images from the D700 are simply superb thanks to the flexible exposure metering systems, exposure modes, and histogram capabilities.

## Metering Systems

The basis for the Nikon D700's exposure meter is a 1,005-segment RGB sensor that meters a wide area of the frame. When this RGB sensor is used with a G or D Nikkor lens containing a CPU, the camera can set exposure based on the distribution of brightness, color, distance, and composition. Most people leave their D700 set to *Matrix metering* and enjoy excellent results. Let's look more closely at each of the Nikon D700's exposure meters.

The *metering selector* is conveniently located on the back of your D700.

*Figures 1* and *2* show the exposure *metering selector* control set to *Matrix* mode. You can turn the small ring surrounding the AE-L/AF-L button to one of the three settings. The right-most setting is *Center-weighted metering* mode, the middle is *Matrix metering* mode, and the left-most is *Spot metering* mode.

(See pages 112–113 in the D700 User's Manual.)

## 3D Color Matrix II Meter

The Nikon D700's *Matrix metering* mode is actually the *3D Color Matrix II* metering system, one of the most powerful and accurate automatic exposure meters in any camera today (see *figure 2*).

There are characteristics for many thousands of images stored in the camera. These characteristics are used (along with proprietary Nikon software and complex evaluative computations) to analyze the image

2

appearing in your viewfinder. The meter is then set to provide very accurate exposures for the large majority of your images.

A simple example of this might be a picture where the horizon runs through the middle of the image. The sky above is bright, and the earth below is much dimmer. By evaluating this image, and comparing it to hundreds of like images in the camera's database, the camera automatically determines the meter setting for you.

The meter examines four critical areas of each picture. It compares the levels of *brightness* in various parts of the scene to determine the total range of EV values. It then notices the *color* of the subject and surroundings. If you are using a G or D CPU lens, it also determines how far away your lens is focused so that it can tell the *distance* to your subject. Finally, it looks at the *compositional* elements of the subject.

Once it has all that information, it compares your image to tens of thousands of image characteristics in its image database, makes complex evaluations, and comes up with a meter value that is usually right on the money, even in complex lighting situations.

However, I'd like to qualify that with the following considerations.

## Fine-Tuning Matrix Metering

Like all digital cameras, the Nikon D700 tends to be a bit conservative when light values get too bright. If the D700 encounters a situation where the light values exceed the range of the sensor, it will tend to expose for the highlights and let the darker areas of the image lose detail. We'll talk more about this in the section "Histogram" of this chapter. In all cases, it tries to keep the bright values from "blowing out" by preventing the meter from fully approaching pure white with no

detail. In my experience, the D700 tries to keep the exposure from ⅓ to ½ stop below the maximum white value.

Fortunately, Nikon has given us a way to fine-tune the *Matrix* meter to closely match our type of shooting. As a stock shooter for **Photoshelter.com**, I'm always concerned about shooting images as noise free as possible. Therefore, I generally try to expose as close to the maximum brightness I can get without completely blowing out the highlights. Underexposure means noise, so I tend toward the highlight or bright edge of normal exposure to keep noise under control. I've found that setting my D700 about ½ stop over what the *Matrix* meter suggests gives me images that have no serious blowout and very little noise. From time to time I have a little problem with white subjects, but I generally do well with a half-stop over.

If you want to experiment with fine-tuning your *Matrix* meter to see what you can get away with, please refer to chapter 6, "Custom Setting Banks", and see the section "Custom setting b6 – Fine tune optimal exposure". This setting allows you to fine-tune each of the exposure meters individually in ⅙ stops. I leave my D700 set to ⅜ stops over exposure, which equals one-half stop. Don't be afraid to experiment with your D700 because you can always change your fine-tuning back to zero.

You might find that ½ stop is too much for your liking or that you don't need any compensation at all. The point is that you are not limited with this camera. You can use the *Matrix* meter with factory settings or fine-tune endlessly.

## Using Flash with Matrix Metering

When you are using flash with matrix metering, you might find that the D700 is especially conservative. I have used the built-in pop-up speedlight, an SB-600, and an SB-800 with my camera, and it consistently underexposes by about ⅓ stop in matrix metering.

To overcome this perceived tendency in my D700, I have reprogrammed my D700's FUNC button to activate the *Spot* meter while I hold the button down (see the section "Custom setting f4 – Assign FUNC button"). With this adjustment, I find that a good spot-reading directly off my subject gives me nearly perfect exposures using flash.

Figure 3 – *Metering selector* set to *Center-weighted*

## Center-Weighted Meter

If you're a bit old-fashioned and were raised on a classic center-weighted meter, and still prefer that type, the D700's exposure meter can be transformed into a flexible center-weighted meter with a variable-sized weighting that you can control (*figure 3*).

The *Center-weighted* meter in the D700 meters the entire frame but concentrates most of the metering into a 12 mm circle in the middle of the frame. If you like, you can make the circle as small as 8 mm or as large as 20 mm. Let's examine the *Center-weighted* meter more closely.

Using *Custom setting b5*, you can change the size of the circle where the D700 concentrates the meter reading (see chapter 6 "Custom Setting Banks"). If you like, you can even completely eliminate the circle and use the entire viewfinder frame as a basic averaging meter.

As mentioned previously, the circle is normally 12 mm in size in your viewfinder.

However, by using *Custom setting b5* you can adjust this size to one of the following:

- 8 mm (.31 inch)
- 12 mm (.47 inch)
- 15 mm (.59 inch)
- 20 mm (.79 inch)
- Avg – Entire Frame

The *Center-weighted* meter is a pretty simple concept. The part of your subject that's in the center of your D700's viewfinder influences the meter more than the edges of the frame.

## Where's the Circle?

You can't see any indication of a circle in the viewfinder, so you'll have to imagine one.

Here's how (*figure 3A*): Locate your current AF sensor in your viewfinder. The distance from the center of one rectangle to the center of the next rectangle in the same row is almost 2 mm (.08 inch) in size. If you imagine about six of these little rectangles side by side, that's about the same size as the default 12 mm

Figure 3A – Series of imaginary red circles on the viewfinder and averaging full frame

circle, which at .47 inch is about ½ inch. The 20 mm maximum size circle, at .79 inch, is about ¾ inch wide.

Primarily, just remember that the center area of the viewfinder provides the most important metering area and you'll do fine. For information on fine-tuning center-weighted metering, see the section "Custom setting b6 – Fine tune optimal exposure" in chapter 6.

Figure 4 – *Metering selector* set to *Spot*

## What About the Averaging Meter?

If you set your meter to *Avg* in *Custom setting b5* (fully averaging), the entire viewfinder's light values are averaged to arrive at an exposure value. No particular area of the frame is assigned any greater importance. The exposure value is an average of the light values in the entire frame (see *figure 3A*, screen 5).

This is a little bit like matrix metering, but without the extra smarts. In fact, on several test subjects, I got remarkably similar meter readings between *Avg* and *Matrix*. *Matrix* should do better in difficult lighting situations since it draws on a database of image characteristics to compare with your current image and it looks at color, distance, and where your subject is located in the frame.

## Spot Meter

Sometimes no meter other than a spot meter will do. In situations where you must get an accurate exposure for a very small section of the frame, or you must get several meter readings from different small areas, the D700 can, once again, be adjusted to fit your needs (*figure 4*).

The D700's *Spot* meter consists of a 4 mm circle surrounding the currently active autofocus (AF) point. That's evaluating less than

Figure 4A – Viewfinder view of the 4 mm spot

1.5% of the frame, so it is indeed a "spot" meter. Since the spot is surrounding the currently active AF point, you can move the *Spot* meter around the viewfinder within the 51 AF points (*figure 4A*).

How big is the 4 mm spot? Well, the *Spot* meter barely surrounds the little AF point rectangle in your viewfinder. It is rather small at .16 inch. When your D700 is in *Spot metering* mode and you move the AF point to some small section of your subject, you can rest assured that you're getting a true spot reading.

In fact, you can use your spot meter to determine an approximate exposure value (EV) range of light values in the entire image. You can do this by metering both the lightest and the darkest spots in the frame. If this value exceeds a four or five stop difference, you've got to decide which part of your sub-ject is most important to you and meter only for it. Something is going to "blow out".

On an overcast day, you can usually get by with no compensation since the range of light values are often within the recording capabil-ity of the sensor. On a bright sunny day, the range of light exceeds what your sensor can record by as much as two times. This range can often be as much as 12 stops total, while your sensor can only record a maximum of six or seven stops!

Don't let the numbers make you nervous. Just remember that spot metering is often a trade-off. You trade the highly specific abil-ity to ensure a certain portion of an image is "spot-on" for the ability of the camera's mul-tiple "averaging" skills to generally get the correct exposure throughout the frame. The choice is yours, depending on the shooting situation.

If you spot-meter a person's face while they are standing in the sun, the shadows around that person will contain little or no data. The shadows will often come out as solid black in the final image. On the other hand, if you spot-meter for the shadows instead, the per-son's face is likely to "blow out" to solid white. We'll discuss this in more detail later in this chapter, when we explore the *Histogram*.

Use your spot meter to get specific meter readings of small areas on and around your subject, make some exposure decisions your-self, and your subject should be well exposed. Just remember that the spot meter evaluates only for the small area that it sees, so it cannot adjust the camera for anything except that one tiny area. Spot metering requires some prac-tice to learn, but it is a powerful tool to bal-ance exposure values in your images.

For information on fine-tuning spot meter-ing, see the section "Custom setting b6 – Fine tune optimal exposure" in chapter 6.

## Exposure Modes

(See pages 114 to 125 in the User's Manual.) I mentioned my old Nikon FM in the begin-ning of this chapter. I remember that camera with fondness, since that was when I got really serious about photography. It's hard for me to imagine that it has already been nearly 30 years since I last used my FM! Things were simpler back then. Now that I think about it, I remember my grandma saying something similar about her Brownie Hawkeye.

When I say simple, I mean that the FM had a basic center-weighted light meter, a manual exposure dial, and manual aperture settings. I had to decide how to create the image in all aspects. It was a camera with only one mode – M or manual.

Later on, I bought a Nikon FE, and was amazed to use its A mode, or aperture prior-ity. I could set the aperture manually and the camera would adjust the shutter speed for me. Luxury! The FE had two modes: M (manual), and A (aperture priority).

A few more years went by, and I bought a Nikon F4. This camera was loaded with fea-tures, and was much more complex. It had four different modes, including the two I was used to, M and A, and two new modes, S (shutter priority), and P (programmed auto). I had to learn even more stuff! The F4 was my first P,S,A,M camera.

This progression leads us to the D700.

The point is that today's cameras are amaz-ingly complex compared to cameras only a few years ago. In fact, the D700 is probably the most complex camera I've ever used! Let's examine how we can use that complexity and express it as flexibility for our benefit. The D700 is also a P,S,A,M camera, which is the abbreviated progression of modes. We'll look at those modes next.

There are two controls that you must use together to set the various modes on the

Figure 5 – *MODE* button, Control Panel CD with *Programmed auto* mode selected, and *Main command* dial

camera: The *MODE* button and the *Main command* dial.

Hold the *MODE* button down with your shutter-release finger, and use your thumb to rotate the *Main command* dial. You'll notice in the upper-left corner of the Control Panel LCD that the mode (P,S,A, or M) scrolls as you turn the command dial (see *figure 5*).

Now, let's discuss each exposure mode in detail.

## P – Programmed Auto Mode

*Programmed auto* mode (P) is designed for those times when you just want to shoot pictures and not think much about camera settings. The camera takes care of the shutter speed and aperture for you and uses your selected exposure meter type to create the

Figure 6 – Control Panel LCD in *Programmed auto* mode

best pictures it can without human intervention. *Figure 6* shows the P for *Programmed auto* mode followed by the shutter speed and aperture to the right of the P.

It is called *Programmed auto* because it uses an internal software program built into the D700. It tries its best to create optimal images in most situations. However, even Nikon's User's Manual on page 116 calls this a "snapshot" mode. P mode can handle a wide variety of situations well, but I personally wouldn't depend on it for my important shooting. When I'm at a party and I just want to enjoy myself, get some nice snapshots, and not think about the camera, then P mode means "P" for party to me.

*P* mode actually comes in two parts: *Programmed auto* and *Flexible program*. *Flexible program* works similarly to A (*Aperture priority auto*) mode. Let me explain.

### From P to P* and Back Again

If you have your D700 in P mode and turn the *Main command* dial to the right, the D700 goes into P* (*Flexible program*) mode and starts counting clicks to the right. In order to get back into normal P mode, you have to turn the *Main command* dial back to the left that same number of clicks (up to 15 clicks).

## Get Down, Grandpa!

You're shooting at a family party and suddenly you see a perfect shot of grandpa dancing on the dinner table and grandma standing on the floor behind him with her hand over her mouth. You (being a well-trained photographer) glance down at your camera and realize that the f/4 aperture showing on the *Control Panel* won't give you enough depth of field to focus on grandpa and still have a sharp image of grandma, who by this time is tugging at grandpa's pant leg. With only seconds to spare you turn your *Main command* dial to the left. The D700 realizes that it is being called upon to leave snapshot mode and give you some control. It throws an asterisk up next to the P on the Control Panel LCD (P*) to let you know it realizes that you are taking over and, since you are turning the dial to the left, it obligingly starts cranking down the aperture. Six clicks to the left and your aperture is now at f/8. As soon as the D700 detected that you were turning the command dial, it started adjusting the shutter speed to match the new aperture. With only milliseconds before grandma starts dragging grandpa off the dinner table, you get the camera to your eye, compose, and press the shutter, and the D700 starts grabbing frames. You get 15 frames off in the three seconds it takes grandma to get grandpa down from the table.

Does that make sense? What you did in my imaginary scenario was invoke *Flexible program* mode in your D700. How? As soon as you turned the *Main command* dial, the D700 left normal P mode and switched to P* mode, otherwise known as *Flexible program*. Before you turned the *Main command* dial, the D700 was happily controlling both shutter speed and aperture for you. When you turned the dial, the D700 immediately switched to *Flexible program* mode, put an asterisk after the P on the Control Panel LCD, and let you

have control of the aperture while it controlled only the shutter speed. In effect the D700 allowed you to exercise your knowledge of photography very quickly and only assisted you from that point.

When you enter P* (*Flexible program*) mode you control only the aperture, and the D700 controls the shutter speed. If you turn the *Main command* dial to the left, the aperture gets smaller. Turn it to the right and the aperture gets larger. Nothing happens if you turn the *Sub-command* dial. Nikon only gave you control of the aperture in *Flexible program* mode. Can you see why I say that *Flexible program* mode acts like A (*Aperture priority auto*) mode?

The reason I know that the D700 is actually counting clicks is that I decided to count along one day.

Here's what I did. I set my D700 to P mode and got into a darker area where it was at maximum aperture. I then started cranking the *Main command* dial to the right, which should increase the aperture. Since I was already at maximum aperture, the D700 could not increase the aperture size, so it just sat there counting clicks instead. In order for me to get back into P mode, and remove the asterisk from the P*, I had to turn back to the left the exact number of clicks I turned to the right (up to 15 clicks). You can also turn the camera off or change modes to get out of the *Flexible program* mode.

## S – Shutter Priority Auto Mode

*Shutter priority auto* mode is for those who need to control their camera's shutter speed while allowing the camera to maintain the correct aperture for the available light. *Figure 7* shows the S for *Shutter priority auto* mode followed by the shutter speed and aperture to the right of the S.

If you find yourself shooting action, you'll probably be concerned about keeping the shutter speed high enough to capture an image without excessive blurring. Shooting sports, air shows, auto races, or anything moving quickly requires careful control of the shutter. Sometimes, too, you might want to set your shutter speed to a very slow setting for special effects or time exposures.

*Figure 7* shows the D700 in *Shutter priority auto* mode (S). To use the S mode, you select a shutter speed that you feel will work for your current shooting situation and set it with the *Main command* dial. The D700 will now assist you by controlling the aperture to maintain correct exposure.

If the light changes drastically and the D700 cannot maintain a correct exposure, it will inform you by replacing the normal aperture reading with either HI or Lo. They mean what they imply: HI means there is too much light for a good exposure, and Lo means there is not enough light for a good exposure.

While you have your camera in S mode, you can set your shutter speed anywhere between 30 seconds and ⅛₀₀₀ of a second. You can also set it at x250, which is one click below the slowest shutter speed on the dial (30s). For more information on x250, see *Custom setting e1* on page 305 of the D700 User's Manual.

## A – Aperture Priority Auto Mode

Nature and macro shooters, and anyone concerned with carefully controlling depth of field, will often leave their D700 set to *Aperture priority auto* mode (A). *Figure 8* shows the A for *Aperture priority auto* mode followed by the shutter speed and aperture to the right of the A.

A (*Aperture priority auto*) mode lets you control the aperture while the D700 takes care of the shutter speed for optimal exposures. With newer AF-S and G lenses, to select an aperture you'll use the *Sub-command* dial. You can control the aperture from maximum to minimum just by using the *Sub-command* dial on the D700.

Depth of field (DOF) is an extremely important concept to understand for photographers. Simply put, it allows you to control the range of sharp focus in your images. Following is a review of DOF.

## Understanding Depth of Field

Depth of field is one of those things that confuses a lot of new DSLR users. Yet, it is very important! I'm going to attempt to explain this concept using pictures. This topic transcends the actual DSLR being used—in fact, my illustrations were created with my trusty Nikon D2X.

Figure 7 – Control Panel LCD in *Shutter priority auto* mode

Figure 8 – Control Panel LCD in *Aperture priority auto* mode

## A Note on Lens Types

If you use an older AF lens with an aperture ring, set it to the smallest aperture on the lens, then use the *Sub-command* dial to change aperture instead of using the ring on the lens. If you have older non-CPU lenses, you'll have to use the aperture ring on the lens to control the aperture.

Figure 8A – Three kids at f/1.8, shutter speed at 1/6000

Let's say you are taking a picture of a friend, who is standing 6 feet (2 m) away from you. About 6 feet behind your friend is another person. There is also a third person standing about 6 feet behind the second person. Three people total, each about 6 feet apart, with the friend in front (see *figure 8A*).

You are shooting with a 50 mm f/1.8 lens. You focus on your friend's face, the young lady in red, and take a picture. It looks like the image in *figure 8A*.

F/1.8 is an aperture number. An aperture is simply an opening in the front of your lens controlled by blades. It lets light come in through the lens to expose your D700's sensor. You can't see the aperture when you look in the front of your lens (usually) since your D700 allows you to focus with the aperture blades wide open and out of the way. The aperture closes down to its selected setting when you press the shutter release to take your picture, or press the depth of field *Preview* button. This is the reason the viewfinder often gets darker when you press the DOF *Preview* button on your camera.

Apertures on your zoom lens probably start at about f/3.5 (big aperture) and stop at f/22 (small aperture). The bigger the aperture can get (the larger the opening), the "faster" the lens is considered. When you hear about a "fast" lens, someone is talking about a lens with

Figure 8B – Three kids at f/8, shutter speed at 1/500

Figure 8C – Three kids at f/22, shutter speed at 1/40

a big maximum aperture opening. The 50 mm f/1.8 lens is a fast lens.

Notice in *figure 8A* that your friend (in red) is in sharp focus. The girl standing behind her, to the right, is not in focus, nor is the young lad even farther away to the left. This is the result of shooting with a big aperture. F/1.8 is a big opening in the front of your lens. It also causes the depth of field, or "zone of sharp focus", to be shallow. Only the girl in front is in focus at f/1.8. Not much else is in focus, so there is very little depth of field. The depth of field in this picture is much less than 3 feet (.91 m) deep; probably more like 1.5 feet (.45 m).

So what would happen if we closed the aperture down ("stopped" down) to a medium aperture like f/8? *Figure 8B* shows what that will do to the depth of field.

Remember, you are focused on the girl in front, and at f/1.8, a big fast aperture, the others were out of focus. Without changing your focus in any way, you adjusted your aperture to f/8. Something changed!

You focused your camera on the girl in front, but now the girl to the right is sharp too, even though you did not change your focus control. The depth of field (or zone of sharp focus) now extends past the girl in front and covers the girl in back. The DOF got deeper.

However, also notice that the boy to the left is still not in focus. The background is not in focus either. The depth of field is deeper but still not deep enough to cover all your subjects.

This image is the result of a medium aperture opening (f/8), not fast (f/1.8) and not slow (f/22). Now, let's consider what happens if we "stop down", or close the aperture, to a small opening like f/22 (*figure 8C*).

Aha! Now everything in the picture is sharp. An aperture as slow and small as f/22 makes it easy to get sharp focus. Remember, you focused on the girl in front in all these pictures. At first only the girl in red was in focus (f/1.8), and as the aperture got smaller, more and more

of the surroundings came into sharp focus (f/8 and f/22).

So, depth of field is simply the zone of sharp focus. It extends in front of and behind your focused subject and gets deeper in both directions, toward the camera and away from it, as you "stop down" your lens. If you set your camera to *Aperture Priority Auto* (or *Manual* mode), you can adjust this powerful functionality to control what is in focus in your pictures. Don't forget that in this case you are also making trade-offs. All three images were shot at ISO 100, and once you started using the smaller apertures, the camera needed to compensate by using longer exposure times. The f1.8 shot was at 1/6000 second. The f/8 shot was at 1/500 second. The f/22 final image required an exposure of merely 1/40 second. This was fairly easy to pull off under sunny skies with stationary subjects, but you can see where the shutter speed exposure compensations could get troublesome if these three subjects were playing ball or jumping around. This is when the experienced photographer takes advantage of the *Manual* mode.

## M – Manual Mode

*Manual* mode takes a big step backwards to days of old. It gives you complete control of your camera's shutter and aperture so that you can make all the exposure decisions, with suggestions from the exposure meter. *Figure 9* shows the M for *Manual* mode followed by the shutter speed and aperture to the right of the M.

Also, in *figure 9*, notice the electronic analog exposure display that's highlighted in red. This display has a plus sign (+) on the left, and a minus sign (−) on the right. Each dot on the scale represents 1/3 exposure value (EV) step and each vertical line represents 1 EV step.

Figure 9 – Control Panel LCD in *Manual* mode, and viewfinder's exposure display highlighted in red

You can control how sensitive the command dials are with *Custom setting b2 – EV steps for exposure cntrl* (see chapter 6). The factory default setting for *b2* is that the command dials change aperture or shutter speed in ⅓ EV steps. If you'd like, you can set *b2* to ½ or 1 EV step instead.

When you are metering your subject, a bar will extend on this display from the zero in the center toward the plus side to indicate overexposure, or toward the minus side to indicate underexposure (see *figure 9A*). You can gauge the amount of over- or underexposure by the number of dots and lines the bar passes as it heads toward one side or the other. The goal in manual mode is to make the bar

disappear. In *figure 9A*, the bar is indicating 2⅓ EV steps (stops) overexposure.

You'll adjust the aperture with the *Sub-command* dial and the shutter speed with the *Main command* dial.

## Histogram

Back in the "good old" film days we didn't have a histogram, so we had to depend on our experience and light meter to get a good exposure. Since we couldn't see the exposure until

### Another Note on Lens Types

With newer G lenses, you can control the aperture from maximum to minimum just using the *Sub-command* dial on the D700. If you use an older AF lens with an aperture ring, set it to the smallest aperture on the lens, then use the *Sub-command* dial to change aperture instead of the ring on the lens. If you have older non-CPU lenses, you'll have to use the aperture ring on the lens to control the aperture.

Figure 9A – Control Panel LCD's exposure display showing 21/3 stops of overexposure

after we had left the scene, we measured our success by the number of correctly exposed images we were able to create. With the exposure meter/histogram combination found in the D700, and the ability to zoom into our images with the high-resolution monitor on the back, the success rate we can experience is very much higher than ever before.

The histogram can be as important, or even more so, than the exposure meter. The meter sets the camera up for the exposure, and the histogram visually verifies that the exposure is a good one.

If your exposure meter stopped working, you could still get perfect exposures using only the histogram. In fact, I gauge my efforts more by how the histogram looks than anything else. The exposure meter and histogram work together to make sure you get excellent results from your photographic efforts.

In *figure 10* is a picture of the D700's histogram screens. The screen on the left is a basic informational screen with only a combined RGB histogram shown in white. It is always available on your camera by scrolling up or down with the Multi Selector during image review.

The second histogram screen in *figure 10* is actually a series of histograms. On the top is the red channel, the middle is the green channel, and the bottom is the blue channel (RGB = red, green, blue). On the left bottom is a white-colored histogram that is all three color channels combined. When you look closely at the "combined" histogram, it looks very similar to the green channel.

Let's discuss the use of a histogram in detail.

## Understanding the Histogram

Using the histogram screens on your D700's Monitor LCD will guarantee you a much higher percentage of well-exposed images. It is well worth spending time to understand the histogram, and it isn't as complicated as it looks.

I'll try to cover this feature with enough detail to give you a working knowledge of how to use the histogram to make better pictures. If you are deeply interested in the histogram, there is much research material available on the Internet. Although this overview is brief, it will present enough knowledge to improve your technique immediately.

### Light Range

The D700's sensor can record only a certain range of light values, which is about five to seven usable EV steps. Unfortunately, many of

Figure 10 – Two D700 histogram screens

the higher contrast subjects we shoot can contain over 12 stops of light values. This is quite a bit more than it is possible to capture in a single exposure. It's important to understand how your camera records light so that you can better control how the image is captured.

Look at *figure 11* closely. The gray rectangular area is a representation of an in-camera histogram. Examine it carefully! Think about it for a minute before reading on.

The histogram basically is a graph that represents the maximum range of light values your camera can capture, in 256 steps (0 = pure black, and 255 = pure white). In the middle of the histogram are the mid-range values that represent middle colors like grays, light browns, and greens. The values from just above zero and just below 255 contain detail.

The actual histogram graph looks like a mountain peak, or a series of peaks, and the more of a particular color, the taller the peak. In some cases the graph will be rounder on top, or flattened.

The left side of the histogram represents the maximum dark values that your camera can record. The right side represents the maximum "lightness" values your camera can capture. On either end of the histogram the light values contain no detail. They are either completely black or completely white.

The top of the histogram (top of mountain peaks) represents the amount of individual colors (a value you cannot control in-camera), so it is for your information only.

We are mostly concerned with the left and right side values of the histogram because we do have much control over those (dark vs. light).

Simply put, the histogram's left-to-right directions are related to the darkness and

Figure 11 – Picture of basic histogram.

Figure 12 – Three histograms – one underexposed, one correct, one overexposed.

lightness of the image, while the up and down directions of the histogram (valleys and peaks) have to do with the amount of color information. I repeated this for emphasis!

The left (dark) to right (light) directions are very important for your picture taking. If the image is too dark, the histogram will show that by clipping off the light values on the left and, if it's too light, by clipping on the right. This will become easier to understand as we look at well-exposed and poorly exposed images. Check out the Histogram Basic Tutorial in *figure 12*, and then we'll look at things in more detail.

When you see the three histograms next to each other, does it make more sense? See how the underexposed histogram is all the way to the left of the histogram window and is clipped mid-peak? Then note the well-exposed histogram and how both edges of the histogram just touch the edges of the histogram window.

Finally, see how the overexposed image's histogram is crammed and clipped on the right. You see how this might be helpful, so let's look at some histogram detail.

### Image and Histogram Shape

Look at the image in *figure 13*. It is well exposed, with no serious problems. The entire light range of this particular image fits within the histogram window, which means that it is neither too light nor too dark and will take very little or no adjustment to view or print. It contains no more than four or five stops of light range.

Compare *figure 13's* histogram to the left side of the histogram graph in *figure 12*. See how the *figure 13* histogram does not cram itself against the dark value side. In other words, the dark values are not clipped off on the left. This means that the camera recorded all the dark values in this image, with no loss of shadow detail.

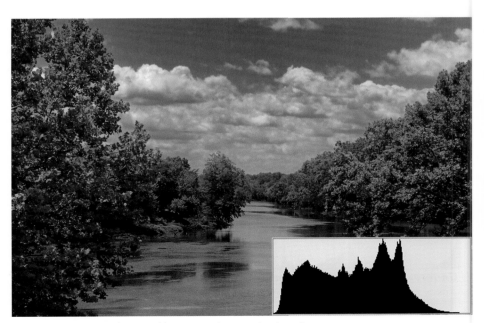

Figure 13 – Image with normal histogram "mountain shape"

Then look at the right side of the histogram and note that it is not completely against the right side, although quite close. The image contains all the light values available. Everything in between is exposed quite well, with full detail. A histogram does not have to cover the entire window for the exposure to be fine. When there is a very limited range of light, the histogram may be rather narrow.

The image in *figure 13* is a relatively bland image with smooth graduations of tone, so it makes a nice smooth mountain peak histogram graph. This will not occur every time, since most images contain quite a bit more color information. Each prominent color will be represented with its own peak on the histogram graph. The most prominent colors will have higher peaks, while the less prominent will have lower or no peaks.

As we progress into images with more color or light information, you'll see that the histogram looks quite different. Look at the image in *figure 14*. This is an image that far exceeds the range of the D700's digital sensor.

Notice that, overall, this image is dark and looks underexposed. The histogram in *figure 14* is crammed to the left, effectively being clipped off. There are no gradual climbs like on a mountain range, from valley to peak and back to valley. Instead, the image shows up on the left side in mid-peak. It is "clipped". This is an underexposed image and the histogram reflects that well.

The most important thing to understand when you see a histogram like the one in *figure 14*, with part of the peak clipped off on the left, is that some or all of the image is significantly underexposed.

Now look at a similar image in *figure 15*. In this image, a larger aperture was used and more light was allowed in. We can now see much more detail. However, once again, the range of light is too great for the sensor, so it is now clipped off on the highlight side (right).

Figure 14 – Wide histogram of an image, showing the histogram to the dark side for an underexposed image

Figure 15 –   Wide histogram of an image, showing the histogram to the light side
            for an overexposed image

The dark-side graph value is not clipped; instead the graph extends to the left dark-side edge but stops there.

The image in *figure 15* shows more detail but is not professional looking and will win no awards. The range of light is simply too great to be recorded fully. Many of the details are overly light, and that can be seen by the histogram's clipping on the right side. The most important thing to remember with this image's histogram is that when you see a histogram that is crammed all the way to the right and clipped, some or all of the image is significantly too light. Overall, a great deal of the image in *figure 15* is recorded as pure white and the detail is permanently gone, or "blown out".

It is important is that you try to center the histogram without either edge being clipped off. This is not always possible, since often there is too much light range and the sensor

or histogram window can't contain it. If you center the histogram, your images will be better exposed. If you take a picture and the histogram is shifted far to the left or right, you can then retake the photograph, exposing in the direction of the opposite light value.

If there is too much light to allow centering the histogram, you must decide which part of the image is more important, the light or dark values. You must expose for the highlights, or you will lose detail in the light areas.

## How Does the Eye React to Light Values?

The D700 camera, with its imaging sensor and glass lenses, is only a weak imitation of our marvelously designed eye and brain functions. There are very few situations where our eyes cannot adjust to the available light range, and we can see well in most cases. So, as photographers, we are always seeking ways to record even a small portion of what the eye and mind can see.

Since our eyes tend to know that shadows are black, and expects that, it is usually better to expose for the highlights. If you see dark shadows, that seems normal. We're simply not used to seeing light that's so bright that all detail is lost. An image exposed for the dark values will look strange because most highlight detail will be burned out.

Your eye can see a range of light in comparison to your digital sensor. The only time you will ever see light values that are so bright that detail is lost is when you are looking directly at an overwhelmingly bright light, like the sun. So, in a worst case scenario, expose the image so that the right side of the histogram graph just touches the right side of the histogram window and the image will look closer to what our eye expects.

Since photography's beginning, we have always fought with being able to record only a limited range of light. But, with the digital camera and its histogram, we can now see a visual representation of the light values and can immediately approve of the image, reshoot it with emphasis on lighter or darker values, or see that we must use a filter or multiple-exposure high dynamic range (HDR) imaging to capture it at all.

## Computer Adjustment of Images

Looking at the image in *figure 16*, taken in mid-day overhead sunshine, we see an example of a range of light that is too great to be captured by a digital sensor but is exposed in such a way that we can get a usable photo later.

Notice in *figure16* how the dark values are clipped off and dark detail is lost. But, look to the right side of the histogram and notice

how the light values are not clipped off. So the camera recorded all the light values but lost some dark values. Since our eye sees this as normal, this image looks okay.

If we were standing there looking at the cabin ourselves, our eye would be able to see much more detail in the front porch area. But, the camera just can't record that much light range. If we want to get a bit more detail in the shadows than this image seems to contain, we can do it. Normally, a camera does not give us enough control to add light values on the fly, so we use the histogram to get the best possible exposure and then adjust the image later in the computer. Some cameras can be "profiled" to capture light ranges more effectively in one direction or the other, but when you push one area, the opposite area must give. So we need a way to take all this light and compress it into a more usable range.

We are now entering the realm of "postprocessing," or of in-computer image manipulation. Look at the image in *figure 17*. This is the exact same image as *figure 16*, but it has been adjusted in Photoshop to cram more image detail into the histogram by compressing the mid-range values. Notice that the entire histogram seems to be farther right toward the light side. Also notice that the mid-range peaks are basically gone. We removed a good bit of the mid-range, but since there was already a lot of mid-range there, our image did not suffer greatly.

How this computer postprocessing was done is outside the scope of this book, but it is not very hard. I do recommend, however, that you buy a program like Nikon Capture NX 2, Photoshop, Photoshop Elements, Lightroom, or another fine graphics program designed for photographers. Your digital camera and your computer are a powerful imaging combination that can create a digital darkroom, where you are in control from start to finish, from

Figure 16 – Cabin picture with correct exposure but dark shadows, and its histogram.

clicking the shutter to printing the image. But, retreating from philosophy, let's continue with our histogram exploration.

Notice in *figure 17* how the histogram edge is just touching the highlight side of the histogram window? A small amount of clipping is taking place, and you can see the slightly blown-out area on the peak of the cabin's roof. Sometimes a very small amount of clipping does not seriously harm the image. The photographer must be the judge.

The greater apparent detail in this image is the result of compressing the mid-range of the light values a bit in the computer. If you compress or make the mid-range light values smaller, that will tend to pull the dark values toward the light side and the light values toward the dark side. So, you will have more apparent detail in your image. It's like cutting a section out of the middle of a garden hose. If you pull both of the cut ends together, the other two ends of the hose will move toward

the middle, and the hose will be shorter overall. Similarly, if you compress or remove the mid-range of the histogram, both ends of the graph will move toward the middle. If one of the ends of the graph is beyond the edge of the histogram window (or is clipped off), it will be less so when the mid-range is compressed.

We are simply trying to make the histogram fit into the frame of its window. If we have to cut out some of the middle, to bring both ends into the window, well, there is usually plenty in the middle to cut out, so the image rarely suffers. Remember, this is being done outside of the camera in a computer. You can't really control the in-camera histogram to compress values, but you need to be aware that it can be done in the computer so that you can expose accordingly with your camera's histogram. Then you will be prepared for later postprocessing of the image in your computer.

In fact, now that we have compressed the mid-range values, the image in *figure 17* more

Figure 17 – Postprocessed cabin picture and its histogram

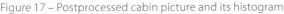

closely resembles what our eye normally sees, so it looks more normal to us.

In many cases, your progression from the shooting site to your digital darkroom can benefit if you shoot RAW (unprocessed) images (Nikon calls it Nikon Electronic Format, or NEF).

A RAW digital image contains an adjustable range of light. With a RAW image you can use controls in Capture NX 2, Photoshop, or even the basic Nikon Picture Project software included with the D700 to select from the range of light within the big RAW image file. It's like moving the histogram window to the left or right over all that wide range of raw image data. You select a final resting place for the histogram window, capture the underlying RAW data, and then your image is ready for use.

This is an oversimplification of the process but, I hope, makes it more understandable. In reality, the digital sensor records a wider

range of light than you can use in one image. While you might be able to use about five stops of light range in a normal image, the digital sensor is recording probably about seven stops of light range. Although you just can't get all of that range into the final image, it is there in the RAW file as a selectable range. I prefer to think of it as a built-in bracket since it works the same way.

This bracketed light range within the image is present to a very limited degree in JPEG, and a bit more so in TIFF images, but is the most pronounced in pure RAW images. That is why many photographers choose to shoot in RAW mode instead of JPEG or TIFF.

## My Conclusions

Your camera meter should be used to get the initial exposure only. Then you can look at the histogram and see if the image's light range is contained within the limited range of the sensor. If it is clipped off to the right or the left, you may want to add or subtract light with your +/- *EV compensation* button or use your *Manual* mode. Expose for the light range with your histogram. Let your light meter get you close, then fine-tune with the histogram.

The Nikon D700 has a Multi Selector that can be pressed right or left to scroll through the images you have already taken. You can also press the Multi Selector up or down to scroll through the various informational modes, such as the histogram screen. When you take a picture of an important subject, find the histogram view of your image. If you can't find the screen with multiple histograms as shown in *figure 10*, see the *Playback Menu – Display mode* and select *RGB histogram*.

There are also other Monitor LCD viewing modes that you can use along with the histogram graph, such as the *Highlights* (blinky) mode for blown-out highlights (*see the Playback Menu – Display mode* and select *Highlights*). This mode will cause your image to blink between light and dark in the blown-out highlight areas. This is a rough representation of a highlight-value clipped histogram,

and it's quite useful for quick shooting. Using your camera's light meter, histogram, and the highlight burnout blinky mode together is a very powerful method to control your exposures.

If you master this method you will have a very fine degree of control over where you place your image's light ranges. This is sort of like using the famous Ansel Adams' black and white Zone System but it is represented visually on the Monitor LCD of your D700.

The manipulation of the histogram "levels" in-computer is a detailed study in itself. It's part of having a digital darkroom. Learn to use your computer to tweak your images, and you'll be able to produce superior results most of the time. Even more important, learn to use your histogram to capture a light-balanced image in the first place!

Your histogram is simply a graph that lets you see at a glance how well your image is contained by your camera. Too far left and the image is too dark; too far right and the image is too light. Learn to use the histogram well and your images are bound to improve!

# Multi-CAM 3500FX Autofocus

As technology has allowed, Nikon has increased the number of focus sensors and area modes in the Autofocus (AF) system.

For instance, the Nikon D100's Multi-CAM 900 AF module has five sensors and two area modes, and the Nikon D200's Multi-CAM 1000 has 11 sensors and four area modes. The D700's Multi-CAM 3500FX has a full 51 autofocus sensors but only three area modes, thereby making the AF system simpler to operate, yet more robust. (The D300 uses a DX-sized Autofocus system, but also has 51 sensors and three area modes.)

What do we gain from all these extra AF sensors and more powerful area modes? Is there anything else new and different? As we progress through this chapter, I'll discuss these questions in detail, along with how your photography will benefit most from the new Multi-CAM 3500FX AF system.

## What Is the Multi-CAM 3500FX Autofocus Module?

It's a thoroughly improved, third-generation version of the excellent Multi-CAM 1000 auto-focus module found in the Nikon D200. Where the Multi-CAM 1000 is limited to only 11 AF sensors, the Multi-CAM 3500FX has 51. In *figure 1* you can see what the new AF module looks like.

As we proceed through this chapter, I'm going to call the Multi-CAM 3500FX

Figure 1 – Picture of Multi-CAM 3500FX autofocus module (Nikon Photo)

autofocus module by the simpler name of AF Module.

The AF Module has three AF-area modes:
- *Single-point AF*
- *Dynamic-area AF*
- *Auto-area AF*

It also has three focus modes:
- Single-servo, or *S* mode
- Continuous-servo, or *C* mode (CL and CH)
- Manual, or *M* mode

What's the difference? Basically, think of the AF-area modes as where the AF Module focuses, and the focus modes as how it focuses.

In addition, the D700 allows you to control how fast and how often a picture is taken. We'll look at how the shutter frame-rate (this was called "motor-drive" on some film-based cameras) works in relation to the AF system.

With the controls built into the D700's body, you'll be able to select whether the AF Module uses one or many of the 51 AF sensors to find your subject. You'll also select whether the camera grabs the focus and "locks" on a static subject or whether it continuously seeks new focus if your subject is moving and how fast in frames per second (FPS) it can capture the images.

Of course, if you want to, you can turn AF off completely and simply use manual focus. This comes in handy when you decide to use older "non-CPU" Nikkor manual-focus lenses, such as the excellent AI/AI-S prime and zoom lenses of yesteryear and the few primes that are available new.

In fact, one of the important features of the near-professional D700 is that the camera will happily use older lenses. Many of us have our old favorites, such as the Nikkor 105 mm f/2.5 portrait lens or the 35mm f/2. We can use AF/AF-S lenses or virtually any of the F-Mount AI/AI-S lenses, with a few limitations.

## Setting Your Lens to Manual Focus

If you'd like, you can use the A-M switch found on most AF Nikkors to set the lens to manual focus, and override the AF system completely. If the AF Nikkor lens supports autofocus with manual priority (M/A), you can use the AF Module to obtain primary focus, and then fine-tune it manually.

Tied in closely with the AF system is *Release* mode. This determines how the camera takes the picture: one at a time or in continuous bursts. You can look through the viewfinder to compose, or use the brand-new *Live View* mode (LV) which allows you to use the large Monitor LCD on the back of the D700, instead of the viewfinder, to compose the image.

The AF Module supports 10 custom settings, *a1–a10*, on the *Custom Settings Menu*. We'll examine each of those custom settings in chapter 6.

Let's consider the various features of the Multi-CAM 3500FX AF Module in detail.

## Understanding the Focus Modes, AF-Area Modes, and Release Modes

The D700 has distinct modes for how and when to focus. We'll examine each of those modes as a starting point in our understanding of autofocus with the Multi-CAM 3500FX AF Module. We'll tie together information about the *Focus* modes, *AF-area* modes, and *Release* modes since they work together to acquire and maintain good focus on your subject.

In fact, this chapter encompasses information found in the User's Manual chapters on *Focus* and *Release* modes (User's Manual pages 71 to 104). It goes deeper than merely

looking at the AF Module alone, since other related camera functions—such as the *Release* modes—directly affect how the AF system performs.

In *figure 2* are four pictures of the controls we'll use in combination to change how the camera focuses and captures images.

Notice in the last picture in *figure 2* how the Multi Selector has a locking ring around it. At the top left of the ring you'll see a dot and an *L*. Move the switch to the dot setting, which unlocks the internal AF "sensor point in use". Otherwise, you won't be able to move the AF sensor point around the viewfinder within the 51 available points.

If you want to use the D700 as a point-and-shoot camera, ensure the AF sensor rectangle is centered in the viewfinder, set the lock on *L*, and the center AF focus is all the camera will use in *Single-point AF* mode. I leave mine unlocked all the time but then I check as I'm focusing to make sure I am using the AF sensor I want to use. I can move a single AF sensor, or a group of sensors, around the array of 51 available sensors with the Multi Selector.

Be aware that 15 of the 51 AF sensors on the D700 are cross-type sensors, which means that they will initiate focus in either a horizontal or

## The D700's Improved Sensor

The sensor is different and improved from the sensors on the D200 camera, on which only its single center sensor is a cross-type sensor. In the D700, the actual underlying AF sensors seem to be well represented by the little rectangles in the viewfinder, although a little less so, as I used sensors closer to the edges on my D700. On older Nikon cameras, the AF sensor was actually considerably wider than the brackets shown in the viewfinder.

Figure 2 – *Focus Mode Selector* switch; *Release Mode* dial and *Lock release*; *AF-area Mode Selector,* and *Multi Selector*

a vertical direction. The center three columns by five rows of AF sensors are cross-type. All sensors outside of the three center columns of sensors are only sensitive in a horizontal direction. *Figure 3* has the sensors that are cross-type colored red.

Figure 3 – Central cross-type sensors

## Focus Modes in Detail

The *Focus* modes allow you to control how the autofocus works with static and moving subjects. They allow your camera to "lock" focus on a subject that is not moving, or moving very slowly. They also allow your camera to "follow" focus on an actively moving subject. Let's consider the two servo-based *Focus* modes to see when and how you might use them best.

### Single-servo AF Mode (S)

*Subject is not moving:* When you press the shutter-release button halfway down, the AF Module quickly locks the focus on your subject and waits for you to fire the shutter. If you don't release shutter button pressure and refocus when your subject starts moving, the focus will be out-of-date and useless. Once you have focus lock, take the picture quickly.

This is perfect for nonmoving subjects, or in some cases even very slowly moving subjects.

*Subject is regularly moving:* This will require a little more work on your part. Since the AF system locks the focus on your subject, if it moves even slightly, the focus is no longer good. You'll have to lift your finger off of the shutter release and reapply pressure halfway down to refocus. If the subject continues moving, you'll need to press the shutter-release button halfway down, over and over, to keep the focus accurate. If your subject never stops moving, is moving erratically, or only stops briefly, *Single-servo AF (S)* is probably not the best mode to use. In this case, *Continuous-servo AF (C)* is better because it never locks focus and you can follow movement better.

### Continuous-servo AF Mode (C)

*Subject is not moving:* When the subject is standing still, *Continuous-servo AF* acts a lot like *Single-servo AF*, with the exception that the focus never locks. If you have camera movement, you may hear your lens chattering a little as the autofocus motor makes small adjustments in the focus position. Since it never locks in this mode, you'll need to be careful that you don't accidentally move the AF sensor off of the subject because it may focus on something in the background instead.

*Subject is moving across the viewfinder:* If your subject moves from left to right, right to left, or up and down in the viewfinder, you will need to keep your AF sensor on the subject if you are using *Single-point AF- area* mode. If you are using *Dynamic-area AF* or *Auto-area AF*, your camera will have the ability to track the subject across a few, or all, of the 51 AF sensors. We'll cover this in more detail in the upcoming section "AF-Area Modes in Detail".

*Subject is moving toward or away from the camera:* If your subject is coming toward you, then another automatic function of the camera kicks in. It is called *Predictive Focus Tracking*, and it figures out how far the subject will move before the shutter fires. Once you've pressed the shutter button all the way down, predictive focus tracking moves the lens elements slightly to correspond to where the subject should be when the shutter fires a few milliseconds later. In other words, if the subject is moving towards you, the camera focuses slightly in front of your subject so that the camera has time to move the mirror and get the shutter blades out of the way. It takes 45 milliseconds for the camera to respond to pressing the shutter release.

## AF-Area Modes in Detail

The *AF-Area* modes are designed to give you control over how many AF sensors are in use at one time, and different ways to track subject movement.

*Figure 4* shows the *AF-area Mode Selector* switch in the *Single-point AF* position.

### Predictive Focus Tracking

Let's say you were playing a ball game and you threw the ball to a running player. You would have to throw the ball slightly in front of the receiving player so that the ball and the player arrive in the same place at the same time. Predictive focus tracking does something similar for you. It saves you from trying to focus your camera in front of your subject and waiting 45 milliseconds for it to arrive. That would be a bit hard to time!

## Example of Use

If you are shooting an air show, for instance, in 45 milliseconds an airplane coming toward you can move enough to slightly change the focus area by the time the shutter opens. If you press the shutter in one smooth motion all the way to shutter release, first autofocus occurs, then the mirror moves up and the shutter starts opening. That takes about 45 milliseconds in the D700. In the time it takes for the camera to respond to your shutter release press, the airplane has moved slightly, which just barely throws the autofocus off. In continuous-servo mode, the camera will predict where the airplane will be when the image is actually exposed and adjusts the focus accordingly.

## Effects of Lens Movement

Lens movement (especially with long lenses) can be interpreted by the camera as subject movement. Predictive focus tracking, in that case, is tracking your camera movement while simultaneously trying to track your subject. Attempting to hand hold a long lens will drive your camera crazy. Use a vibration reduction (VR) lens or a tripod for best results. Nikon says that there are special algorithms in predictive focus tracking that notice sideways or up and down movement and shuts it down. So, predictive focus tracking is not activated by the D700 for sideways or up and down subject movement, or panning.

### Single-point AF

This mode uses a single AF sensor out of the array of 51 sensors to acquire a good focus. As mentioned before, you can control which sensor by selecting it with the Multi Selector.

Figure 4 – *AF-area Mode Selector* switch set to *Single-point AF*

In *figure 5* notice how the center AF sensor point (of the 51 sensor points) is the one that provides focus information.

If I have two people standing next to each other, but with a gap in the middle, I can do one of two things.

One, I could get the focus first by pointing the center sensor at the face of one of my subjects, pressing the shutter-release button halfway to get a focus, then holding it down while recomposing the image. When I have recomposed the shot, I finish pressing the shutter release the rest of the way and take the picture.

Two, I can compose the picture first by centering it however I like, then use the Multi Selector to move the single AF sensor until it rests on the face of one of my subjects. With the sensor repositioned, I press the shutter-release button halfway down to get good

Figure 5 – *Single-point AF* sensor with center sensor selected

3

focus, and the rest of the way down to take the picture.

### Single-Point AF Example of Use

If a subject is not moving, like a tree or a standing person, then *Single-point AF* and *Single Frame Release* will allow you to acquire focus. Once the focus is acquired, the AF Module will "lock" focus on the subject, and it will not change. If the subject moves, your focus will be out-of-date, and you'll need to recompose while releasing and then pressing the shutter-release button halfway again. Often, if the subject is moving very slowly or sporadically, I'll not even use *CL* release mode, but will leave it in *S* release mode. I'll press the shutter-release button halfway to acquire focus when the subject moves and tap it again as needed. When I'm ready, I simply press the shutter-release button the rest of the way down and I've got the shot!

Either of these methods will solve the age-old autofocus problem of having a perfectly focused background with out-of-focus subjects because the center AF sensor was looking at the background between them.

Many of us will use *Single-point AF* mode most of the time. It works particularly well for static or slowly moving subjects. When I'm out shooting beautiful nature images or at a party snapshooting pictures of my friends,

### Main Point

Any time I'm shooting a static or slowly moving simple subject, I'll use *Single-point AF* along with *S* or *CL* release modes. (See pages 74 and 84 of your D700 User's Manual.)

### Note on Priority Modes

Anytime you switch your D700 out of single frame release mode, you must be aware of how *Custom settings a1* and *a2* are configured. These two custom settings are *Focus Priority* and *Release Priority*. These are not the same thing as the release modes, so don't get confused. It is critical that you understand these two release "priorities" before you start using your D700 on critical shoots or some of your images may not be in focus at all. I won't cover that information in this *Single-point AF* section, but in chapter 6 we'll look at them in detail. Please, be very sure that you understand what *Custom settings a1* and *a2* do!

I'll use *Single-point AF*, along with *Single frame (S) Release* mode, almost exclusively. If I'm shooting a wedding, where the bride and groom are walking slowly up the aisle, *Single-point AF* and *Continuous low speed (CL) Release* mode seem to work well for me.

Now, we move on to *Dynamic-area AF* and see what benefits it brings us.

### Dynamic-Area AF

This mode is best used when your subject is moving. Instead of a single AF sensor alone for autofocus, several sensors surrounding the one you have selected with your thumb switch are also active. In *figure 6* is a picture of the *AF-area Mode Selector* switch with *Dynamic-area AF* selected.

You can select the three different sensors patterns in *Custom setting a3*. The three primary patterns are represented in *figure 7*. The first image shows nine points or AF sensors in use.

The second shows 21 points, and the third, all 51 points.

Figure 6 – *AF-area Mode Selector* switch set to *Dynamic-area AF*

See *figure 8* for the *Custom setting* screens used to set the patterns.

You can, of course, move the first two patterns (nine and 21 points) around the viewfinder with your Multi Selector. Unfortunately, the camera does not show you more than the center AF sensor of the pattern, even though you have *9, 21,* or *51 points* selected. The sensor you can see in the viewfinder is providing the primary autofocus, but the surrounding sensors (in the pattern you've selected in *Custom setting a3*) are also active.

If the subject moves and the primary AF sensor loses its focus, one of the surrounding sensors will grab the focus quickly.

If the subject is moving slowly or predictably, then you can use a smaller pattern, such as the *9 points* selection in *Custom setting a3*. If the subject's movement is more erratic or unpredictable, then you might want to increase the number of AF sensors involved. If nine won't do it, try 21, and finally even 51 for subjects that are very unpredictable and move quickly.

Can you see how flexible the *Dynamic-area AF* mode is, especially when adjusting the patterns in *Custom setting a3*? If your subject will only move a short distance (or slowly), you can simply select a pattern of nine points. Maybe you're doing some macro shots of a bee on a flower and it is moving around the flower. Or, you might be photographing a tennis game and use 21 points to allow for more rapid side-to-side movement without losing the focus. You'll have to decide which pattern

Figure 7 – Three *Dynamic-area AF* sensor patterns (left to right) – 9, 21, 51

Figure 8 – *Custom setting a3 – Dynamic AF area* screens

**3**

best fits your needs for the current shooting situation.

We'll talk more about the 9, 21, and 51 points later in this chapter, and we'll even discuss another pattern called *51 points (3D-Tracking)*, which allows your D700 to pay attention to the color of the subject to improve tracking accuracy with some subjects.

We'll also examine *Custom setting a4* later in the chapter. This setting allows you to

### Capture a Bird in Flight

Let's imagine that you are photographing a bird perched in a tree, but you want some shots of it in flight. You are patiently waiting for it to fly. You have *Dynamic-area AF* selected with all 51 points active, so that autofocus never fully locks and will track the bird instantly when it starts flying. You've already established focus with the sensor you selected using the Multi Selector, and are holding the shutter release half way down to maintain focus. You've also previously set the release mode to *CH (Continuous High)* so that you can fire off rapid bursts of images (up to five per second). Suddenly, and faster than you can react, the bird takes to flight. By the time you can get the camera moving, the bird has moved to the left in the viewfinder, and the focus tracking system has reacted by instantly switching away from the primary sensor you established focus with, and is now using other AF sensors in the pattern of 51 to maintain focus on the bird. You press the shutter release all the way down, and the images start pouring into your CF card. You are panning with the bird, firing bursts, until it moves out of range. You've got the shot!

enable *Focus Tracking with Lock-On*, which affects what happens if something briefly gets between your camera and subject while you're following the subject with your D700.

### Auto-Area AF

This mode turns the D700 into an expensive point-and-shoot camera. Use this mode when

> **Main Point**
>
> Using *Dynamic-area AF* and *Custom setting a3*, you can more accurately track and photograph all sorts, sizes, and speeds of moving subjects.

you simply have no time to think but would still like to get great images. The AF Module decides what the subject is and selects the AF sensors it thinks work best. In *figure 9* is a picture of the *AF-area Mode Selector* switch with *Auto-area AF* selected.

If you are using *Single-servo AF (S)*, you'll have an idea what is going to be in focus, because the AF sensors in use will flash on the screen in red, and then turn black for a period of one second. If, however, you are using *Continuous-servo AF (C)* nothing, will appear on the viewfinder screen to give you a clue of what is going to be in focus. In *Continuous-servo AF (C)*, your camera is operating like a very expensive Nikon Coolpix point-and-shoot!

According to Nikon, if you are using a D or G lens, there is a bit of "human recognition technology" built into this mode, similar to the Coolpix. Since most of us will only be using *Auto-area AF* when we want to shoot for fun, a human subject that is closest to the camera is the most likely subject anyway. Your D700, using *Continuous-servo AF (C)*, can usually detect a human and help you avoid shots with

Figure 9 – *AF-area Mode Selector* switch set to *Auto-area AF*

Figure 10 – *Release Mode* dial on *CH*, with its *Lock release* button at the upper left

perfectly focused backgrounds and blurry human subjects.

We've covered the *Focus* and *AF-area* modes pretty well, so now we move on to the *Release* modes.

## Release Modes in Detail

The D700 has several *Release* modes, which decide how many images can be taken, and how fast. In *figure 10*, we see the *Release Mode* dial with its *Lock release* button (press the lock button, turn the dial).

Here is a look at each *Release* mode in more detail:

- *S* – Single Frame
- *CL* – Continuous low speed
- *CH* – Continuous high speed
- *LV* – Live View
- Self-timer
- *MUP* – Mirror Up

In the good-old-film days, some of the *Release* modes would have been called "Motor-Drive" settings, since those modes are concerned with how fast the camera is allowed to take pictures.

We've already talked about these modes to some degree in the consideration of the *AF-area* modes.

### Single Frame (S) Mode

This is the simplest frame rate since it takes a single picture each time you depress the shutter release fully. No speed here. This is for shooting a few frames at a time. Nature shooters will often use this mode since they are more concerned with correct depth of field, and precise composition.

### Continuous Low Speed (CL) Mode

This mode allows you to select an image taking between one frame per second and five frames per second (FPS). If you have an MB-D10 Battery Pack mounted on your D700, you can also select seven FPS. The camera cannot shoot over five FPS without the MB-D10 Battery Pack, although it will allow you to select seven FPS. The default frame rate from the factory is three FPS, which seems about right for most of us. If you want more or less speed, simply adjust *Custom setting d4* (see D700 User's Manual page 299) and select your favorite frame speed.

### Continuous High Speed (CH) Mode

This high-speed mode is designed for when you want to go fast always! The camera will attempt to capture five frames per second every time you hold the shutter-release button down. The manual states "up to" five FPS as the default without the MB-D10 Battery Pack mounted and eight FPS when you do have the battery pack on your camera. So, if you're a high FPS junkie, buy the battery pack!

### Requirements for Fast Frame Rates

All of the settings for fast frame rates (high FPS) are based on the assumption that you are shooting at least ¹⁄₂₅₀ of a second shutter speed, have a fully charged battery, and have some buffer space left in your camera's memory.

### Live View (LV) Mode

This was a brand new mode with the release of the D3 and D300 cameras, and the D3X and D700 offer the feature as well. Normally, one would not use the Monitor LCD to compose an image since this is not as stable as holding the camera close to your body and could result in shaky images.

However, in some instances a live view through the Monitor LCD is quite useful. For instance, what if you want to take an image of a small flower growing very close to the ground? You could just lie down on the

ground and get your clothes dirty, or you can use LV mode instead. LV mode allows you to see what your camera's lens sees, without using the viewfinder.

Anytime you need to take pictures high or low, or even on a tripod, the D700 will happily give you that power with its new LV mode. Let's look at some camera screenshots for setting Live View on your camera. First, you'll use your camera's *Release mode* lock button and dial (top left when viewed from the rear) to set the LV mode. The LV icon is to the right of the CL and CH mode icons.

Then, you'll need to set the *Shooting Menu's Live View* selection to *Hand-held* or *Tripod* (defaults to *Hand-held*). Finally, you'll set the *Release* mode for *Single frame, Continuous low-speed,* or *Continuous high-speed* using the selection screens. You normally would use the *Release mode* dial to do that, but since it is already set to LV mode, you'll have to use the shooting menus instead.

Figure 11 – *Release mode* dial at *LV,* and *Live View* menu settings

*Figure 11* shows the *Release mode* dial and the screens involved in the process.

Here are the steps to use the Live View mode after you've set the LV setting on the *Release mode* dial and configured the selection screens:

### LV Hand-Held Mode

1. Point your camera toward your subject.
2. Press the shutter release halfway down to activate Autofocus. The Monitor LCD will not come on yet. Give the camera just a moment to focus. This saves time later!
3. Raise the mirror by fully pressing the shutter-release button.
4. The Monitor LCD now comes on, so you can compose the picture.
5. Press the shutter release fully again. The mirror will drop, Autofocus will reactivate, and the shutter will fire. If you don't fully press the shutter release, but go only halfway, the mirror will drop and Autofocus will reactivate, but no picture will be taken, which is a good way to refocus if your subject has moved. (This can take a second or so in lower light levels.)
6. Repeat as necessary. Be sure to set the camera back to normal viewfinder mode using the *Release mode* lock and dial when you are done with Live View.

### LV Tripod Mode

(Uses contrast-detection AF instead of normal phase-detection AF)

1. Frame your image in the viewfinder and press the *AF-ON* button to initiate Autofocus. The shutter release will *not* cause AF to happen in *Tripod* mode. You must use the *AF-ON* button.
2. Press the shutter-release button fully to raise the mirror.
3. The Monitor LCD now comes on, so you can compose the picture.

4. Use the normal zoom button to enlarge the image enough that you can see how well the focus looks. (The zoom button looks like a magnifying glass with a plus sign in it. It's right above the *OK* button, on the lower-left of the Monitor LCD.)
5. Press the *AF-ON* button to top off the focus. This can take some time (especially in low light) since it is using contrast detection to find the best focus. You will see the image on the monitor focus before and past correct focus and then finally settle on the correct focus. Be patient!
6. Without moving the camera, press the shutter-release button fully to take the image. (The mirror will go up and down twice to take the picture. It sounds entirely weird but it works!) The D700 really should be on a tripod to make the *Tripod* mode work successfully.

In *Hand-held* mode, I've learned to lightly press the shutter release halfway down so that AF can function while the mirror is briefly down. It can take a moment to refocus, but once I feel sure that the camera is fully focused, I'll press the shutter-release button all the way down to take the picture. The Monitor LCD is nice and big, so you can see focus detail pretty well. So far, it seems to be

### Consider It a Tripod "Only" Mode

Don't look at the Live View mode as a replacement for a Coolpix shooter. It has speed limitations that makes the best of the Coolpix cameras seem like speed demons in comparison. In *Hand-held LV* mode, it's not too bad. However, *Tripod* mode should really be considered a tripod-only mode, or you probably won't get pictures in focus. Contrast-Detection AF is painfully slow, but gets the job done, eventually.

3

fine and actually usable. Hats off to Nikon on this one. Pretty cool!

### Self-Timer Mode

The factory default time-out on the self-timer is 10 seconds. You can configure *Custom setting c3* to set 2, 5, 10, or 20 seconds. (See page 297 in your D700 User's Manual.)

If you like to hear that little "beep beep beep" when it is counting down the seconds to firing the shutter, you can control that sound with *Custom setting d1*, by selecting *High*, *Low*, or *Off*. If either a *High* or *Low* beep is selected, a small musical note will appear in the top-right of the Control Panel LCD on the camera's top. (See page 298 in your D700 User's Manual.)

Here are the three steps to use the self-timer after it has been configured (or left on factory defaults):

1. Use the *Release mode* lock and dial to select *Self-timer* mode. That's the little symbol between *LV* mode and *MUP* mode.
2. Frame the photograph and focus the camera. If *Focus Priority* is selected, you will not be able to start the self-timer unless the little round green focus light is on in the viewfinder.

### Tips on Stopping the Self-Timer

If you want to stop the self-timer, all you have to do is raise the flash. If the flash is already raised, just lower it and raise it again. Or, you could just turn the camera off. (Of course, that's like turning off your home computer while the operating system is busy with some task, and will probably result in your compact flash card bursting into flames, your lens elements unseating, or some other ugly thing happening. I think I'll just raise, or lower and raise, the flash instead!)

3. Press the shutter-release button all the way down and run like the wind for your position in the group. (Or, if you are using the self-timer as a cheap cable release, just stand there looking cool instead.) The AF-Assist light will blink once per second, and the beeping will start too. The last two seconds arrive and the AF-Assist light stops blinking, while the beeping doubles in speed. You are out of time once the beep gets fast! The image is taken about the time the beeping stops.

### Mirror Up (MUP) Mode

This mode is very simple and very effective. I use this constantly when I am doing nature photography. Instead of having to find a lever to press, as on the older film cameras, all you have to do to use *MUP* mode are follow these simple steps:

1. Use the *Release mode* lock and dial to select *MUP* mode. It's past the *CL*, *CH*, *LV*, and self-timer settings on the *Release mode* dial.
2. Frame your picture, focus, and press the shutter release the rest of the way down to raise the mirror.
3. Press the shutter release again fully to take the picture.

For a complete consideration of *Custom settings a1* to *a10*, please see chapter 6 "Custom Setting Menus".

It is very important that you read the information in chapter 6 concerning *Custom settings a1* and *a2*, especially the section called "Special Section on the Usage of *a1* and *a2*". If you do not read and understand this special section, you may get quite a few out-of-focus images as a result.

### Don't Touch That Shutter Release!

Please buy yourself an electronic shutter release cable so that you're not using your finger to press the shutter release when on a tripod and in *MUP* mode. Touching the camera seems a bit silly after going to all that trouble to stabilize the camera and raise the mirror. A finger press could shake the entire tripod! If you do not have an electronic cable release, simply wait for 30 seconds after raising the mirror and the camera will fire on its own. It has a built-in 30-second delay, after you've raised the mirror, then the shutter will fire. This could be used as a slow but high-quality self-timer.

## My Conclusions

I've followed the development of the Nikon autofocus systems since back in the late 1980s. My first camera with autofocus was the Nikon F4 professional film SLR. Down through the last 20 years I've experienced each new level of autofocus released by Nikon. It's gotten better and better with each new generation!

In the digital bodies, the first-generation D100 set new standards followed by the second-generation D200. With the generation of the D700, my reaction has been "Wow!"

This is a powerful leap forward. Autofocus with the D700 is a real pleasure. Nikon has really learned how to make excellent technology. The D700 has a more powerful AF system than most cameras before it and yet is somewhat simplified in its operation in comparison.

The system can still come across as complex, but if you spend some time with this chapter, you should come away with a much greater understanding of the D700's AF Module. You'll better understand how you can adapt your camera to work best for your style of photography.

Enjoy your D700's excellent Multi-CAM 3500FX autofocus system!

# White Balance

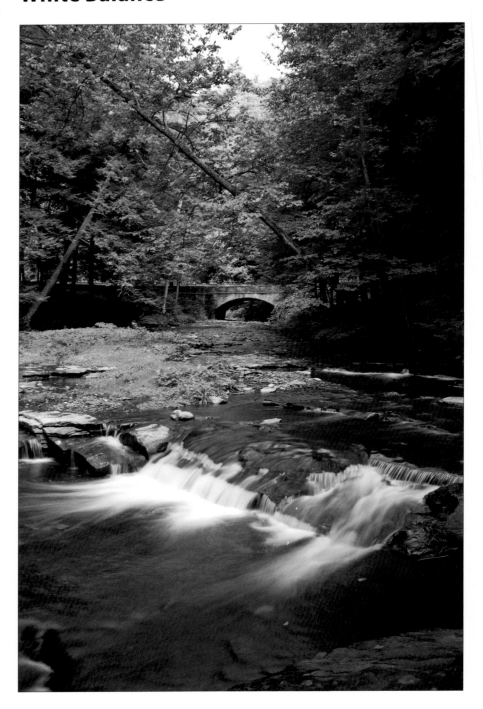

Back in the "good old days" we'd buy special rolls of film or filters to meet the challenges of color casts that came from indoor lighting, overcast days, or special situations.

The D700's method for balancing the camera to the available light comes with the *White balance* (WB) controls.

## How Does White Balance (WB) Work?

Normally the WB is used to adjust the camera so that whites are truly white and other colors are accurate under whatever light source you are shooting. You can also use the *White balance* controls to deliberately introduce color casts into your image for interesting special effects.

Camera WB color temperatures are exactly backwards from the Kelvin scale we learned in school for star temperatures. Remember that a red giant star is "cool" while a blue/white star is "hot". The WB color temperatures are backwards because the WB system is adding color to make up for a deficit of color in the original light of the subject.

For instance, under a fluorescent light, there is a deficit of blue, which makes the image appear greenish yellow. When you add blue, the image is balanced to a more normal appearance.

Another example might be shooting on a cloudy, overcast day. The ambient light could cause the image to look bluish if left unadjusted. The WB control in your camera sees the "cool" color temperature and adds some red to "warm" the colors a bit. Normal camera WB on a cloudy, overcast day might be about 6,000K.

Just remember that we use the real Kelvin temperature range in reverse: warm colors are considered reddish while blue colors are cool. Even though this is backwards from what we were taught in school, it fits our situation better. Blue seems cool while red seems warm to photographers! Just don't let your astronomer friends convince you otherwise.

> **Main Point**
>
> Understanding white balance in a fundamental way is simply realizing that light has a range of colors that go from cool to warm. We can adjust our cameras to use the available light in an accurate and neutral "balanced" way that compensates for the actual light source or allows a color cast to enter the image by unbalancing the settings.

We will discuss this from the standpoint of the D700's camera controls and how they deal with WB.

## Color Temperature

The D700 WB range can vary from a very cool 2,500K to a very warm 10,000K. (See pages 139–158 in your D700 User's Manual for more details. )

Figure 1 – Same image with different white balance settings

In *figure 1* is the same picture adjusted in Photoshop to three WB settings manually with the use of Photo Filters. Notice how the image in the center is about right while the same shots to the left and right are bluer (cooler) or warmer (more of an orange cast).

As mentioned before, the same adjustments we made with film and filters can now be achieved with the hard-coded white balance settings built into the D700.

To achieve the same effect as daylight film and a warming filter, simply select the *Cloudy* white balance setting while shooting in normal daylight. This sets the D700 to balance at about 6,000K, which makes nice warm-looking images. If you want to really warm the image up, set the controls to *Shade*, which sets the camera to 8,000K.

On the other hand, if you want to make the image appear cool or bluish, try using the *Fluorescent* (4,200K) or *Incandescent* (3,000K) settings in normal daylight.

Remember, the color temperature shifts from "cool" values to "warm" values. The D700 can record your images with any color temperature from 2,500K (very cool or bluish) to 10,000K (very warm or reddish), and any major value in between. There's no need to carry different film emulsions or filters to deal with light color range. The D700 has very easy-to-use color temperature controls and a full range of color temperatures available.

Following are two separate methods of setting the WB on the D700:

1. Manual WB using the WB button and selecting options.
2. Manual WB using the Monitor LCD's *Shooting Menu* and selecting options.

We'll consider each of these methods since you may prefer to use different methods according to the time you have to shoot and the color accuracy you want. Most critical photographers will use method number two; the PRE measurement method.

## Method 1 – Manual White Balance Using the WB Button

Sometimes we might simply want to control the WB in a totally manual way. This method and the next are basically the same thing, only one is set using a button and dial and the other by menu changes.

Each of these methods will allow you to set a particular WB temperature. If you want your image to appear cool, medium, or warm, you can set the appropriate color temperature and take the picture; then look at the image on the Monitor LCD. In *figure 2*, we see the external camera controls used to adjust WB.

### Manually Selecting a Color Temperature Between 2,500 and 10,000K

The *K*, or *Choose Color Temp,* selection is a flexible one that allows you to select a WB value manually between 2,500 K and 10,000 K. Once you have selected the *K* symbol by holding down the *WB* button and

Figure 2 – White balance external controls: *WB* button (top); *Main command* dial (rear); *Sub-command* dial (front)

## WB Button

Here is how to manually choose a WB color temperature value using the WB button, the *Main command* dial, and the Control Panel LCD:

1. Press and hold the WB button on the top left of your D700 (see *figure 2*).
2. Rotate the *Main command* dial. Each click of the dial will change the display to one of the symbols in the chart below. They'll appear in sequence on the Control Panel LCD. (See pages 140–142 of the D700 User's Manual.) These symbols, options, and their Kelvin values are as follows:

 AUTO   Auto White Balance: 3,500–8,000K

   Incandescent: 3,000K

   Fluorescent: 4,200K

   Direct Sunlight: 5,200K

   Flash: 5,400K

   Cloudy: 6,000K

   Shade: 8,000K

 **K**   K: Choose your own color temperature from 2,500 to 10,000K.

**PRE**   PRE: Use to measure WB for the actual ambient light. If no measurement is taken, the value used is whatever was last stored in camera memory location *d-0*.

rotating the *Main command* dial; you rotate the *Sub-command* dial to select the actual WB temperature you desire.

### Measuring Actual Ambient Light and Using *PRE* (PrE)

This method allows you to measure ambient light values and set the camera's WB. It's not hard to learn and is very accurate since it's an actual through-the-lens measurement of the Kelvin temperature of the source light. (See pages 148–153 of the D700 User's Manual.) You'll need a white or gray card to accomplish this measurement. *Figure 3* shows the popular WhiBal pocket card, which is a product of PictureFlow LLC and is available exclusively from **RawWorkflow.com**.

Figure 3 – The WhiBal pocket card in its case

How to select the PrE white balance measurement method:

1. Press and hold the *WB* button.
2. Rotate the *Main command* dial until PrE shows in the lower right of the Control Panel LCD. You'll also see *d-0* in the top-left corner of the Control Panel LCD, unless you have previously stored a WB value.
3. Release the *WB* button.
4. Press and hold the *WB* button again until the PrE starts flashing.
5. Point the camera at a white or neutral gray card in the light source in which you will be taking pictures. It does not have to focus

on the card; it can just be pointed at it so that it fills the frame.

6. Press the shutter release fully as if you were photographing the white card. It will fire the shutter, but nothing will appear on the Monitor LCD.

7. Check the Control Panel LCD on top and see if *GOOD* is flashing. If you see *No Gd* flashing (instead of *GOOD*), then the operation was *not* successful. Your available light may not be bright enough to take an accurate reading.

The PrE measurement is very sensitive because it is using the light coming through the lens to set the WB. Unless you are measuring in an extremely low light level it will virtually always be successful.

In step 2 above, I mention *d-0* in the top-left corner of the Control Panel LCD during a WB measurement. This *d-0* is where the current WB value is stored. The other memory locations, *d-1* to *d-4*, are four locations that you can use to store WB values you regularly use. Later you can copy a value stored in *d-1* to *d-4* back into *d-0*.

### Storing White Balance Values for Future Use

If you have previously used the manual "measured" PRE method to set the WB, you will have a value already in WB memory location *d-0*. You can keep up to five WB values stored in your D700. In *d-0* you'll find the current "PRE" WB, and in *d-1* through *d-4* you'll find any stored WB values. They appear as tiny images, as shown in *figure 4*.

If you shoot under a certain light source on a frequent basis, such as in a studio, you may want to store one or more of your PRE set white balance values in one of the four permanent storage areas in your camera (*d-1 to d-4*).

Figure 4 – The *PRE* screen

I tried to do a white balance measurement directly into *d-1* to *d-4* by selecting one of the memory locations before doing the light measurement. However, my values did not show up in *d-1* to *d-4*, but instead overwrote the value in *d-0* each time. It is only possible to *copy* a value from *d-0* into one of the other four storage locations. I suppose Nikon was concerned that one might accidentally overwrite a carefully prepared white balance setting, so they added a copy step between the measurement and long-term storage.

In effect, you may have up to five white balance values stored in your camera. One is the current temporary setting, and the other four are in memory for longer term reuse. In *figure 5* are the steps and shooting menus used to copy the current white balance value in memory location *d-0* to one of the other four areas (*d-1 to d-4*). You'll see a visual representation—a tiny picture—of the stored WB values. If there is nothing stored in *d-1* through *d-4*, there will only be a blank spot above the number.

### Saving a Current WB Reading to Memory Locations *d-1* to *d-4*:

1. Use *Method 1* to obtain a *GOOD* PRE white balance reading. It will automatically be placed in memory location *d-0*.

Figure 5 – Screens to access *d-0* through *d-4*

2. Use the screens shown in *figure 5* to find the current *d-0* value.
3. Select a blank memory location (*d-1* to *d-4*), or one that you want to overwrite, and press the Multi Selector's center button (*figure 6*).
4. Select the menu selection *Copy d-0*, and press the *OK* button. You'll then see that *d-0* has written a copy of itself into the memory location you selected.
5. *Optional*: As shown in *figure 7*, rename the memory location that you just stored by selecting it with the Multi Selector's center button and then selecting *Edit*

*comment* from the menu. Change the name of the memory location to something that will remind you of its use, if you'd like.

When you have the character-selection panel open (see *figure 7*), use the Multi Selector to navigate between letters and numbers; then press the Multi Selector's center button to add the character to the name. To scroll through characters already in the new name, hold the *Checkered Thumbnail* button on the left of the Monitor LCD while navigating to the left or right with the Multi Selector. Press the *Delete* button (garbage can on top left of camera) to

Figure 6 – Select a memory location *d-1* to *d-4*, then copy *d-0* to it

Figure 7 – Renaming a memory location by using *Edit comment*

delete the current character. Press the *OK* button to save the memory location name.

### Using the Values Stored in Memory Locations *d-0* to *d-4*

Once you've written a WB value to one of the memory locations *d-1* to *d-4*, it will remain there for future use as needed. You can access any of the saved WB values by selecting PRE with the WB button, then rotating the front *Sub-command* dial until you find the one you want (*d-0* to *d-4*). Also, you can use the menus to directly select the named memory location (see *figure 5*).

### Storing and Selecting the White Balance from a Previously Captured Image

It is also possible to select a white balance value from an image you have already successfully taken. This image's value can be applied to the image you are about to take, or the value can be copied to *d-1* through *d-4* (using the method described previously) for later use.

Here are the steps and shooting screens to recover the white balance from an image already taken and stored on your Compact Flash (CF) memory card (*figure 8*):

1. Use the shooting menu screens shown in *figure 5* to get to the *d-0* through *d-4* memory location screen.
2. Use the Multi Selector to select the memory location you want to set with the value from an image. You must select *d-1* through *d-4* only. You can't use *d-0* for this operation. Press the Multi Selector's center button to select the memory location you want to replace.
3. As shown in *figure 8*, screen 2, scroll down and choose *Select image*. It will be grayed out if there are no images on your current CF card.
4. Scroll to the right on *Select image* and you'll see the image selection screen, as shown in *figure 8*, screen 3.
5. Navigate through the available images until you find the one you want to use for white balance information.

Figure 8 – Screens to recover a white balance setting from an image

6. Press the Multi Selector's center button and a small picture of the image will show under the selected white balance memory location (*d-1* to *d-4*).

## Method 2 – **Manual White Balance Using the Monitor LCD's Shooting Menu**

This method is similar to *Method 1*, but it uses camera *Shooting Menu* screens to select the Kelvin range. Instead of using the WB button and *Sub-command* dial, you'll open up your menus and set the color temperature by selecting from them.

In *figure 9* are the steps to set the WB selection using your D700's *Shooting Menu*.

Normally you will use only the first two screens to set one of the "preset" WB values such as *Cloudy*, *Shade*, or *Direct sunlight*, and then you'll just press the *OK* button for the final screen, without changing anything. *Figure 9* uses *Direct sunlight* as an example.

Note that the *Fluorescent* selection provides for choosing one of seven different light sources, covering a wide spectrum.

If you choose to fine-tune any of the color temperature settings after you have selected one of the preset WB values, the last menu screen in *figure 9* allows you to do so by "mired" clicks. Each scrolling press of the Multi Selector is equal to 5 mired in each of the four color directions. Up is green (*G*),

down is magenta (*M*), left is blue (*B*), right is amber (*A*).

If you aren't familiar with adjusting the preset's default color temperature, or don't want to change it (most won't), then simply press the *OK* button without moving the little square from the center. If you've accidentally moved it, simply move it back with the Multi Selector until it's in the middle again, then press *OK*. That will select the preset WB value you wanted to use, without modifying its default value. (Example default value is *Flash* at 5,400K.)

In review, the steps to set the preset you want to use are as follows (see *figure 9*):

1. Select *White balance* from the *Shooting Menu*, and then scroll right to the next screen.

2. Select one of the preset values, such as *Flash* or *Cloudy*, and then scroll right to the next screen.

3. Press *OK* immediately, without moving the little square from its center position.

That is all there is to selecting a preset from within the menu system. The only difference by doing it this way is that you can fine-tune the color temperature values in the third screen of *figure 9*. I normally do not use *Method 2*, since *Method 1* allows me to select a preset WB value without accidentally modifying the settings of its default color temperature and doesn't require me to use the menus.

I find that *Method 1* is much faster, since I am using external camera controls, and it

Figure 9 – Menu screens to set *White balance* via camera menus

takes only seconds to set the values, or even do a PRE reading of ambient light.

## White Balance Bracketing

You can also do WB bracketing in a way similar to flash or exposure bracketing. If you want to use bracketing, you must change *Custom setting e5* from *AE & flash* to *WB bracketing*. This means that flash or

### Customizing Your White Balance

If you feel that one of the D700's preset values is not exactly what you would like it to be, you can experiment with the color temperature values for that preset by adjusting it along the horizontal or vertical color directions. (See pages 143–145 in your D700 User's Manual for more information.)

exposure bracketing will not work during the time that e5 is set to *WB bracketing*.

Personally, I prefer to use RAW mode and make minor or major adjustments in the computer post-processing stage of the image's preparation. However, you may want to use WB bracketing, so let's consider it.

WB bracketing works similarly to exposure bracketing (see User's Manual pages 135–138). *WB bracketing does not work when your camera is in RAW mode!*

In *figure 10* we see the controls and menus used to set up WB bracketing.

Here are the steps to set it up:

1. Set *Custom setting e5* to *WB bracketing* (see *figure 10*, and User's Manual page123).
2. As shown in *figure 10*, choose the number of shots in the bracket by pressing and holding the function (*Fn*) button on the right front of the D700, and turning the *Main command* dial to select the number

Figure 10 – *Fn* button, *Main command* dial, *Sub-command* dial, and *Custom setting e5* screen of shots in the bracket. (Look for the WB-BKT symbols to appear on the Control Panel LCD, along with lines below the +/– scale to show the number of shots you've selected, up to nine shots total.)

3. Select the WB color temperature increment by pressing and holding the function (*Fn*) button and rotating the *Sub-command* dial. Choose 1, 2, or 3. (1=5 mired, 2=10 mired, 3=15 mired.) The D700 will expose the sequence of shots over and under according to what you've selected in step 2. You can only adjust the bracket along the blue (*B*) to amber (*A*) values (cool to warm). The shots to the + side are toward blue, and to the negative side toward amber.

4. Take the WB bracketed picture series. Be sure to set your D700 back to normal bracketing in *Custom setting e5* when you're done.

## AUTO White Balance

*Auto* WB works pretty well in the D700. As the camera's RGB meter senses colors, it does its best to balance to any white or mid-range grays it can find in the image. However, the color will vary a little on each shot. If you shoot only in *Auto* WB mode, your camera considers each image a new WB problem and solves it without reference to the last image taken. Therefore, you may see a variance in the color balance of each image with *Auto* WB.

The *Auto* WB setting also has the fine-tuning screen mentioned in *Method 2* earlier. When you select *AUTO* in the *Shooting Menu*, you can toggle to the next screen and fine-tune the colors. I don't see how that is particularly useful since each image is likely to have slightly different color temperatures to deal with, which would mean the fine-tuning

would have little value for more than an image or two. If you were shooting in the exact same light for a period of time, I suppose the fine-tuning would be useful; however, wouldn't it make more sense to do a PRE reading of the light for exact WB? This choice will depend on your shooting style and personal preferences.

## Should I Worry about White Balance if I Shoot in RAW Mode?

The quick answer is no, but it may not be the best answer. When you take a picture using RAW mode (creating .NEF files) the sensor image data has no WB, sharpening, or color

### My Opinion about Auto WB

If you are concerned with a series of images having the same color settings so that they look similar and require no extra post-processing, it is best to actually adjust the WB to one of the preset or measured values. Then, each image taken will have the same color balance. *Auto* WB takes control of the image away from you! The D700 is very good at *Auto* WB, but I still shoot at a predefined WB setting most of the time. Call me old-fashioned!

If I'm at a party, shooting images of friends for small snapshot prints, I'll often put my camera in *Auto* WB and Program (*P*) exposure mode. Then, I'll just take lots of pictures without worrying about a thing. However, if I'm shooting for commercial reasons, or if I'm concerned with maximum image quality, I use a gray or white card and balance my camera to the available light. I only rebalance if the light source changes. Use *Auto* WB for when you are not overly concerned about absolutely correct WB. It'll be close enough for average use and will return great images most of the time.

saturation information applied. Instead, the information about your camera settings is stored as "markers" along with the RAW black-and-white sensor data. Color information is only applied permanently to the image when you postprocess and save the image in another format, like JPG, TIF, or EPS.

When you open the image in Nikon Capture, or another RAW conversion program, the camera settings are applied to the sensor data in a temporary way so that you can view the image on your computer screen. If you don't like the color balance or any other setting you used in-camera, you simply change it in the conversion software and the image looks as if you used the new settings originally when you took the picture.

Does that mean I am not concerned about my WB settings, since I shoot RAW most of the time? No. The human brain can quickly adjust to an image's colors and perceive them as normal, even when they are not. That is one of the dangers of not using correct WB. Since an unbalanced image on-screen is not compared to another correctly balanced image side by side, there is a danger that your brain may accept the slightly incorrect camera settings as normal and your image will be saved with a color cast.

As a rule of thumb, if you use your WB correctly at all times, you'll consistently produce better images. You'll do less post-processing if the WB is correct in the first place. As RAW shooters, we already have a lot of post-processing work to do on our images. Why add WB corrections to the work flow? It's just more work, if you ask me!

Additionally, you might decide to switch to JPEG mode in the middle of a shoot, and if you are not accustomed to using your WB

controls, you will be in trouble. When you shoot JPEGs, your camera will apply the WB information directly to the image and save it on your card...permanently. Be safe; always use good WB technique!

## White Balance Tips and Tricks

*Tips for using a white/gray card:* When measuring WB with a gray or white card, keep in mind that your camera does not need to focus on the card. In PRE mode, it will not focus anyway, since it is only trying to read light values, not take a picture. The important thing is to put your lens close enough to the card to prevent it from seeing anything other than the card. Three or four inches (about 75 mm–100 mm) away from the card is about right for most lenses.

Also, be careful that the source light is not casting a shadow from the lens onto the card in a way that lets your lens see some of the shadow. This will make the measurement less accurate. Also, be sure that your source light does not make a glare on the card, which is a little harder to do since the card has a matte surface, but it still can be done. You may want to hold the card at a slight angle to the source light if it is particularly bright and might cause glare.

Finally, when the light is dim, use the white side of the card since it has more reflectivity. This may prevent a *No Gd* reading in low light. The gray card may be more accurate for color balancing, but might be a little dark for a good measurement in dim light. If you are shooting in normal light, the gray card is best for balancing. You might want to experiment in normal light with your camera and see which you prefer.

## My Conclusions

Pages 139–158 of your D700's User's Manual have extensive WB information. With the simple tips we've covered and a little study of the manual, you can become a D700 WB expert. Learn to use the color temperature features of your camera to make superior images.

You'll be able to capture very accurate colors, or make pictures with color casts reflecting how you feel about the image. Practice a bit, and you'll find it easy to remember how to set your WB in the field.

# Shooting Menu Banks

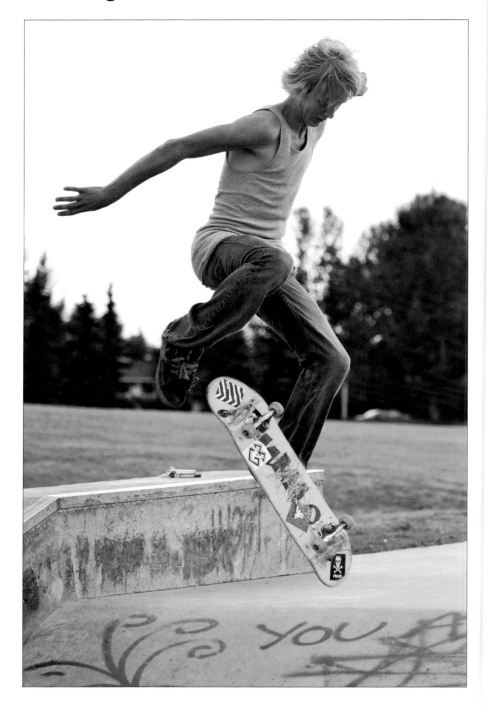

Using the four *Shooting Menu* banks, your D700 can change from a pro camera to a snap-shooter with just a few presses of the buttons.

This camera can shoot RAW files, using ISO 200, in Adobe RGB *Color space*, and with the *Fn* button assigned to *Spot metering* for serious professional shooting, and then can quickly change to good-quality JPEGs, at ISO 400, in sRGB *Color space*, and with high image sharpening for that party where you don't want to think about anything but having a good time. These are only two variations of the many available combinations of "bank" settings you can use.

The D700 has four *Shooting Menu* banks (and four *Custom Setting* banks that are covered in the next chapter). You can easily set the functionality of these banks, name them, and use them to quickly change the way your D700 behaves.

Why not get your D700 now and let's examine how to set the *Shooting Menu* banks. When you're done with this chapter, you'll be able to configure your D700 to be your own personal, multifunction camera.

The *Shooting Menu* banks allow you to set up functions such as file naming, image quality modes (RAW, JPEG, etc.), white balance, ISO, sharpening, and color space. You have a total of 20 separate menu items to configure in the *Shooting Menu*. Each bank can be configured with different settings and you can switch between the banks.

There are four default bank names—banks A, B, C, and D. You can rename any of these.

In this chapter, we'll assume that your camera banks have not yet been adjusted and that you are not entirely familiar with the process. Let's learn how to rename bank A to a more useful name and set its individual features. When you've done this once, you'll be ready to set your camera up for special uses and switch between them quickly.

## Setting Up Shooting Menu Bank A

Press the *MENU* button on the back of your D700, and use the Multi Selector to scroll to the left, then up or down until you find the *Shooting Menu* icon (looks like a small camera on the left of the menus). Now, use the Multi Selector to scroll to the right (which will select *Shooting Menu*), then scroll down to find the *Shooting menu bank* item.

Notice in the first screen of *figure 1* that there's a selection called *Shooting menu bank* with an *A* after it (unless it has been previously changed to a different bank, in which case it might be any letter *A* through *D*). This means that your D700 is using *Shooting menu bank A*. If any letter other than A is showing, you are in a different *Shooting menu bank*.

Let's set the D700's *Shooting menu bank* to *A* and add a bank name, so that you'll be able to see at a glance what this particular bank is set up to accomplish.

Scroll the Multi Selector to the right once. The screen will change to look like screen two of *figure 1*. Assuming that you have not yet renamed any of your *Shooting menu banks*,

Figure 1 – First three screens used to select and rename a *Shooting Menu* bank

you'll see the four default *Shooting menu banks* called *A, B, C, D,* and a selection called *ABC Rename*. Scroll down to *ABC Rename* and then scroll to the right. Your screen will now look like the third screen in *figure 1*. This is the bank *Rename* screen.

The factory default for an unnamed bank is simply a blank field. In other words, if you haven't yet named your banks, you'll simply see the big letter *A, B, C,* or *D,* followed by a blank field.

We'll rename our bank by selecting the top bank *A* and then scrolling to the right. The screen will now look like the menu screen in *figure 2*.

Figure 2 – Screen with characters for creating a *Shooting menu bank* name

Figure 2A – Camera controls for renaming *Shooting Menu* banks

You'll see a series of symbols, numbers, and letters on top, with a line of dashes at the bottom. The dashes are where we'll put our text we rename the bank. In the upper-left corner of the character area is a blank spot which represents a blank for insertion in the line of text. This space is good for separating words. If you scroll down past the uppercase letters, you'll find some lowercase letters too. I use "NEF Uncompressed" as the name for my bank A.

Below are a series of steps to use while creating the new bank name. Refer to *figure 2A* for the camera controls to use in renaming:

**Steps to input new characters:**

1. Use the Multi Selector to scroll through the numbers and letters to find the characters you want to use. Scroll down for lowercase letters.
2. Press the Multi Selector's center button to select a character. Keep selecting new characters until you have the entire new bank name in place.
3. If you make a mistake, hold down the *Checkered Thumbnail* button while using the Multi Selector to move to the position of the error. Push the garbage can (delete) button on the top-left of the back of the D700. The unwanted character will disappear.
4. Press the *OK* button to save the new name. Congratulations! You have named bank A to a more meaningful name so that you can identify it quickly.

Now, scroll the Multi Selector to the left until the *Shooting Menu* appears, or just press the *MENU* button to return to the start.

**Setting up Your Menu Bank**
You are now using bank A and now must set up the camera functionality for this bank. Using

the Multi Selector, scroll down and set each individual line item available under the *Shooting Menu*. They will each be saved as part of bank A, which we just renamed. Be sure to set, at least, the following:

- Image quality
- JPEG compression (if you are using JPEG mode)
- RAW compression (if you are using RAW mode)
- White balance
- ISO sensitivity
- Image sharpening
- Color space

These items are a subset of 20 items that can be set for each bank. These form the basis for how your D700 functions when you are using a particular bank. The ones listed here are the ones I personally consider most important. However, you should look at the complete list and consider which are most important to you.

Each bank can be completely configured with these items having different settings.

## Shooting Menu Banks

The *Shooting Menu* items *Multiple exposure* and *Interval timer shooting* affect all four *Shooting menu banks* at once. So, if you change either of these settings, they will affect all four banks (A–D) simultaneously. The other 18 settings affect only the bank your camera is currently using.

Your D700 can act like four different cameras because you can select four different banks, each having different settings.

When you have finished modifying the items that affect what type of shooting you will do with any bank, your D700 now has a certain "personality" for that bank. This facility gives you a very flexible camera.

On pages 269–279 of the D700 User's Manual, you will find extensive information on each of the 20 *Shooting Menu* items. We will briefly consider what each of these items does so that you can decide how to set your *Shooting menu bank A*. You can, of course, configure each of these same items in a completely different way using *Shooting menu banks B* through *D* and give each a different name to identify the special configuration.

## Shooting Menu's 20 Item Review

Having just discussed the *Shooting menu bank* item, let's move on to the remaining 19 configurable items in the *Shooting Menu* and discuss each one of them. Pay careful attention to the items that are essential to your style of shooting.

### Reset shooting menu
(User's Manual page 271)
Be careful with this selection. It does what it sounds like and resets the *Shooting Menu* for the currently selected bank back to factory default settings. Page 419 of the User's Manual

Figure 3 – *Reset shooting menu* screens

shows the default settings, in case you are interested.

This is a rather simple process. As seen in screen three of *figure 3*, simply scroll to *Yes* or *No* , then press the *OK* button or scroll to the right. That's about it. If you select *Yes*, the *Shooting menu bank* you're currently using will be reset to factory defaults.

### Active folder

(User's Manual pages 272–273)
The D700 defaults to creating a folder on your Compact Flash (CF) card with a name of 100ND700. This folder can contain up to 999 images. If you want to store images in separate folders on the current CF card, you might want to create a new folder, such as 102ND700 or 200ND700.

Each of these folders can hold 999 images and, using *Active folder*, you can select any one of these folders as the default folder. This is a way to isolate certain types of images on a photographic outing. Maybe you'll put landscapes in folder number 300ND700 and people shots in 400ND700. Whenever the D700 senses that the current folder contains 999 images, a new folder is created and named by incrementing the value in the first three digits of the current folder's name by one. Therefore, when manually creating folder names, you may want to leave room for the D700's dynamic folder creation and automatic naming.

As shown in *figure 4*, to create a new folder, scroll to the right when *Active folder* is selected. Now select *New folder number* by scrolling to the right. You'll now see a screen that allows you to create a new folder with a number from 100 through 999. Choose a number using the Multi Selector, then press the *OK* button when you are done.

You cannot create a folder numbered 000, or any other number less than 100. Remember that the three digit number you select will have ND700 appended to it and will finally look something like 101ND700 when you have finished.

Once you have created a new folder, you can select it for receiving images or, in other words, make it the current folder. Refer to screen one in *figure 5*, and scroll down to *Select folder*, then scroll right. You'll see the available folders displayed in a list that looks like screen two in *figure 5*.

Figure 4 – *Active folder* screens

Figure 5 – *Select folder* screens

Simply select the folder you want to use, and press the *OK* button. All images will now be saved to this folder until you change it to another. You can tell at a glance which folder is active by looking at screen one in *figure 4*. To the right of the words *Active folder*, you'll see the first three characters of the current folder. Folder number 101ND700 will display as *Active folder 101*.

If you are in folder 999ND700 and the camera records the 999th image (or if it records image number 9999), the shutter release will be disabled until you change to a different folder.

### File naming

(User's Manual page 274)
This feature allows you to change the first three letters of the image name for each of the images created by your camera. The camera defaults to using the following file naming conventions for your images (*figure 6*):

- sRGB color space:  DSC_1234
- Adobe RGB color space:  _DSC1234

According to which color space you are using, the D700 adds an underscore character to the end of the three DSC characters in sRGB or to the beginning in Adobe RGB, as shown above.

I use this feature on my Nikon D700 in a special way. Since the D700 can count its images in a *File number sequence* that continues from 0001 to 9999 (see *Custom setting d6*), I use *File naming* to help me classify my images in sequence. Here's how I do it.

When I first got my D700, I changed the three default characters from DSC to 1DY. The 1 is purely arbitrary, and DY are the initials of my name (you could certainly replace the DSC characters with your three initials), thereby helping me protect the copyright of my image in case it is ever stolen and misused. This allows me to use filenames 1DY0001 through 1DY9999 in the current folder, as long as there are no more than a total of 999 files in the folder.

Since the camera's *File number sequence* counter rolls back over to 0001 when you exceed 9999 images, there needs to be a way to keep from accidentally overwriting images from the first set of 9999 images you took. Fortunately, the D700 will create a new folder when the image number in the current folder is 9999 (or even when there are 999 images in the current folder).

### File Number Sequence

If *Custom setting d6* is set to *Off*, the D700 will start the *File number sequence* back over at 0001 each time you format your CF card. I verified that *Custom setting d6* was set to *On* as soon as I got my D700 so that it would remember the sequence. I want to know exactly how many images I've shot with this camera!

Figure 6 – *File naming* screens

If Nikon ever gives us just one extra digit in our image counting, this would be a moot point since we could count in sequences of just under 100,000 images, instead of 10,000 images. I suppose that many of us will have traded on up to the next Nikon DSLR before we reach enough images that this really becomes a constraint. On my Nikon D2X, which I've used for over four years, I am now about to break 30,000 images.

This is merely the way I'm utilizing this useful feature in the D700. If you don't want to add your initials, you could use the three characters to classify your image names in all sorts of creative ways.

To rename your three characters from DSC to a sequence of your choosing, please refer to *figure 6*. From the second screen of *figure 6*, scroll to the right until you see the third screen. This works just like the method for naming the *Shooting menu banks* discussed in the earlier section "Setting Up Shooting Menu Bank A", except that you only have uppercase characters and numbers from which to select.

**Steps to input new characters:**
1. Use the Multi Selector to scroll through the numbers and letters to find the characters you want to use.
2. Press the Multi Selector's center button to select a character.
3. To correct an error, hold down the *Checkered Thumbnail* button and use the Multi Selector to scroll. Use the garbage can *Delete* button to delete a character.
4. Press the *OK* button to save.

Now you've customized your camera so that the image names it creates reflects your personal needs.

*Image quality, Image size, Image area, JPEG compression, and NEF (RAW) recording*

(User's Manual pages 58–70)

This section outlines five items in the *Shooting Menu*. All five of these are related to how *Image quality* is set, so they must be discussed as a unit.

There are three camera controls we'll use to adjust the image quality parameter: the *QUAL*

Figure 7 – *QUAL* button (1), *Control Panel* LCD (2), and *Main command* dial (3)

button, *Main command* dial, and Control Panel LCD (*figure 7*).

The D700 supports the following image types:

- NEF (RAW) Uncompressed or Compressed (two types)
- TIFF (RGB)
- JPEG Fine, Normal, and Basic
- Combination of NEF and one of the three JPEG types at the same time (two images at once)

Let's look at each of these formats and see which you might want to use regularly. Following this section is a special supplement called "Notes on the Image Formats: RAW, TIFF, and JPEG". That special section will go beyond just how to turn the different formats on and off and discusses why you might want to use one particular format over another (*figure 8*).

## NEF (RAW) Format

This format stores raw image data directly to the camera's CF memory card. You must use conversion software, such as Nikon ViewNX or Capture NX 2, or a photo editing product such as Photoshop CS3 or CS4, to later change your Nikon Electronic Format (NEF) RAW file into a format like TIFF or JPEG. You may not be able to view NEF files directly on your computer unless you have the conversion software

installed. (Be aware that some older versions of these software products may not have been updated to support the NEF file format used in the D700.)

Some operating systems provide downloadable "patches" that let you at least view NEF files as small thumbnails. Before you go out shooting in NEF's RAW format, I recommend that you install your conversion software of choice so that you'll be able to view and adjust these images.

There are three NEF formats available:

- NEF (RAW) Lossless Compressed (20–40% size reduction)
- NEF (RAW) Uncompressed
- NEF (RAW) Compressed (40–55% size reduction)

***NEF (RAW) Lossless Compressed*** – The factory default for NEF (RAW) format is *NEF (RAW) Lossless Compressed*. According to Nikon, this compression will not affect image quality since it is a "reversible" compression algorithm. Since this lowers the stored file size by 20 to 40% with no data loss, it's a good one to consider.

To set your camera to *NEF (RAW) Lossless Compressed*, do the following:

1. Select *Image quality* from the *Shooting Menu* (*figure 8*).
2. Select *NEF (RAW)* from the list of formats (*figure 8*).

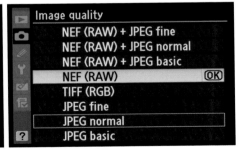

Figure 8 – Two *Shooting Menu* screens for setting *Image quality*

Figure 9 – *Shooting Menu* screens for setting *NEF (RAW) recording*

Once you have selected *NEF (RAW) recording*, you'll need to complete the following steps, referring to *figure 9*:

1. Scroll down to *NEF (RAW) recording* and then scroll right.
2. Select *Type* and scroll right.
3. Select *Lossless compressed* and press the *OK* button.

Your D700 is now in *NEF (RAW)* mode and is using lossless compression to save a lot of CF card and computer hard drive storage space. If you do not complete the steps shown in *figure 9*, your camera will probably still be using lossless compression, since that is the factory default for NEF (RAW).

**NEF (RAW) Compressed** – Before the newest generation of cameras, including the D700, this mode was known as "visually lossless". Compression is applied to the image, which reduces it by 40 to 55%, depending on the detail in the image. There is a small amount of data loss involved in this compression method. Most people won't be able to see the loss since it doesn't affect the image visually. I have never really seen any loss in my images. However, I've read that some have noticed slightly less highlight detail, so there may be a small amount of dynamic range loss toward the highlights.

Nikon says that this is a "nonreversible" compression, so once you've captured an image using this mode, it is permanently compressed, and any small amount of compression data loss is permanent. If this concerns you, then use the *Lossless compressed* method discussed earlier.

## Your CF Card's Storage Capacity

Why does my CF card's remaining image capacity seem to stay the same in NEF compressed modes as it is in uncompressed mode? Shouldn't it show lots more capacity in compressed modes since they make the image smaller by 20 to 55%? Good questions! The reason your D700 does not show any increased image capacity in the Control Panel LCD in compressed modes is because the D700 has no idea how well it will be able to compress a particular image. Images with large amounts of blank space (such as a sky) will compress much more efficiently than an image of a forest with lots of little leaves. The D700 shows a certain amount of image storage capacity in NEF (RAW) modes like the 320 images you can expect with an 8-gigabyte CF card. What you'll find is that, in the compressed modes, the D700 does not decrease the image capacity by one for each picture taken as it does in uncompressed mode. This means that the D700 will only decrease the number of available images every two or three shots, according to how well it could compress the images. When the card is filled up, it might have more than twice as many images stored as it initially reported that it could hold. Basically, your D700 deliberately under-reports storage capacity when you are shooting in either of the NEF (RAW) compressed modes.

It won't compress the image quite as much, at 20 to 40%, but it's guaranteed by Nikon to be a reversible compression that in no way affects the image.

*NEF (RAW) Uncompressed* – When I'm out shooting nature images, I use this mode exclusively. No compression is applied to the image. This mode provides the absolutely best image your camera can capture. The only drawback to this mode is that your images will be quite large to store. Each 14-bit image will be in the 25-megabyte range (or about 20 megabytes if you're using 12-bit color depth), so it will take larger storage media to contain your images in quantity.

In 14-bit color depth, shooting in FX-format, an 8-gigabyte CF card will hold about 310 images in this mode, so your D700 is not overly limited in image capacity while shooting. With hard drive prices dropping quickly, and even terabyte-sized hard drives becoming quite affordable, using the *Uncompressed* mode is not such a concern anymore. I use this mode, and shoot at 14-bit color depth, when I am very serious about my images, such as when I am out shooting premium stock. Maximum quality!

*NEF (RAW) Bit Depth* – When shooting in NEF (RAW) mode, the D700 has a special feature for those of us concerned about storing the maximum amount of color information.

The D700 has the ability to manage the bit depth, or number of colors per channel, stored in an image. The default is 12 bits, or 4,096 colors per RGB channel. Or, you can

switch it (as shown in *figure 10*) to 14 bits, or 16,384 colors per RGB channel. This is further explained in the short "Bit Depth Tutorial" following this section.

As mentioned above and as seen in *figure 10*, the D700 has the following two bit depths available:
- *12-bit*
- *14-bit*

Referring to *figure 10*, select one of the bit depth settings. I always use 14 bits because I want all the color my camera can capture, for the best pictures later. After reading the bit depth tutorial in the next section, you'll understand why I feel this way.

### 14-Bit Color Depth and Frame Rates

If you choose 14-bit, be aware that your camera's file sizes will be larger than they would have been in 12-bit—1.3 times larger for uncompressed RAW images, and slightly less for compressed RAW images. Lots more color information is being stored, after all. Unlike the D300, though, the D700 is capable of maintaining its high CH-mode frame rate, regardless of the bit depth setting.

### Bit Depth Tutorial

What does all the 8-bit, 12-bit, and 14-bit talk mean? In NEF (RAW), why would I change my camera to 14-bit depth instead of the default of 12-bit?

Figure 10 – *NEF (RAW) recording* screens for setting *NEF (RAW) bit depth*

Here is a short tutorial on bit depth and how it affects color storage in an image.

An image from your D700 is an RGB image. RGB stands for red, green, blue (R=red, G=green, B=blue). Each of the colors has its own "channel". There is a red channel, a green channel, and a blue channel.

If you are shooting in 12-bit mode, your D700 will record up to 4,096 colors for each channel. Therefore, there will be up to 4,096 different reds, 4,096 different greens, and 4,096 different blues. An extravaganza of color! In fact, almost 69,000,000,000 colors.

However, if you set your camera to 14-bit mode, instead of 4,096 different colors per channel, the camera can now store 16,384 different colors in each channel. Wow! That's quite a lot more color. Four times more for each color channel, to be exact, which totals almost 4,400,000,000,000 colors, or 64 times as many colors as 12-bit mode .

Is that important? Well, it can be, since the more color information you have available, the better for the image. I always use the 14-bit mode, now that I have it available. Later, that allows me to have smoother color changes, when a broad range of color is actually in the image.

Of course, once you save your image as a JPEG or TIFF, most of those colors are "compressed" or thrown away. Shooting in-camera as a TIFF or JPEG means that the D700 converts from a 12- or 14-bit RGB file down to an eight-bit file. An 8-bit file can only hold 256 different colors per RGB channel. So, there's a big difference in the number of colors stored in the image going from a RAW file to an in-camera JPEG or TIFF. That's why I always shoot in RAW, so that later I can make full use of all those potential extra colors.

If you shoot in RAW and later use an image editor such as Photoshop to save your image as a 16-bit TIFF file, you can store all the colors you originally captured. The D700

will not create a 16-bit TIFF. It is limited to an 8-bit TIFF. However, if you shoot RAW, and in 14-bit color depth, you can later save the file into the 16-bit TIFF and not lose any color information. 16-bit files can contain 65,536 different colors in each of the RGB channels. Many people save their files as 16-bit TIFFs during postprocessing of the RAW file. TIFF gives us a known and safe industry standard format that will fully contain all the image color information from a RAW file.

**JPEG Format**

As shown in *figure 11*, the D700 has three JPEG modes. Each of the modes affects the final quality of the image. Let's look at each mode in detail:

- *JPEG fine* (compression approximately 1:4)
- *JPEG normal* (compression approximately 1:8)
- *JPEG basic* (compression approximately 1:16)

Each of the JPEG modes provides a certain level of lossy image compression. The human

### ViewNX and Capture NX 2

Nikon ViewNX RAW conversion software is supplied free with the D700, while Nikon Capture NX 2 requires a separate purchase. Capture NX 2 has become my favorite conversion software, along with Adobe Photoshop. I use ViewNX to look at my images, since it has an excellent browser-type interface, and then push them to Capture NX 2 for final postprocessing. If I need to remove an ugly tree branch from the edge of an otherwise spotless image, or a blemish from a person's face, I'll use Photoshop's Clone and Healing tools.

eye compensates for small color changes quite well, so—for images intended for other than fine-art printing—the JPEG compression algorithm works efficiently enough. A useful thing about JPEG is that one can vary the file size of the image, via compression, without significantly reducing quality.

*JPEG fine* (or fine quality JPEG) uses a 1:4 compression ratio, so there is a large difference in the file size, with it being as small as 25% of the original size. In this mode, a normal 20 megabyte D700 file can be compressed down to as little as five megabytes, without significant loss of image quality. If you decide to shoot in JPEG, this mode will give you the best-quality JPEG your camera can produce. With *Image area* (which is covered very soon) set for *FX format*, where a *RAW Uncompressed* setting only allows 400 12-bit images on an 8-gigabyte CF card, the *JPEG fine* setting raises that to about 1,100 files when *JPEG compression* is set to *Size priority*. (If *Image area* is set for *DX format*, then 900 RAW uncompressed 12-bit images can be stored, or 2,500 JPEG fine images when *JPEG compression* is set to *Size priority*).

*JPEG normal* (or normal quality JPEG) uses a 1:8 compression ratio. This makes a 20-megabyte D700 image file as small as 2.5 megabytes. The image quality is still very acceptable in this mode, so if you are just shooting at a party for 4 × 6 inch image

size, this mode will allow you to store a large number of images. In FX-format, an 8-gigabyte CF card will hold about 2,200 *JPEG normal* image files when *JPEG compression* is set to *Size priority*.

*JPEG basic* (or basic quality JPEG) uses a 1:16 compression ratio, so the 20-megabyte D700 file stores as a 1.25-megabyte JPEG file, so you can surely take a lot of pictures. If you are shooting for the Web, or you just want to document an area, this mode has sufficient quality. My D700 tells me that in FX-format, it can store a whopping 4,300 *JPEG basic* files on my 8-gigabyte CF card when *JPEG compression* is set to *Size priority*.

**JPEG Compression Menu**

There is one more menu that we need to discuss. Remember how the NEF (RAW) mode has an additional menu screen called *NEF (RAW) recording (figure 9)* that allows you to select the type of RAW compression you'd like to use?

Well, the JPEG mode has a similar menu called *JPEG compression*, as shown in *figure 12*.

There are two types of compression available with JPEGs:

• *Size priority*
• *Optimal quality*

These two modes affect the final file size and image quality of the picture.

Figure 11 – *Image quality* screens for setting *JPEG fine*

*Size priority* is designed to keep the images within a relatively consistent file size. It will sacrifice image quality to keep the image small. If you need to keep your images within a certain file size for storage purposes, then use this selection. If any one image is five megabytes in size, nearly all the images will be close to that size.

*Optimal quality* is not concerned with file size. It is going to protect the quality of the image, even if that means the file size will vary a great deal. If one image is 5 megabytes because it has lots of sky and is easily compressed, and another has trees and leaves that are not easy to compress, the latter's file size might be 10 megabytes. *Optimal quality* means just that!

Personally, I always use *Optimal quality* when I shoot JPEGs since the whole JPEG concept is one of lossy image compression. Size priority just adds more potential "lossiness" (is that a word?), so I avoid it.

## TIFF Format

The TIFF mode is probably one of the least used modes in the D700 because it drops storage capacity on an 8-gigabyte card to just a little over 200 images when using FX-format with *Image size* set to *Large*. Plus, it slows the

image writing process to the CF card (*figure 13*).

Personally, I would rather shoot in NEF (RAW) mode, since I can get almost double the number of images (at 12-bit color depth) on my CF card and they are 12 or 14 bits instead of the TIFF mode's 8 bits.

However, since the TIFF mode creates images that do not have to be postprocessed later (but easily can be if desired), some people will use TIFF mode for initial shooting. TIFF is not a lossy compressed mode, although there is a conversion from 12- or 14-bit to 8-bit initially. The image loses 4 or 6 bits from each color channel during the conversion so there is color data loss, but—for non-fine-art printing—it is not enough to make a big difference in the image. Use TIFF mode if you do not want the lossy compression of a JPEG and you'd rather not adjust the images later in your computer.

## Combined NEF and JPEG Shooting

(*Two Images at Once*)

Some photographers use a clever storage mode whereby the D700 takes two images at the same time. It's called *NEF (RAW) + JPEG*. This gives you the best of both worlds in that

Figure 12 – Two *Shooting Menu* screens for setting *JPEG compression*, with the second screen set to *Optimal quality*

Figure 13 – *Image quality* screens for setting *TIFF*

you shoot a RAW file and a JPEG file each time you press the shutter button. In *NEF (RAW) + JPEG fine*, my camera's 8-gigabyte CF card storage drops to about 295 images since it is storing both an uncompressed 14-bit RAW and a high-quality JPEG file at the same time for each picture taken (*figure 13A*).

You can use the RAW file to store all the image data and later to postprocess it into a masterpiece, or you can just use the JPEG file immediately with no adjustment. Many people use this combination quite often. You can have a JPEG to give others immediately and later work on the RAW file for special purposes. Here are the three available modes:

- *NEF (RAW) + JPEG fine*
- *NEF (RAW) + JPEG normal*
- *NEF (RAW) + JPEG basic*

There is no need to go into any amount of detail about these modes other than what

**Storage Capacity for Combined Modes**

Note the previous section, "JPEG Compression Menu", and *figure 12*. If you are using the NEF (RAW) + JPEG modes, please be aware that the JPEGs created by these "combined" modes all use *Size priority* as a default. User's Manual page 64 seems to imply that one cannot change this since it does not mention a way to do so. However, I have noted that even when I am shooting in FX-format and using the NEF (RAW) + JPEG modes, the number of files stored changes when I select *Size priority* and then change to *Optimal priority*. For instance, *NEF (RAW) + JPEG fine* stores 240 files on an 8-gigabyte card when using *JPEG compression* set to *Size priority*. Then, when I change to *Optimal quality*, the file storage drops to 220 files.

Figure 13A – *Image quality* screens for setting *NEF (RAW) + JPEG fine*

we have already discussed. The NEF + JPEG modes have the same features as their individual modes. In other words, the NEF (RAW) file works just like a NEF (RAW) file if you were using the standalone NEF (RAW) mode. The JPEG in a NEF + JPEG mode works just like a standalone JPEG shot without a NEF (RAW) file.

If you need more information, just refer to the NEF (RAW) or JPEG information found earlier in this chapter.

Now, let's consider which of these formats might become your favorite and the benefits each might bring to your photography.

## Notes on the Image Formats: RAW, TIFF, and JPEG

### NEF (RAW) Notes

There are innumerable discussions on Internet camera forums on the subject of which image format is best. As a primarily RAW-shooting photographer, I have strong opinions on that and will do my best not to be overbearing about it.

Yes, I am a NEF (RAW) photographer about 99% of the time. I think of a RAW image the way I thought of my slides and negatives a few years ago: this is my original file that must be saved and protected. The only problems I can think of for the RAW format are the following:

- You must postprocess and convert every image you shoot into a TIFF or JPEG (or other viewable format).
- There is no industry standard RAW image format, and Nikon can change the NEF (RAW) format each time it comes out with a new camera.

Despite those drawbacks, I—and many others—shoot NEF (RAW) for maximum image quality.

It is important that you understand something very different about NEF (RAW) files. They are not really images ... yet. Basically, a RAW file is composed of sensor data and camera setting information markers. The RAW file is saved in a form that must be converted to another image type to be used in print or on the Web.

When you take a picture in RAW, the camera records the sensor data and markers for how the camera's color, sharpening, etc. are set, but it does not apply the camera setting information to the image. In your computer's postprocessing software, the image will appear on-screen using the settings you initially set in your D700. However, they are only applied in a temporary manner.

If you do not like the white balance you had selected at the time you took the picture, simply apply a new white balance and the image will be just as if you had used the new white balance setting when you took the picture. If you had low sharpening set in-camera and change it to normal sharpening in-computer, then the image will look just like it would have looked if you had used normal in-camera sharpening when you took the image.

This is quite powerful! Virtually no camera settings are applied to a RAW file in a permanent way. That means you can change the image to completely different settings, and the image will be as if you had used the new settings when you first took the picture. This allows a lot of flexibility later. If you initially shot the image in what you might think of as "Color Mode I" and now want to use "Color Mode II", all you have to do is change the image to "Color Mode II" and it will be as if you used "Color Mode II" when you first took the picture. Complete flexibility!

NEF (RAW) is generally used by individuals concerned with maximum image quality and who have time to convert the image in the computer after taking it with the camera.

### NEF (RAW) Pros:

- Allows the manipulation of image data to achieve the highest quality image available from the camera.
- All original detail stays in the image for future processing needs.
- No conversions, sharpening, sizing, or color rebalancing will be performed by the camera. Your images are untouched and pure!
- Can convert to any of the other image formats by using your computer's much more powerful processor instead of the camera processor.
- You have *much* more control over the final look of the image because *you* (not the camera) are making decisions as to the final appearance of the image.
- Supports 12-bit or 14-bit color depth for maximum image data.

### NEF (RAW) Cons:

- Not compatible with publishing industry, except by conversion to another format.
- Requires postprocessing by special proprietary software as provided by the camera manufacturer or third-party software programmers. (This is generally included with the camera.)
- Large file sizes; you must have sufficient storage media. (Although, not as large as TIFF.)
- No accepted industry standard RAW mode. Each camera manufacturer has its own proprietary format. Adobe has recently introduced a new RAW format called DNG (Digital Negative) that might become an industry standard. We'll see!
- 12-bit or 14-bit color-depth is not really in use, since 8-bit is industry standard.

### JPEG Notes

JPEG (.JPG) is used by individuals who want excellent image quality but have little time or interest in later postprocessing or converting images to another format. They want to use the image immediately when it comes out of the camera, with no major adjustments. (The initials *JPEG* stand for Joint Photographic Experts Group. )

The JPEG format applies whatever camera settings you have chosen to the image when it is taken. It comes out of the camera ready to use, as long as you have exposed it properly and have all the other settings set in the best way for the image.

Since JPEG is a lossy format, one cannot modify and save it more than a time or two before ruining the image from compression losses. However, since there is no postprocessing required later, this format allows much quicker use of the image. A person shooting a large quantity of images who may not have the time, patience, or software to convert RAW images will usually use JPEG. This describes a large number of photographers.

While a nature photographer might want to use RAW, since he has more time for processing images and wringing the last drop of quality out of them, an event or news editorial photographer may not have the time or interest in processing images, so he'll use JPEG.

### JPEG Pros

- Maximum storage of images on camera card and later on computer hard drive storage.
- Fastest writes from camera memory buffer to memory card storage.
- Absolute compatibility with everything and everybody in imaging.
- Uses the industry standard 8-bit color depth.
- High-quality first-use images.

- No special software needed to use the image right out of the camera (no post-processing).
- Immediate use on websites with minimal processing.
- Easy transfer across Internet and as email attachments.

*JPEG Cons*

- JPEG is a lossy format, which means that it permanently throws away image data from compression algorithm losses as you select higher percentages of compression.
- You cannot use JPEG to manipulate an image more than once or twice before it degrades to an unusable state.
- Every time you modify and resave a JPEG image it loses more data.
- May not be as sharp out of the camera as TIFF or RAW modes due to initial camera compression.

**TIFF Notes**

Finally, let's consider the TIFF format. It is used by those who want to be able to work with their images over and over without throwing away data from compression as JPEG does.

You can shoot in TIFF if you'd like since the D700 allows it and you'll get excellent 8-bit images. When you shoot TIFF the camera does not compress the image, but it does apply the camera settings to the image file immediately. Since the camera shoots natively in 12-bit or 14-bit color depth, there is some initial data loss in using the TIFF format since some data is thrown away when converting down to 8-bit TIFF. The primary problem with TIFF files is that they are huge and will slow your camera down while it saves them.

Here are the pros and cons of the TIFF format.

*TIFF Pros*

- Very high image quality.
- Excellent compatibility with the publishing industry.
- Is considered a lossless format since the image normally uses no compression and loses no more data than the initial conversion from 12 or 14 bits to 8 bits in the camera's software.
- Can modify and resave the images an endless number of times without throwing away image data.
- Does not require software postprocessing during or after download from camera, so the image is immediately usable.

*TIFF Cons*

- Very large files in camera memory, so your ability to take a lot of images requires very large CF storage cards.
- Must have large hard drives on your computer to store these larger images.
- In-camera image processing is slower, so you will be limited in the number of fast pictures you can take.
- Unless you have a high-speed Internet connection, don't even consider sending one of these monsters across the Internet. Even then, you may find you are constrained by your ISP's file-size limitations.

**Final Image Format Ramblings**

Which format do I prefer? Why, RAW, of course! But, it does require a bit of a commitment to shoot in this format. The D700 is simply an image capturing device, and you are the image manipulator. You decide the final format, compression ratios, sizes, color balances, etc. In RAW mode, you have the absolute best image your camera can produce. It is not modified by the D700 and is ready for your personal touch. No in-camera processing allowed!

If you get nothing else from this chapter section, remember this: By letting your camera process the images in *any* way, it is modifying or throwing away image data. There is only a finite amount of data for each image that can be stored on your camera and later on the computer. With JPEG or TIFF mode, your camera is optimizing the image according to the assumptions recorded in its memory. Data is being thrown away permanently in varying amounts.

If you want to keep all the image data that was recorded in the image, you must store your originals in RAW format. Otherwise you'll never again be able to access that original data to change how it looks. RAW format is the closest thing to a film negative or a transparency that your digital camera can make.

This is important if you would like to use the image later for modification. If you are a photographer who is concerned with maximum quality, you should probably shoot and store your images in RAW (or even TIFF) format. Later, when you have the urge to make another masterpiece out of the original RAW image file, you will have ALL of your original data intact for the highest quality.

If you are concerned that the RAW format may change too much over time to be readable by future generations, then you might want to convert your images into TIFF or JPEG files. TIFF is best if you want to modify them later. I often save a TIFF version of my best files just in case RAW changes too much in the future. Why not do a little more research on this subject and decide which you like best.

## Image area
(User's Manual page 58)
*Image area* is the D700's means of determining whether to use the full (36 × 24 mm) FX-format image dimension, or the smaller (24 × 16 mm) DX-format image dimension. Be careful: don't confuse *Image area* with *Image size*.

In addition to all the so-called "full-frame" lenses that will work with the D700, the camera can also accept and work with the large collection of DX lenses that have come onto the market in the last few years. However, as the DX lenses were designed to work with a smaller image sensor, the image they create on the D700 image sensor is correspondingly smaller, generating an image the same dimension in the D700 as in the earlier DX-format DSLRs from Nikon.

As shown in *figure 14*, you can select *Auto DX crop*, which will cause the camera to automatically recognize when a DX-format lens is attached and set the image dimension accordingly. This reduced image dimension is shown in the viewfinder as an orange frame. If you prefer, you can select the *Choose image area* option, allowing you to specify that the camera is to use either FX-format or the DX-format, regardless of the mounted lens. Note that when a DX lens is mounted, but *Image area* has been set to *FX format*, the DX-format frame is not displayed and the edges of the recorded image will generally show significant deterioration in the area beyond the normal DX-format dimension.

## Image size
(User's Manual page 69)
This menu selection applies only to images captured in TIFF or JPEG modes. If you are shooting with your D700 in NEF + JPEG modes, it applies only to the JPEG image in the pair.

The support for both FX-format and DX-format image dimensions also affect your selection of *Image size*. Once you have set *Image area* (or let the camera determine

Figure 14 – *Image area* screens

*Image area* based on the type of lens mounted), specifying *Image size* is relatively simple, since it just affects the megapixel (MP) size of the image.

When *Image area* is set to *FX format*, the three settings under *Image size* are as follows:

- *Large:* 4,256 × 2,832 = 12.1 megapixels
- *Medium:* 3,184 × 2,120 = 6.7 megapixels
- *Small:* 2,128 × 1,416 = 3.0 megapixels

Similarly, when *Image area* is set to *DX format*, the three settings under *Image size* are as follows:

- *Large:* 2,784 × 1,848 = 5.1 megapixels
- *Medium:* 2,080 × 1,384 = 2.8 megapixels
- *Small:* 1,392 × 920 = 1.2 megapixels

I've been playing around with these settings for the fun of it. I'm personally not interested in using my D700 for images smaller than the maximum allowed by the mounted lens, but you may have special uses for these settings.

If I set *Image quality* to *JPEG basic*, *Image size* to *Small*, *Image area* to *FX format*, and *JPEG compression* to *Size priority*, my D700 will capture 15,600 images on an 8-gigabyte card. The images are 3.0 MP in size (2,128 × 1,416 = 3,013,248), and compressed to the maximum the D700 will create, but there are a large number of them.

If I were to set off today to walk completely around the earth, and I had only one 8-gigabyte CF card to take with me, well, my

Figure 14A – FX *Image size* screens

Figure 14B – DX *Image size* screens

D700 in FX-format will give me over 15,000 images on the one card, so I can at least document my trip very well.

### White balance

(User's Manual pages 140–158)
We have devoted an entire chapter of this book to white balance. Please turn to chapter 4, "White Balance", for detailed information on this important subject.

### Set Picture Control

(User's Manual pages 160–167)
As shown in *figure 15*, there are a series of *Set Picture Control* screen selections that modify how your D700 captures an image.
- *SD,* or Standard
- *NL,* or Neutral
- *VI,* or Vivid
- *MC,* or Monochrome

Each of these settings has a different and variable combination of the following settings:
- Sharpening
- Contrast (does not apply when the *Active D-Lighting* option is set)
- Brightness (does not apply when the *Active D-Lighting* option is set)
- Saturation (does not apply to *MC* – Monochrome)
- Hue (does not apply to *MC* – Monochrome)
- Filter Effects (only applies to *MC* – Monochrome)
- Toning (only applies to *MC* – Monochrome)

You can select one of the controls (*SD, NL, VI,* or *MC*) and leave the settings as they are set at the factory or you can modify the settings (*figure 15* screen 3) and completely change how the D700 captures the image. If you are shooting in RAW mode, the D700 does not apply these settings to the image but stores them with the image so that you can later change them in-computer.

Let's examine each of the picture controls, and then we'll look at the settings.

## Picture Controls

*SD*, or Standard, is Nikon's recommendation for getting "balanced" results. Nikon recommends *SD* for most situations. Use this if you later want a balanced image and don't want to postprocess it to get it there. It has what Nikon calls "standard" image processing (*figure 16*).

*NL*, or Neutral, is best for an image that will later be extensively postprocessed in the computer. It too is a balanced image but has minimal camera processing so that you'll have room to do more with the image in the computer.

*VI*, or Vivid, is for the Fuji Velvia lovers among us! This setting places emphasis on saturating primary colors for intense imagery. The contrast is higher for good highs and lows, and the sharpness is higher too. If you are shooting JPEGs and want to try to imitate a saturated transparency film like Velvia, this mode is for you!

Figure 15 – *Set Picture Control* screens for setting *SD, NL, VI,* or *MC*

Figure 16 – Four images of the same subject with settings of *SD*, *NL*, *VI*, and *MC*

*MC*, or Monochrome, allows the black-and-white (B&W) lovers among us to shoot natively in toned B&W.

As shown in *figure 17*, there are *Filter effects* available that simulate the effect of yellow, orange, red, and green filters on a monochrome image. Yellow, orange, and red each change the contrast of the sky in B&W images. Green is often used in B&W portrait work to change the appearance of skin tones. You don't have to buy these filters because they are included in your D700! (See *figure 17*.)

In addition to the basic *B&W Toning* selection, there are nine variable *Toning* effects available, varying from *Sepia* and *Cyanotype* to *Red*, *Yellow*, *Green*, *Blue Green*, *Blue*, *Purple Blue*, and *Red Purple* (*figure 18*). Each of the *Toning* effects is variable within itself. You can adjust the saturation of the individual tones. You can shoot a basic B&W image, use filters to change how colors appear, or tone the image in experimental ways.

If you press the *Checkered Thumbnail* button while viewing one of these settings, the camera will show you a grid of settings that is for informational use only (as far as I can tell). You have to adjust the individual settings, such as *Sharpness*, *Contrast*, or *Saturation*, in the controls shown in *figure 15*. If you modify the settings, a small underline character will appear where the previous setting was originally.

Figure 17 – *Filter effects* controls

*Manage Picture Control*
(User's Manual pages 168–171)
This section of your D700's *Shooting Menu* allows you to store Picture Control settings for future use. If you modify them under the "Picture Control" section (just before this one), you are simply creating a one-off setting. If you'd like to set up different combinations of picture controls that you can use later, the D700 is happy to oblige.

There are six screens involved in modifying a default picture control and storing the results for later usage. In *figure 19*, we see the

Figure 18 – *Toning* controls

screens involved to modify and save a Picture Control setting. Here are the steps:

1. Select *Manage Picture Control* from the *Shooting Menu*.
2. Highlight and select *Save/edit* by scrolling to the right.
3. Highlight and select a picture control that you want to use as a base for your new settings; scroll right.
4. Make your adjustments to the items such as *Sharpness*, *Contrast*, etc., and when you are done, press the *OK* button.
5. Select one of the nine storage areas (named *C-1* through *C-9*) and scroll to the right.
6. You should now be on the *Rename* screen, which works just like the other screens you've used to rename things. See the section "Setting Up Shooting Menu Bank A" at the beginning of this chapter to see how to use the *Rename* controls.
7. Press the *OK* button when you have entered the name.

Your camera is now set to your custom Picture Control settings. You can create up to nine of these in *C-1* through *C-9*, and switch between them at will.

Figure 19 – *Manage Picture Control* screens

### Color space

(User's Manual pages 181–182)

Color spaces are an interesting and important part of digital photography and help your images fit into a much broader range of imaging devices. Software, printers, monitors, and other devices all recognize which color space is attached to your image and use it (along with other color profiles) to help balance the image to the correct output colors for the device in use. The two available color spaces have different gamuts or range of colors (*figure 20*).

The Nikon D700 camera uses these two color spaces:

* *sRGB*
* *Adobe RGB*

Both of these color spaces have an equal number of available colors within them. The difference is that *Adobe RGB* has a wider color gamut. It's not that *Adobe RGB* has more colors than *sRGB*, they are just different colors from a wider selection in the total color range available to the camera.

To make it simple, let's imagine that there are only 1,000 colors available to us. Let's say that *sRGB* uses colors 1 through 256. *Adobe RGB* would use colors from a broader selection in the range of 1,000 colors. Instead of 1 through 256, *Adobe RGB* might use 1 through 128, then colors 250 to 255, 300 to 305, 415 to 420, 550 to 560, 895 to 900, and so on. They both use the same number of colors, but the colors come from different places in the color temperature spectrum. *Adobe RGB* uses colors from a broader selection of the total color range; therefore, it has a wider gamut.

I personally always use *Adobe RGB* since I predominantly shoot nature with a wide range of color. I want the colors to be as accurate as my camera will give me.

There are some drawbacks to using *Adobe RGB* though. The *sRGB* color space is widely used in printing and display devices. If you try to print directly to some inkjet printers using the *Adobe RGB* color space, the colors may not be as brilliant as with *sRGB*. If you aren't going to modify your images out-of-camera and just take them directly to print, you may want to use *sRGB*. If you shoot only JPEGs, it might be better to stay with *sRGB* for everyday shooting.

If you are a RAW shooter and regularly postprocess your images, you should use *Adobe RGB*. You will then have that wider gamut of colors to work with and can optimize your images. Later, you can convert your carefully crafted images to print with a good color profile and get great results from inkjet printers and other printing devices.

Figure 20 – *Color space* screens

So, here's a rough way to look at it:
- JPEG shooters use *sRGB*.
- RAW shooters use *Adobe RGB*.

These are not hard and fast rules, but most people use these settings according to their style of shooting.

### Active D-Lighting

(User's Manual pages 179–180)
Often the range of light around our image subject is broader than the D700's sensor can capture. Where the D700 might be able to capture four to six stops of light, the light out in the world on a bright summer day might equal 12 stops in range. The contrast is so high!

Since the D700 cannot grab the full range of light, and most people use the histogram to expose for the highlights, some of the image detail will be lost in the shadows. The D700 allows you to "D-Light" the image and bring out additional shadow detail or (in other words) lower the image contrast (*figure 21*).

*Active D-Lighting* has these settings:
- *Auto*
- *High*
- *Normal*
- *Low*
- *Off* (no *Active D-Lighting*)

If you are familiar with Nikon Capture NX or NX 2, you may already know how D-Lighting works, since you can use it to bring up "lost"

shadow detail at the expense of adding noise in the darker areas recovered.

*Active D-Lighting* will bring out detail in areas of your image that are hidden in shadow due to excessive image contrast. *Figure 22* shows a series of four images with *Active D-Lighting* set to its various levels.

You'll need to experiment with the *Active D-Lighting* settings to see which you like best. It has the effect of lowering contrast, and some people do not like low-contrast images. Also, anytime you recover lost detail from shadows, there will be extra noise in the areas recovered. So watch the noise!

There is a great deal of processing required for *Active D-Lighting*, depending on the particular image. This could have a negative impact on CH-mode frame rates.

### Vignette control

(User's Manual page 276)
Now, this is a harbinger of things to come....
Today's cameras have so much computing power built into the camera body that we can expect to see even more sophisticated image enhancement being applied before the image is even written to the CF card.

This option applies to Nikon's G and D lenses (no DX-format lenses are supported), but for that set of lenses, vignetting (the drop-off in brightness that is so common as a

Figure 21 – *Active D-Lighting* screens

Figure 22 – *Active D-Lighting* images, showing effects of all four settings

lens approaches maximum aperture) can be significantly reduced. There are many factors that impact on the accuracy of this process, so you will probably want to take some test shots for critical situations to ensure you are getting what you expect.

As shown in screen 2 of *figure 22A*, there are three levels of control available; the third screen is the result of pressing the *Help* button (just below the *MENU* button, on the back of the camera) while the first screen is displayed.

### Long exposure NR
(User's Manual page 277)

Nikon knows its sensors well. It feels that images taken at exposures longer than one second may exhibit more noise than is acceptable for normal use. The D700 provides two settings for long exposure noise reduction, as shown in *figure 23*.

The two choices are as follows:

- *On*
- *Off*

*On:* When you select *On*, and your exposure exceeds one second, the D700 will take two exposures with the exact same time for each.

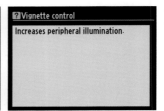

Figure 22A – *Vignette control* screens

Figure 23 – *Long Exposure NR* screens

The first exposure is the normal picture-taking exposure. The second is a "black frame subtraction" exposure in which an image is made for the same length of time as the first one but with the shutter closed. The noise in the second "black frame" image is examined and subtracted from the original image. It's really quite effective and beats having to blur the image to get rid of noise. I've taken images of around 30 seconds and had perfectly usable results. The only drawback is that the exposure time is doubled since two images are taken.

When the second "black frame" image is being taken, the words *Job nr* will blink in the Control Panel LCD and in the viewfinder. During this second exposure (while *Job nr* is flashing), you cannot use the camera. If you turn it off while *Job nr* is flashing then the camera still keeps the first image but does not apply any noise reduction on it.

If *Long Exposure Noise Reduction* is *On*, the frame-advance rate may slow down and the capacity of the in-camera memory buffer will drop.

*Off:* If you select *Off*, then of course you will have no noise reduction with long exposures above ISO 1600, unless you exceed ISO 6400, as discussed in the next section.

### High ISO Noise Reduction
(User's Manual page 278)
The D700 has better noise control than most cameras, so it is able to capture images at higher ISO values with little increase in noise. However, no digital camera is completely without noise (that I know of), so it is a good idea to use some noise reduction above a certain level of exposure gain. With the D700 the ISO can go up to 1600 without noise reduction. For ISO values of 2000 through 6400, you must choose to allow or disallow *High ISO*

Figure 24 – *High ISO NR* screens

Figure 25 – ISO 6400 images at all four High ISO Noise Reduction settings

*Noise Reduction* (NR). *Figure 24* shows the selections:

- *High*
- *Normal* (factory default)
- *Low*
- *Off*

For any of these settings (except *Off*), *High ISO Noise Reduction* will be performed starting at ISO 2000. You'll need to shoot some high ISO exposures and decide for yourself whether you are comfortable with *High*, *Normal*, *Low*, or even *Off*. *Figure 25* shows

the result of using each of the four High ISO Noise Reduction settings. The two arrows in the upper-left image point out the areas in which grain becomes most apparent, when the image is magnified.

Regardless of the *High ISO Noise Reduction* setting, the D700 will still apply noise reduction when you exceed ISO 6400. The official starting point for forced noise reduction is HI 0.3, which is ISO 8000, with HI 0.3 being ⅓ stop above ISO 6400. There are two other ⅓ stop levels above HI 0.3, namely HI 0.7 and

HI 1, followed by a full-stop increment of HI 2, which should approximate ISO 25600. The mount of noise reduction at these forced levels is roughly equivalent to that applied at the *Low* setting.

It seems like a good idea to have High ISO Noise Reduction turned on, at least at the *Low* level. I leave mine on *Normal*.

### ISO Sensitivity Settings

(User's Manual pages 106–109)

An ISO number, such as ISO 200 or ISO 3200, is an agreed-upon sensitivity for the image capturing sensor. Virtually anywhere in the world, all camera ISO numbers will mean the same thing. With that fact established, camera bodies and lenses can be designed to take advantage of the ISO sensitivity ranges they will have to deal with. Standards are good!

In the D700, the ISO numbers are sensitivity equivalents. Consider ISO "sensitivity" as the digital equivalent of film speed. The higher the ISO sensitivity, the less light needed for the exposure. A high ISO set-

ting allows faster shutter speeds and smaller apertures.

In *figure 26*, we see the external camera controls used to adjust ISO quickly. This is the easiest method to change the camera's ISO setting.

You can also use the *Shooting Menu's ISO sensitivity settings* screens. *Figure 27* shows the screens used to change the camera's ISO.

Notice in screen three of *figure 27* that you have a scrollable list of ISO values, starting from LO 1 (ISO 100) all the way to HI 2 (ISO 25600). The normal ISO range for the D700 is ISO 200 to ISO 6400. Select your needed ISO from the list of available ISOs.

The standard minimum *ISO sensitivity setting* for the D700 is ISO 200. You can adjust the camera in a range from ISO 100 through ISO 12800, in ⅓ steps.

The D700 is very flexible in the number of increments allowed while adjusting the ISO sensitivity. According to how you have *Custom setting b1* set, the ISO numbers can be adjusted in ⅓, ½, or 1 EV steps.

Figure 26 – ISO external controls: *ISO* button and *Main command* dial

Figure 27 – *ISO sensitivity settings* screens, with *Custom setting b1* set to *1/3 step*

Figure 28 – Screens to set ISO-AUTO

To the right is a chart that shows the ISO ranges for all the *Custom setting b1* settings.

Select your favorite ISO setting from these values, either with the external camera controls, or with the *Shooting Menu's ISO Sensitivity Settings* screens.

### *ISO sensitivity auto control* (ISO-AUTO)
(User's Manual pages 108–109)
The *ISO sensitivity auto control* allows your camera to automatically select the ISO. Let's consider this often misunderstood feature in detail.

You may have noticed in screen two of *figure 27* that there is another setting available, *ISO sensitivity auto control*, which defaults to *Off*. This was known on earlier Nikon cameras as ISO-AUTO.

This setting is used to allow the camera to control the ISO according to the light levels sensed by the camera meter. In *figure 28*, we see the *Shooting Menu* screens used to enable and configure ISO-AUTO.

Once you've turned ISO-AUTO on you should set the following two values, according to how you shoot:

- *Maximum sensitivity*
- *Minimum shutter speed*

*Maximum sensitivity* – This setting is a safeguard for you. If you would prefer that ISO-AUTO not exceed a certain ISO, simply select from the list shown in *figure 29*.

You'll note that there are only seven available settings ranging from ISO 400 through

### ISO Ranges for *Custom setting b1*

**⅓ EV Step ISO Range**
(*Custom setting b1* factory default)

LO 1, LO 0.7, LO 0.3, 200, 250, 320, 400, 500, 640, 800, 1000, 1250, 1600, 2000, 2500, 3200, 4000, 5000, 6400, HI 0.3, HI 0.7, HI 1, HI 2

**½ EV Step ISO Range**

LO 1, LO 0.5, 200, 280, 400, 560, 800, 1100, 1600, 2200, 3200, 4500, 6400, HI 0.5, HI 1, HI 2

**1 EV Step ISO Range**

LO 1.0, 200, 400, 800, 1600, 3200, 6400, HI 1, HI 2

HI 2. Whichever one of these settings you choose will be the maximum ISO the camera will use to get a good exposure when the light drops.

*Minimum shutter speed* – Since shutter speed controls how sharp an image can be, due to camera shake and subject movement, you'll need some control over the minimum shutter speed allowed while ISO-AUTO is turned on. See *figure 30* (screen 3) for a list of shutter speeds.

You can select a shutter speed from the list, and it will be set as the minimum shutter

Figure 29 – Setting ISO-AUTO *Maximum sensitivity*

speed the camera will allow when the light gets darker.

When you have enabled ISO-AUTO, the Control Panel LCD and viewfinder will show and blink the words *ISO-AUTO*. The blinking is a reminder to turn it off when not needed so that you don't get unnecessarily noisy images.

**When and Why Should I Use ISO-AUTO?**
How much automation do you need to produce consistently excellent images?

Normally you will set your camera to a particular ISO number, such as 200 or 400, and shoot your images. As the light diminishes or you find yourself in the deep shade, you might increase the ISO number to allow handheld images to continue being made.

If you are in circumstances where you absolutely must get the shot, ISO-AUTO will work nicely. Here are a few scenarios.

**Scenario # 1**
Let's say you are a photojournalist and you're shooting flash pictures of an important news personality as he disembarks from his airplane, walks into the terminal, and drives away in his limousine. Under those circumstances you will have little time to check your ISO settings or shutter speeds and will be shooting in widely varying light conditions.

**Scenario # 2**
You are a wedding photographer in a church that does not allow the use of flash. As you follow the bride and groom from the dark inner rooms of the church, out into the lobby, and finally up to the altar, your light conditions will be varying constantly. You have no time to deal with the fluctuations in light by changing your ISO since things are moving too quickly.

**High ISO Noise Reduction**

It might be a good idea to enable *High ISO Noise Reduction,* as discussed a few pages back, when you enable ISO-AUTO. This is especially true if you leave the camera set to the default maximum ISO value of 6400. Otherwise, you may have excessive noise when the light drops.

Figure 30 – Selecting ISO-AUTO *Minimum shutter speed*

## Scenario # 3

You are at a party and you want some pictures. You want to use flash but the pop-up Speedlight may not be powerful enough to reach across the room at low ISO settings. You really don't want to be bothered with camera configuration at this time but still want some well-exposed images. Light will vary as you move around the room, talking and laughing and snapping pictures.

These scenarios are excellent environments for ISO-AUTO. The camera will use your normal settings (such as your normal ISO, shutter speed, and aperture) *until* the light will not allow those settings to provide an accurate exposure. Only then will the camera raise or lower the ISO value to keep functioning within the shutter/aperture parameters you have set.

Look at ISO-AUTO as a "failsafe" for times when you *must get the shot* but have little time to deal with camera settings or when you don't want to vary the shutter/aperture settings but still want to be assured of a well exposed image.

Unless you are a private detective shooting handheld telephoto images from your car, or are a photojournalist or sports photographer who *must get the shot every time* regardless of the level of quality, I personally would not recommend leaving your camera set to ISO-AUTO. Use it only when you really need to get the shot under any circumstances!

Of course, if you are unsure of how to use the "correct" ISO for the light level, don't be afraid to experiment with this mode. At the very worst all you might get are noisier than normal images.

## Are There Any Drawbacks to Using ISO-AUTO?

Maybe, but it really depends on how widely varying the light conditions will be when you are shooting. Most of the time your camera will maintain normal ISO range settings in ISO-AUTO so your images will be their normal low-noise, sharp, masterpieces. However, at times the light may be so low that the ISO may exceed the "normal" range of ISO 200 through ISO 1600 and will start getting into the noisier ranges above ISO 1600.

Just be aware that ISO-AUTO can— and will—push your ISO into a range that causes noisier images when light levels drop. Use it with this understanding and you'll do fine. ISO 25600 is the maximum in ISO-AUTO, unless you have set the maximum to a lower number. Make sure you understand this, or you might get some noisy images.

ISO-AUTO is yet another feature in this powerful Nikon camera. Maybe not everyone needs this "failsafe" feature, but for those who do, it must be there. I will use it myself in circumstances where getting the shot is the most important thing and where light levels may get too low for normal ISO image making.

Even if you think you might only use it from time-to-time, do learn how to use it for those times. Experiment with ISO-AUTO. It's fun and can be useful!

### Live view

(User's Manual page 90)

The *Live View* mode is covered in great detail in chapter 3, "Multi-CAM 3500FX Autofocus". Please refer to that chapter for information on setting and using *Live View*.

Figure 31 – *Multiple exposure* set up screens

## Multiple Exposure

(User's Manual pages 198–202)

Multiple exposure is the process whereby you take more than one exposure on a single frame, or picture. Most of us will only do double exposures, which are two exposures on one frame. It requires you to figure the exposure values carefully for each exposure so that, in the end, all the combined exposures equal one normal exposure. In other words, if you are going to do a nonmasked double exposure, your background will need two exposures at one-half the normal exposure value to equal one normal exposure.

The D700 allows us to figure our own exposure settings and do them manually or gives us *Auto gain* to help us with exposure calculations.

There are really only three steps to setting up a multiple-exposure session. However, there are six *Shooting Menu* screens we'll use to do these three steps, which are as follows:

1. Select the *Number of shots* you want to take from the *Shooting Menu* screens.
2. Turn *Auto gain* on or off according to how you want to control exposure.
3. Take the picture.

Let's consider each of the screens we see in *figure 31* and discover how to set up the *Multiple exposure* system.

Using *figure 31* as a reference, do the following:

1. Select *Multiple exposure* from the *Shooting Menu* (screen 1).
2. Select *Number of shots* from screen 2, and scroll right.
3. Select a number of shots on screen 3 (any number from 2 through 10).
4. Press the *OK* button to lock in the number of shots.
5. Select *Auto gain* from screen 4, and scroll right.
6. Select *On* in screen 5.
7. Press the *OK* button to turn *Auto gain* on.
8. Select *Done* from screen 6 and press the *OK* button.
9. Shoot your images from a tripod.

Once you've selected a value for *Number of shots*, the camera remembers the value and comes back to it for the next session. To repeat another series of multiple exposures with the same settings, you'll have to use screen 2 again (*figure 31*) and select *Done*, then press the *OK* button. These steps prepare the camera to do the multiple exposures in the same way as last time, by remembering the previous *Number of shots* and other settings until you reset them (using screen 2).

If the D700's *Release mode* dial is set to either *CH* or *CL*, the shutter is triggered *Number of shots* in a single burst; otherwise, you will need to press the shutter-release button for each of the *Number of shots* exposures.

### Understanding Auto Gain

*Auto gain* defaults to *On*, so you need to understand it well.

*Auto gain* applies only if you want to make a number of exposures with the exact same exposure value for each. If you want to make two exposures, the camera will meter for a normal exposure and then divide the exposure in half for the two shots. For three shots, it will divide the exposure by three, four shots by four, eight shots by eight, and so forth.

In other words, it will take the normal exposure for a single shot and divide it by the number of shots so that when you are done, you have the equivalent of a single good exposure.

Here is another way of looking at it: If I want a two-shot multiple exposure, I normally want the background to get one-half of the normal exposure in each shot so that it will appear normal in the final image. *Auto gain* does that automatically. If I need four shots, I want only the background to get one-fourth of a normal exposure for each shot so that I'll have a normally exposed background when the four shots are taken.

The reason I mentioned this in such a repetitive fashion is that it took me a little while to wrap my brain around the confusing presentation of this issue in the User's Manual. Whoever heard of "gain" meaning dividing something into parts? What I think the

manual writers were trying to say is that each shot "gains" a portion of the normal exposure so that in the end the exposure is complete and correct. I hope this makes sense to you!

*Auto gain* is, therefore, like an automatic normal exposure "divider-upper" for multiple exposures. It divides up the exposure into appropriate sections so you won't have to fool with it.

When should you use *Auto gain*? Only when you have no need for controlling exposure differently on each frame but, instead, can use an exact division of similar exposures.

*Auto gain* works fine if you're not using masks. When you use a mask, you want a full normal exposure for each of the uncovered (nonmasked) sections of the image, so *Auto gain* will not work for this. In this case, you should use *MANUAL* exposure with *Auto gain* turned off instead.

### *Interval timer shooting*

(User's Manual pages 203–209)
*Interval timer shooting* allows you to set up your D700 to shoot a series of images over time. Make sure you have a full battery (or are connected to a full-time power source) for images taken over long periods of time.

The first step in using *Interval timer shooting* is to make sure that your *World time* (where you are located on the earth), and time and date are set correctly in the *Setup Menu* of your D700. The *Setup Menu* is two menus below the *Shooting Menu*. It is right below the *Custom Settings* menu. If you don't have your *World time* set on the D700, your *Interval timer* screen will be grayed out and you won't be able to use it.

*Figure 32* shows the *Shooting Menu* screens used to set *Interval timer shooting*.

The screens look a little daunting, so it might help you to understand that the bottom half of screen 2 in *figure 32* is informational in nature. It shows the settings you will create with the top half of the screen.

There are four steps to setting your camera for *Interval timer shooting*:
1. Choose a *Start time*.
2. Choose an *Interval*.
3. Choose the number of intervals.
4. Choose the number of shots per interval.

So, if you wanted to take a series of images starting at *Now* (starting time) and shoot for every 10 seconds (*Interval*), making two images per interval (number of shots), over a period of 30 seconds (number of intervals), you would set the following:

1. In screen 2 of *figure 32*, you could select *Now* under *Choose start time*, and the timer would start three seconds after you complete the rest of these five steps. If you would rather start at a future time, instead of *Now*, simply select *Start time* from screen 2, then scroll right. If you select *Now*, please skip step 2 and go directly to step 3.
2. You will now see a *Start time* screen (see screen 3 in *figure 32*) with the time in military 24 hour format looking like this:

**00:00**

Since you want to set this for a future time to start the process, choose a time. If you want to start at 3:30 p.m., insert the following in the fields:

**15:30**

This is in 24-hour "military" time instead of the normal 12-hour time with which we are more familiar.

3. You will now see the *Interval* screen with hours, minutes, and seconds in the following format:

**00 : 00' 00"**

Since you want to start out with an *Interval* of 10 seconds, set the screen to look like this:

**00 : 00' 10"**

The first pair of digits represents the hours, the second pair represents minutes, and the last pair represents seconds. Since you have chosen an *Interval* of 10 seconds, the number in the third pair of digits should be *10* representing 10 seconds (see screen 4 in *figure 32*). Scroll to the right.

4. Now we'll select the number of Intervals, using screen 5 in *figure 32*.

Figure 32 – *Interval timer shooting* setup screens

This screen will say *Select intvls × no. of shots*. The formula below that heading is in the following format:

**Number of intervals × Number of shots = Total shots:**

**000 × 0 = 0000**

Use the Multi Selector to set your D700 so that it looks like this instead:

**003 × 2 = 0006**

This means that there will be 003 intervals of 10 seconds each (set in step 3) and that the camera will take two pictures in each interval for a total of 0006 pictures. In other words, two pictures will be taken every 10 seconds over a period of 30 seconds for a total of six images. Now scroll to the right to the next screen.

5.  Using screen 6 of *figure 32*, select *On* and press the *OK* button. A *! Timer Active* message will appear briefly on your Monitor LCD. If you look at the Control Panel LCD, you will see the word *INTERVAL* flashing. This will keep flashing as long as the interval timer is in operation.

To pause or stop an interval from being timed and cease timer operations, simply select the *Interval timer shooting* screen and scroll to the right. You can select *Pause* or *Off* from the next screen. It will also show you the *Starting Time, Current Time, Number of Intervals* and *Number of Shots* remaining (in case you don't want to pause or stop it but just want to see how things are going).

During timed-interval operations, while the word *INTERVAL* is flashing on the Control Panel LCD, the number of intervals remaining will be displayed in the same spot the shutter speed is normally displayed on the Control Panel LCD, and the place that normally displays the aperture will instead display the number of shots remaining in the current interval (see page 194 of your User's Manual under the subheading "During Shooting").

Congratulations! You've fully configured *Shooting Menu* bank A.

Now, set up another bank or all the shooting banks, and rename them by repeating the steps above in the section "Setting Up Shooting Menu Bank A". Remember that you have four *Shooting Menu* banks and we've configured only one of them.

### The Eyepiece Shutter

If you are shooting this timed interval in daylight hours, be sure to close the D700's eyepiece shutter. Otherwise, changes in the light from behind the camera could cause the exposure to be inaccurate.

## My Conclusions

Using the D700's four *Shooting Menu* banks allows you a great deal of flexibility in how your camera operates. By selectively configuring each bank, you can essentially switch between four different cameras.

When you combine the use of the four *Shooting Menu* banks with the four *Custom Setting* banks (covered in the next chapter), you'll have an expanded number of ways to configure your camera for specific, personally defined purposes.

# Custom Setting Banks

In chapter 5, we carefully considered the configurability of the Nikon D700 and its *Shooting Menu* banks. Now we will continue with this process by going over the *Custom setting* banks in great detail.

Each of those settings can be configured in different ways. When combined with the *Shooting Menu*, the *Custom Setting Menu* allows you to configure your D700 in a variety of ways.

This chapter will help you develop a much better understanding of your favorite digital shooter. Without further ado, let's dive right into the settings and see what they each do.

## Setting Up Custom Setting Bank A

First, we'll consider the process of renaming bank A on our D700 so that we'll know what style of shooting this bank is configured to support.

In chapter 5, we discussed how to rename a *Shooting Menu* bank to a name

that describes its functionality. You change the name of a *Custom setting* bank the same way. If you are familiar with the process, you can just name your bank and skip this first section.

### Renaming Custom Setting Bank A

Press the *MENU* button on the back of your D700, and use the Multi Selector to scroll to the left, then up or down until you find the *Custom Setting Menu* (looks like a small pencil on the left of the Monitor LCD), then scroll to the *Custom setting bank* line.

Notice, in the first screen of *figure 1*, that *Custom setting bank* has an *A* after it. This means that your D700 is using bank A. If any letter other than *A* is showing, you are in a different *Custom setting* bank. Let's set the D700 bank to *A* and add a bank name so that you'll be able to see at a glance what this particular bank is set up to accomplish. Scroll the Multi Selector to the right. The Monitor LCD will change to look like screen two of *figure 1*.

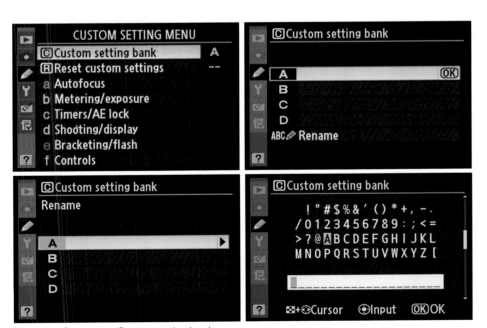

Figure 1 – Renaming *Custom setting* banks

Assuming that you have not yet renamed any of your *Custom setting* banks, you'll see the four default banks called A, B, C, and D, and a selection called *ABC Rename*. Scroll down to *ABC Rename* and then scroll to the right. Your screen will now look like the third screen in *figure 1*. This is the bank rename screen. The factory default for an unnamed bank is simply a blank field. In other words, if you haven't yet named your banks, you'll simply see the single capital letter for that bank, followed by a blank field. Let's rename our bank by selecting bank A and then scrolling to the right. The screen will now look like the fourth screen in *figure 1*.

You'll see a series of symbols, numbers, and letters on top, with a line of dashes at the bottom. The dashes are where we will put our text to rename the bank. In the upper-left corner of the characters area is a blank spot which represents a blank character for insertion in the line of text, which is helpful for separating words. If you scroll down past the uppercase letters, you'll find some lowercase letters too.

Here is a series of steps to use while creating the new bank name. Refer to *figure 2* for the camera controls to use in renaming.

**Steps to input new characters:**

1. Use the Multi Selector to scroll through the numbers and letters to find the characters you want to use. Scroll down for lowercase letters.
2. Press the Multi Selector's center button to select a character. Keep selecting new characters until you have the entire new bank name in place.
3. If you make a mistake, hold down the *Checkered Thumbnail* button while using the Multi Selector to move to the position of the error. Push the garbage can (delete) button on the top left of the back of the D700. The unwanted character will disappear.
4. Press the *OK* button to save the new name.

Excellent! You have named bank A to a more meaningful name so that you can quickly recognize the custom set of functions.

Now, scroll the Multi Selector to the left until the *Custom Setting Menu* appears, or press the *MENU* button to return to the start.

## Configuring the Custom Settings

Let's start by looking at the *Reset custom settings* screen. Then we'll proceed through all 50 of the individual custom settings.

### Reset custom settings
(User's Manual page 282)
Be careful with this selection. It does what it sounds like and resets the menu for the currently selected *Custom setting* bank back to factory default settings. Page 420 of the User's Manual shows the default settings.

This is a rather simple process. As seen in screen two of *figure 3*, simply scroll to *Yes* or *No* and press the *OK* button or scroll to the right. That's about it. If you select *Yes*, the *Custom setting* bank you're currently using will be reset to factory defaults.

Figure 2 – Camera controls for renaming banks: The *Multi Selector*, and the *Checkered Thumbnail*, *Delete*, and *OK* buttons

Figure 3 – *Reset custom settings* screens

## Autofocus

Custom settings a1 to a10
(User's Manual pages 283–291)

***Custom settings a1** and **a2** – **AF-S** and
**AF-C priority selection***
Shown in *figure 4A* and *figure 4B* are the
screens used to configure *Custom settings a1*

and *a2*. I have combined these two settings
into one section since they are closely related
and work basically the same way.

These particular settings help control how
your camera's autofocus works in *Continuous-
servo AF* or *Single-servo AF*. (For a review of
these focus modes, see chapter 3, "Multi-CAM
3500FX Autofocus".)

Figure 4A – AF-C *Autofocus* screens

Figure 4B – AF-S *Autofocus* screens

*Focus* – This setting is designed to prevent your D700 from taking a picture with the viewfinder's green in-focus indicator off. In other words, if the picture is not in focus, the shutter will not release. It does not mean that the camera will always focus on the correct subject. It simply means that when your camera has focused on something out there, it allows the shutter release to activate. Nikon cameras do a very good job with autofocus, so you can usually depend on the AF Module to perform well. *Focus* will drastically increase your chances that your image is in correct focus.

*Release* (AF-C and AF-S) or *Release + focus* (AF-C only)
If the image must be taken, no matter what, then you will need to set *a1* and/or *a2* to *Release*, or *Release+focus* (AF-C only). *Release* allows the shutter to fire every time you press it, even if the image is not in focus. *Release+focus* slows the frame rate for improved focus when the light is low or the subject has little contrast with its surroundings, but still allows the shutter to fire even if it cannot find a good focus point. Just be aware that if you select either of these settings, your D700 will take the picture even if the focus is not sharp. If you are well aware of the consequences of shooting without a focus guarantee, then use these settings to make your camera take a picture every time you press the shutter release or *AF-ON* button (*see Custom setting a5*). Your camera will shoot at its maximum frames per second (FPS) rate since it is not hampered by validating that each picture is in correct focus. You'll need to decide whether taking the image is more important than whether the image is in focus.

*Custom setting a1 –*
*AF-C priority selection*
(User's Manual page 283)
- *Release* (default) – Photo can be taken at any time, even if not in focus.
- *Release+focus* – Photo can be taken at any time, even if not in focus. The camera will slow down its maximum FPS rate when the subject is in low light or low contrast.
- *Focus* – The image must be in focus or the shutter will not release. This also means that the shutter will not release unless the little green viewfinder light is on. This is the closest thing to a guarantee that your image will be in focus when you press the shutter-release button.

*Custom setting a2 –*
*AF-S priority selection*
(User's Manual page 284)
- *Release* – Photo can be taken at any time, even if not in focus.
- *Focus* (default) – The image must be in focus, or the shutter will not release. This also means that the shutter will not release unless the little green viewfinder light is on. This is the closest thing to a guarantee that your image will be in focus when you press the shutter-release button.

**Important Note Regarding Custom Settings *a1* and *a2***

Please read the following section, *"Special Section on the Usage of a1 and a2"*. Configuring *a1* and *a2* correctly will affect how many in-focus images you can capture. It is very important that you understand why, or you may get either quite a few out-of-focus images or entirely missed images.

## Special Section on the Usage of *a1* and *a2*

Before we proceed to the next *Custom setting*, (*a3*), please consider the following special information.

### Release priority vs. Focus priority *(Custom settings a1 and a2)*

Two of the more important settings in the *Custom settings* list are *a1* and *a2*. I am adding this special section so you'll understand why to pay very close attention to these two settings.

The two settings, *a1* and *a2*, are very important because they can affect how many images you get that are truly in sharp focus. These two set the camera to either *Focus* priority or *Release* priority. These apply to *Continuous-servo AF* and *Single-servo AF*. *Continuous-servo AF* uses *Custom setting a1*, while *Single-servo AF* uses *Custom setting a2*.

*Focus* priority simply means that your camera will refuse to take a picture until it can reasonably focus on something. *Release* priority means that the camera will take a picture when you decide to take it, whether anything is in focus or not!

Now, you might ask yourself, "Why is there such a setting as *Release* priority"?

Well, many professional photographers are shooting high-speed events at high frame rates, taking hundreds of images, and are using depth of field (or experience and luck) to compensate for less than accurate focus. They are in complete control of their camera's systems, having a huge amount of practice in getting the focus right where they want it to be.

There are valid reasons these photographers have for not using *Focus* priority. However, most of those same photographers do not let the shutter-release button start the autofocus either, since the focus would change every time the shutter-release button is pressed. They set *Custom setting a5* so that the autofocus doesn't even activate until the *AF-ON*

button is pressed. They then use the *AF-ON* button for their autofocus and the shutter-release button to take the picture. They separate the two functions instead of using the shutter-release button for both.

You need to ask yourself, "What type of a photographer am I"? If you are a pro, shooting hundreds of pictures of fast race cars, *Focus* priority may not be for you. But, for the average photographer taking pictures of his kids running around the yard, a deer jumping a fence, beautiful landscapes, flying birds, or a bride tossing a bouquet, *Focus* priority is the best choice. For most of us, it's better to have the camera refuse to take the picture unless it's able to focus on your subject.

When shooting at a high frame rate, *Focus* priority may cause your camera to skip a series of out-of-focus images. *Focus* priority will also slow down your camera's frame rate so that it may not reach the maximum five frames per second in some cases. But, I have to ask, what is the point of five out-of-focus images and five in-focus images? Why waste the card space and then have to weed through the slightly out-of-focus images?

I wanted you to pay special attention to these two settings. You will need to decide, based on your style of shooting, whether you want your D700 to refuse to take an out-of-focus image. If you set *a1* and *a2* to *Focus* priority and you try to take an out-of-focus image, the D700's shutter release will simply not respond. The little round green in-focus indicator in the viewfinder will have to be on before the shutter will release.

Personally, I set both *a1* and *a2* to *Focus* priority. I am not a high-speed shooter, so I don't need my camera to take a picture "no matter what" if that includes a series of out-of-focus images. What good are out-of-focus images?

6

**Custom setting a3 – Dynamic AF area**
(User's Manual page 285)
*Figure 5* shows the screens used to configure
*Custom setting a3.*

This custom setting is designed to assist
you with how *Dynamic-area AF* works. See
the section "AF-Area Modes in Detail" in
chapter 3 for more information on *Dynamic-
area AF.*

• **9 points** (default) – Use this setting when
your subject is moving predictably. This
uses an array of eight AF sensors surrounding your selected and viewable AF
sensor in the viewfinder. Examples might
be subjects in a car race or airshow.
• **21 points** – If your subject is moving
unpredictably, this may be your best
choice. This uses 20 sensors surrounding
your viewable sensor in the viewfinder.
A good example for this pattern setting
might be players in a football or basketball
game.
• **51 points** – This is for worst-case scenario
subjects that are small or moving rapidly
and unpredictably, to the point that it is
even hard to keep them in the viewfinder.
All 50 sensors surrounding your selected
sensor are active. An example might be a
bird in flight.
• **51 points (3D-tracking)** - This mode is
intended for the most extreme cases, such
as when the subject is unpredictably moving back and forth (think of a tennis player

in a singles match). Using the colors of
the focused subject, the camera will track
those colors to follow the subject.

In *figure 5*, notice the asterisk above the
a3 menu listing. Such an asterisk is used
in *Custom Setting Menus* to indicate that
option has been set to a value other than
the default.

**Review**

*Dynamic-area AF* works by allowing you
to control a single AF sensor and initiate
good focus with it. You can move your AF
sensor selection around among the 51 sensors in the viewfinder by using the Multi
Selector. Once sharp focus has been
achieved with your selected AF sensor, the
camera can track the subject, even if it loses
focus on the subject with your selected sensor. It does this by allowing you to select
extra sensors surrounding your selected
sensor, in patterns. The patterns are nine
points, 21 points, and 51 points. Of course,
if you select 51 points, all the AF sensors are
in use. If you've selected nine points, or 21
points, you can move this entire pattern in
the viewfinder by using the Multi Selector.
Unfortunately, you can only see the primary
AF sensor you selected, not the pattern. Let's
see how to set up the "points" pattern you
decide to use.

Figure 5 – *Custom setting a3* screens

**Very important!** Please review the next section (*Custom setting a4*) about *Focus tracking with lock-on*. *Custom setting a4* is critical for working with sensor patterns and *Dynamic-area AF*. If you do not set *a4* to one of the enabled options, you may not be able to track your moving subject if an object comes between you and the subject briefly.

## Custom setting a4 – Focus tracking with lock-on
(User's Manual page 287)
*Figure 6* shows the screens used to configure *Custom setting a4* and its "Lock-On" time-out period.

*Custom setting a4* allows you to select the length of time that your camera will ignore an intruding object that blocks your subject. The *a4* setting specifies the following:

- *Long* (about two seconds)
- *Normal* (about 1.5 seconds). This is the default setting
- *Short* (about one second)

This allows you to fine-tune how you want *Focus tracking with lock-on* to work. It can ignore an intruding subject for a second or more.

With *Single-point AF*, the camera will start the lock-on time-out as soon as the single AF sensor is unable to detect the subject.

With *Dynamic-area AF* or *Auto-area AF* and *Focus tracking with lock-on* enabled, I was amused at how adamant the camera was about staying with the current subject. I'd focus on a map on the wall and then cover most of the focusing sensors with the D700 manual. As long as I allowed at least one or two AF sensors to remain uncovered so it could see the map, the focus did not switch to the manual. I could just hear the D700 muttering, "Hah, you can't fool me. I can still see a little edge of that map there, so I'm not changing focus!"

Only when I stuck the D700 manual completely in front of the lens, covering all the sensors, did the D700 decide to start timing the *a4* lock-on time-out. After a second or two, the D700 would give up on the map and focus on the manual instead.

Try this yourself! It's quite fun and will teach you something about the power of your camera's AF system.

## Custom setting a5 – AF activation
(User's Manual page 287)
*Figure 7* shows the screens used to configure *Custom setting a5*.

This setting allows you to choose whether you want the shutter-release button to actually release the shutter. If you leave this setting at the factory default, the AF system will be activated when you press the

Figure 6 – *Custom setting a4* screens

## Special Section on the Usage of *a4*

*Focus tracking with lock-on* is a focus algorithm that allows your D700 to maintain focus on a subject and ignore anything that comes between the camera and the subject for a period of time. It will "lock on" and track where that subject is on the array of focus sensors. It is controlled by configuring *Custom setting a4* to a duration period or to *Off*.

This is a technology that has some misunderstanding surrounding it. Since it is designed to cause the autofocus to hesitate for a variable time period before seeking a new subject, it may seem to make the camera seem sluggish to some users.

But, this "sluggishness" is really a feature designed to keep you from losing your subject's tracked focus. Once the camera locks on to a subject's area of focus, it tries its best to stay with that subject even if it loses the subject briefly. That keeps the lens from racking in and out and searching for a new subject as soon as the previous subject is no longer under an AF sensor.

It also causes the camera to ignore other higher-contrast, or closer intruding subjects while it follows your original subject. You will have to judge the usefulness of this technology for yourself. I suggest that you go to some event, or down to the lake, and track moving objects with and without lock-on enabled. Your style of photography has a strong bearing on how you'll use (or whether you'll use) *Focus tracking with lock-on*.

*Custom setting a4* has little to do with *how well* the D700 focuses. Instead, it is concerned with what it is focused on. Here are some good reasons to leave *Custom setting a4* enabled in your D700.

*Dynamic-area AF* and *Auto-area AF*, with *Custom setting a4* set to *Off*, will instantly react to something coming between your subject and the camera. When you enable *Custom setting a4*, the camera will ignore anything that briefly gets between you and your subjects. If you turn *a4* off, your camera will happily switch focus to a closer subject even if it only appears in the frame for a moment. A good example of this is when you are tracking a moving subject and just as you are about to snap the picture a closer or brighter object enters the edge of the frame and is picked up by an outside sensor. The camera will instantly switch focus to the intruding subject.

If you turn off *Custom setting a4*, you'll have a camera that doesn't know how to keep its attention on the subject you are trying to photograph if something interferes. When using *Dynamic-area AF* or *Auto-area AF* modes, I call turning off *Custom setting a4* "focus roulette!"

Configuring *Custom setting a4* is not difficult but first you'll need to decide just how long you want your camera to lock onto a subject before it decides that the subject is no longer available.

shutter-release button half-way down or if you press the *AF-ON* button. You can also select the setting that only allows the *AF-ON* button to initiate autofocus and the shutter release will not cause autofocus to happen.

- **Shutter / AF-ON** (default) – Autofocus will happen if you press the shutter-release

button halfway or if you press the *AF-ON* button.

- **AF-ON Only** – Autofocus only works when you press the *AF-ON* button. The shutter-release button will not cause autofocus but will only start metering and release the shutter.

Figure 7 – *Custom setting a5* screens

## Custom setting a6 –
## AF point illumination
(User's Manual page 288)
*Figure 8* shows the screens used to configure
*Custom setting a6.*

This is a control that helps you see the little
AF sensor when you first start autofocus. You
have seen this little square in your viewfinder
when it briefly highlights itself in red and then
turns black. Sometimes the background is
dark, and it might be difficult to see the black
square. If that is the case, and setting *a6* is
turned off, you will still have the black square,
showing your selected AF sensor, but may not
be able to see it. I leave this set to *Auto* on my
D700, which is the factory default. See the following descriptions:

• *Auto* (default) – If your background is
  dark, so that it might be difficult to see
  your AF sensor in use, it will briefly flash
  red when you start autofocus by pressing
  the shutter release or *AF-ON* button. If the

background is bright, and you'll have no
trouble seeing your AF sensor's little black
square, it does not flash red when you start
autofocus.

• *On* – The selected AF sensor is always
  highlighted in red when you start autofocus, regardless of the light level of the background.

• *Off* – The selected AF sensor does not
  light up in red when you start autofocus. It
  always stays black.

## Custom setting a7 –
## Focus point wrap-around
(User's Manual page 288)
*Figure 9* shows the screens used to configure
*Custom setting a7.*

When you are scrolling your selected AF
sensor to the right or left, or even up and
down, in the array of 51 sensors, eventually
it will come to the edge of the sensor area.
The setting allows you to set whether the

Figure 8 – *Custom setting a6* screens

Figure 9 – *Custom setting a7* screens

AF sensor simply stops when it gets to the edge or scrolls to the other side. So if you are scrolling the AF sensor to the left and come to the edge, it will stop, unless you have *a7* set to *Wrap*, in which case it will not stop and will reappear on the right side of the screen. It "wraps" around. It works the same way in an up and down motion. If you scroll off the top of the sensor area, the AF sensor will reappear on the bottom.

- **Wrap** – This setting allows the selected AF sensor to scroll off of the viewfinder screen and then reappear on the other side.
- **No wrap** (default) – If you scroll the AF sensor to the edge of the viewfinder screen, it stops there! You'll have to press the thumb button in the opposite direction to go back toward the middle.

**Custom setting a8 – AF point selection**
(User's Manual page 289)
*Figure 10* shows the screens used to configure *Custom setting a8*.

If you scroll your AF sensor often, it might get tiring to scroll through the full 51 focus points. In our older Nikon cameras, we had a maximum of 11 sensors to scroll through, so it wasn't too bad. However, with 51 AF sensors, it could take longer than you want to scroll from one side of the viewfinder to the other. Or, you might just like the old ways better! Nikon has given you a choice. If you'd rather not scroll through 51 sensors, you can set *a8* to 11 sensors instead.

This does not modify the fact that there are 51 sensors available in *Dynamic-area AF* or *Auto-area AF*. It just means that your Multi Selector will make the selected sensor move

Figure 10 – *Custom setting a8* screens

farther with each press. It skips over sensors when you scroll in *Single-area AF* and *Dynamic-area AF*. This means that you cannot select "in-between" sensors as selected AF points, so you have a limited choice of sensors to start autofocus.

If you are not happy scrolling through 51 sensors, change it to 11. You can always change it back! Here are the details:

- **51 points** (default) – Choose from any of the 51 focus points (AF sensors) when you are scrolling through them.

- **11 points** – Choose from only 11 focus points (AF sensors) when you are scrolling through them. The other AF sensors are still available for autofocus, you just can't scroll directly to them as some are skipped. That means the Multi Selector will move the selected AF sensor around more quickly.

### Custom setting a9 – Built-in AF-assist illuminator

(User's Manual page 290)

*Figure 11* shows the screens used to configure *Custom setting a9.*

You've seen the little autofocus assist light on the front of the D700, near the grip. Well, this setting allows you to control when that little light comes on. Nikon calls this the *Built-in AF-assist illuminator*, and it lights

up when low-light conditions are sensed, and when using certain AF-area modes (not all) to help with autofocus.

- **On** (default) – If the light level is low, the AF-assist illuminator lights up to help light the subject enough for autofocus. This only works in certain modes, though:

  a) *Single-servo AF* as a Focus mode at any time it's needed

  b) *Auto-area AF* as an AF-area mode any time it's needed

  c) *Single-point AF* and *Dynamic area AF* as an AF-area mode if you are using only the center AF sensor as the selected sensor

- **Off** – The AF-assist illuminator does not light up, so it cannot help you in low-light autofocus situations. The camera may not be able to autofocus in low light.

### Custom setting a10 – AF-ON for MB-D10

(User's Manual page 291)

*Figure 12* shows the screens used to configure *Custom setting a10.*

This custom setting will only be used by those who have an MB-D10 Battery Pack attached to their D700 camera bodies. It modifies how the *AF-ON* button on the MB-D10 works and provides some additional and useful functionality for MB-D10 users. This setting does not modify the functionality of the *AF-ON* button found on the D700 body.

Figure 11 – *Custom setting a9* screens

Figure 12 – *Custom setting a10* screens

Be aware that using the *AF-ON* button on the MB-10 Battery Pack will not activate the vibration-reduction feature on a VR lens.

- **AF-ON** (default) – This setting means that the *AF-ON* button on the MB-D10 Battery Pack will work exactly like the regular *AF-ON* button on the D700 body.
- **AE/AF lock** – Selecting this means that the MB-D10's *AF-ON* button executes focus and exposure lock instead of normal *AF-ON*.
- **AE lock only** – Selecting this means that the MB-D10's *AF-ON* button executes exposure lock instead of normal *AF-ON*.
- **AE lock (Reset on release)** – When the MB-D10's *AF-ON* button is pressed, it executes an exposure lock. The exposure lock stays active until the *AF-ON* button is pressed a second time, the exposure meter shuts off, or the shutter is released.
- **AE lock (hold)** – When the MB-D10's *AF-ON* button is pressed, it executes an exposure lock. The exposure lock stays active until the *AF-ON* button is pressed a second time or the exposure meter shuts off.
- **AF lock only** – Focus locks while the MB–D10's *AF-ON* button is held down.
- **Same as FUNC button** – The MB-D10's *AF-ON* button performs whatever function has been selected in *Custom setting f5* (see User's Manual page 320).

**The Low-Down on EVs**

What is an EV? EV simply means *exposure value*, which is an agreed-upon value of exposure metering. It is spoken of in full or partial EV steps, like ⅓, ½, or 1. It simply means different combinations of shutter speeds and apertures that give similar exposures. An EV step corresponds to a standard base-2 logarithmic exposure step, commonly referred to as a "stop". So, instead of saying "1 EV" you could substitute "1 stop". EV 0 (zero) corresponds to an exposure time of 1 second at an aperture of f/1.0, or 15 seconds at f/4. EV can be positive or negative. EV -6 equals 60 seconds at f/1.0. EV 10 equals ¹⁄₁₀₀₀ at f/1.0 or ¹⁄₆₀ at f/4. The EV step system was invented in Germany back in the 1950s. Interesting, huh?

**Metering/exposure**
Custom settings b1 to b6
(User's Manual pages 292–295)
The next three custom settings (*b1, b2, b3*) affect how your camera views steps in its EV sensitivity. Most people might like to have their camera work very precisely, so they will use the *1/3 step* EV selection of *b1, b2*, or *b3*.

Others might not be as selective, and would prefer to change sensitivity in ½ EV, or even whole EV steps.

**Custom setting b1 –
ISO sensitivity step value**
(User's Manual page 292)
*Figure 13* shows the screens used to configure *Custom setting b1*.

The D700's ISO "step" value is set with this custom setting. As mentioned above, you can control the steps in the following values:

- *1/3*, or ⅓ step EV (ISO steps 200, 250, 320, 400, etc.)
- *1/2*, or ½ step EV (ISO steps 200, 280, 400, 560, etc.)
- *1*, or 1 step EV (ISO steps 200, 400, 800, 1600, etc.)

If you are concerned with maximum ISO sensitivity, then use the ⅓ step setting. It takes longer to scroll through the ISO selections if you manually set your ISO value in ⅓ steps. The *1/3 step* setting is the factory default value for *b1*.

With *b1* set to *1/3 step*, hold down your D700's ISO button on the top left of the camera and turn the rear *Main command* dial to the right. If your camera was set to ISO 200 initially, you'll see that the ISO number in the Control Panel LCD changes in this pattern:
**200, 250, 320, 400, 500, 640, etc.**
These are ⅓ steps of ISO sensitivity.

Now, if you set *b1* to 1/2 *step* instead, the pattern changes to:
**200, 280, 400, 560, 800, 1100, etc.**
These are ½ step sensitivity changes.

Finally, if you set *Custom setting b1* to *1 step*, the pattern of changes are like this:
**200, 400, 800, 1600, 3200, 6400, HI 1 (12800), and HI 2 (25600).**
Clearly, these are full step (or stop) changes in ISO sensitivity values.

You can be as precise as ⅓ step EV, or as loose as 1 step EV when you change sensitivity.

**Custom setting b2 –
EV steps for exposure cntrl**
(User's Manual page 292)
*Figure 14* shows the screens used to configure *Custom setting b2*.

*EV steps for exposure cntrl* refers to the number of the steps in your shutter speed and aperture, since those are your main exposure controls. It also encompasses the exposure bracketing system.

Here are the three settings available for exposure control:

- *1/3*, or ⅓ step (EV is ⅓ step, bracketing can be ⅓, ½ or 1 EV).
- *1/2*, or ½ step (EV is ½ step, bracketing can be ½ or 1 EV).
- *1*, or 1 step (EV and bracketing are 1 EV each).

All this really means is that when you are adjusting the shutter speed or aperture manually, they will work incrementally in the following steps:

Figure 13 – *Custom setting b1* screens

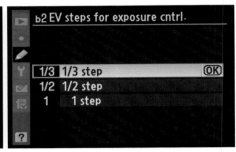

Figure 14 – *Custom setting b2* screens

## Shutter and Exposure

(starting at a random shutter speed or aperture)

**1/3 EV step:**
- Shutter: ¹⁄₁₀₀, ¹⁄₁₂₅, ¹⁄₁₆₀, ¹⁄₂₀₀, ¹⁄₂₅₀, ¹⁄₃₂₀, etc.
- Aperture: f/5.6, f/6.3, f/7.1, f/8, f/9, f/10, etc.

**1/2 EV step:**
- Shutter: ¹⁄₉₀, ¹⁄₁₂₅, ¹⁄₁₈₀, ¹⁄₂₅₀, ¹⁄₃₅₀, ¹⁄₅₀₀, etc.
- Aperture: f/5.6, f/6.7, f/8, f/9.5, f/11, f/13, etc.

**1 EV step:**
- Shutter: ¹⁄₆₀, ¹⁄₁₂₅, ¹⁄₂₅₀, ¹⁄₅₀₀, ¹⁄₁₀₀₀, ¹⁄₂₀₀₀, etc.
- Aperture: f/4, f/5.6, f/8, f/11, f/16, f/22, etc.

## Bracketing

- **1/3 EV step** – Bracket: 0.3, 0.7, 1.0 (or ⅓, ⅔, 1 EV steps)
- **1/2 EV step** – Bracket: 0.5, 1.0 (or ½ and 1 EV steps)
- **1 EV step** – Bracket: 1.0 (or 1 EV step)

Nikon chose to lump shutter speed, aperture, and bracketing all under this one custom setting. *1/3 step* is the factory default value for setting *b2*.

### Custom setting b3 – Exp comp/fine tune

(User's Manual page 292)

*Figure 15* shows the screens used to configure *Custom setting b3*.

*Custom setting b3* is concerned with exposure compensation or flash compensation. Most of us will, at one time or another, use the exposure compensation or flash compensation system. The exposure compensation adjustments are made with the *Exposure compensation* button on the top right of the D700. The *Flash compensation* button is right below the button that opens the pop-up Speedlight flash on the D700 (*figure 15A*).

Figure 15 – *Custom setting b3* screens

Figure 15A – *Flash compensation* button

Holding the *Exposure compensation* button and turning the *Main command* dial allows you to adjust the exposure compensation. Holding the *Flash compensation* button and turning the *Sub-command* dial allows you to adjust flash compensation.

Maybe *Matrix Metering*, or your pop-up flash, is giving you a little less exposure than you'd like, so you "fine-tune" by adding a little extra exposure with the *Exposure compensation / Flash compensation* buttons. These buttons can be configured by setting *b3* so that they work in a finer or coarser way for the exposure fine-tuning. Compensation can be added or subtracted in ⅓, ½, or 1 EV steps, up to 5 EV (five stops).

### Exposure or Flash Compensation

*1/3 step:*
- +/- Exposure/Flash EV compensation of 0.3, 0.7, 1.0, 1.3, 1.7, 2.0, 2.3, 2.7, 3.0, etc. (up to 5.0), plus or minus

*1/2 step:*
- +/- Exposure/Flash EV compensation of 0.5, 1.0, 1.5, 2.0, 2.5, 3.0, 3.5, 4.0, etc. (up to 5.0), plus or minus

*1 step:*
- +/- Exposure/Flash EV compensation of 1.0, 2.0, 3.0, 4.0, 5.0, plus or minus

The factory default for *Custom setting b3* is *1/3 step*. Most shooters will leave it set to ⅓, since that allows fine control over the amount of exposure or flash compensation.

### Custom setting b4 – Easy exposure compensation
(User's Manual page 293)
*Figure 16* shows the screens used to configure *Custom setting b4*.

It took me a bit of thinking to wrap my brain around this particular series of settings. The bottom line is that you can set the D700's exposure compensation without using the +/- *Exposure compensation* button.

There are three settings in *b4*, as follows:
- *On (Auto reset)*
- *On*
- *Off*

If you set the D700 to *On (Auto reset)* or simply to *On,* you can use the command dials to do exposure compensation instead of the normal +/- *Exposure compensation* button. *Off* means what it says. If you use the normal +/- *Exposure compensation* button, it overrides the settings of b4.

Each exposure mode (*P,S,A,M*) reacts somewhat differently to *Custom setting b4*. Let's consider how the *P-Program*, *S-Shutter Priority*, and *A-Aperture Priority* modes act when you use the three settings above. The *M-Manual* mode does not seem to be affected by *Custom setting b4*, although it does work with the normal +/- *Exposure compensation* button.

Notice in *figure 16A* how the Control Panel LCD uses the +/- icon to show the compensation value you've dialed into the D700. Here are the values, and how they work.

### On (Auto reset)
Using the *Sub-command* dial in *P-Program* or *S-Shutter Priority* mode or the *Main command* dial in *A-Aperture Priority* mode, you

Figure 16 – *Custom setting b4* screens

can dial in exposure compensation without using the normal +/− *Exposure compensation* button.

Once you allow the meter to go off, or turn the camera off, the compensation value you dialed in is "reset" back to 0. That's why it's called "Auto reset".

If you already have a compensation value set, using the normal +/− *Exposure compensation* button, then the process of dialing in compensation with the *Sub-command* dial simply adds more compensation to what you originally put in with the +/− *Exposure compensation* button. When the meter resets, it only returns back to the compensation value you added with the normal compensation button and not to 0.

**On**

This works the same way as *On (Auto reset)* except that the compensation you've dialed in does not reset but stays in place, even if the meter or camera is turned off.

**Off**

Only the normal +/− *Exposure compensation* button applies exposure compensation.

**Note on Custom Settings**

*Custom setting b5 – Center-weighted area*

(User's Manual page 294)

*Figure 17* shows the screens used to configure *Custom setting b5*.

Years ago, our cameras didn't have matrix metering. Back in the good old days, we all had averaging, or partially averaging meters or none at all. If you prefer not to use Nikon's built-in database of image scenes, otherwise known as matrix metering, and you only use spot metering as needed, you are most likely using the center-weighted area meter. It's cool that Nikon gives us a choice. You have three

Figure 16A – Control Panel LCD with compensation dialed in

The granularity of *Custom setting b4*'s EV step fine-tuning is affected by *Custom setting b3*'s ⅓, ½, or 1 step setting. Also, the command dials used to set compensation can be swapped in *Custom setting f9*, which we will consider later in this chapter (pages 293 and 326 of your D700 User's Manual).

meter styles in your D700, thereby adding to its chameleon status.

*Figure 17A* is a picture of the control used to set the metering mode types.

The center-weighted meter can be configured to use a central area of the viewfinder to do most of its metering, with less attention paid to subjects outside this area, or it can be set up to simply average the entire frame.

Here are the five settings used by the D700's *Center-weighted area* metering system:

- *8,* or 8 mm
- *12,* or 12 mm
- *15,* or 15 mm
- *20,* or 20 mm
- *Avg,* or Average

Using this mode, the metering system uses an invisible circle in the center of the viewfinder to meter the subject. Setting it down to 8 mm makes it almost small enough to be a spot meter, since the real spot metering mode of the D700 uses a 4 mm circle surrounding the currently selected AF sensor.

The center-weighted meter does not appear to move around with the currently selected AF sensor point as the true spot meter does. Instead, it assigns the "greatest weight" to the center of the viewfinder frame, and everything outside the circle in the center is not as important.

How large is the invisible circle? Well, from my own experimentation, I've noticed

Figure 17A – *Metering mode* control, surrounding the *AE-L / AF-L* button

that the 20 mm setting brings the edges of the best metering to about where the big circle shows in the viewfinder. Experiment for yourself to see if your D700 notices when brighter light passes that circle in 20 mm mode. So, the 8 mm setting would be about 40% of the diameter of that big visible circle on the viewfinder. Each size increase from 8, 12, 15, to 20 will of course increase the sensitivity of the center of the screen, so that more emphasis is given to a larger area in the middle.

Except when *Custom setting b5* is set to *Avg,* if a non-CPU lens is attached to the camera, the center-weighted area is set to 12 mm, regardless of any settings for non-CPU lens data in the *Setup Menu.*

If you select the *Avg – Average* setting, then the entire viewfinder frame is used to meter the scene. The D700 takes an average of the entire frame by including all light and

Figure 17 – *Custom setting b5* screens

dark areas mixed together for an averaged exposure.

Personally, I use 3D matrix metering, and have my *FUNC* (Fn) button set up to switch to the spot meter temporarily. That way, I am using Nikon's incredible *3D Color Matrix* system, with its ability to consider brightness, color, distance, and composition. It gives me the best metering I've had with any camera yet!

### Custom setting b6 –
### Fine tune optimal exposure
(User's Manual page 294)
Nikon has taken the stance that most major D700 systems should allow the user to fine-tune them. The exposure system is no exception. *Custom setting b6* allows you to fine-tune the matrix, center-weighted, and spot metering systems by +1/–1 EV in ⅙ EV steps.

In other words, you can force the three metering systems to add or deduct a little exposure from what it normally would use to expose your subject. This stays in effect with no further notice until you set it back to zero.

It is indeed fine-tuning, since the maximum 1 EV step up or down is divided into six parts (⅙ EV). If you feel that your D700 is too conservative with the highlights, mildly underexposing, and you want to force your D700 to add ½ step exposure, you simply add ³⁄₆ EV to the compensation system for that metering system.

This works like the normal compensation system, except it only allows you one EV of compensation. As screen three of *figure 18* shows, an ominous looking warning appears, telling you that your D700 will not show a compensation icon as it does with the normal *+/- Exposure compensation* button when you use the metering fine-tune system. This simply means that while you have this fine-tuning system dialed in for your light meter, the D700 will not keep reminding you that it is fine-tuned by showing you a compensation icon. If it did turn on the compensation icon (+/- on the Control Panel LCD and in the viewfinder), then how could it show you the same icon when you were using normal compensation at the same time as meter fine-tuning?

Figure 18 – *Custom setting b6* screens

This light meter fine-tuning applies only to the custom setting bank you are currently working with. If you are working in bank A, banks B through D are not changed.

In *figure 18* we see the steps to fine-tune your favorite metering system.

1. Select setting *b – Metering/exposure* from the *Custom Setting Menu*.
2. Select *b6 – Fine tune optimal exposure* from the screen.
3. Select *Yes* from the warning screen and scroll right.
4. Select the metering system you want to adjust. In *figure 18*, I have *Matrix metering* selected.
5. Scroll up or down in ⅙ EV steps until you reach the fine-tuning value you would like to use.
6. Press the *OK* button.

That's all there is to it! Since the D700 will not remind you, just remember that you have "optimal exposure" fine–tuning turned on. Watch your histogram to make sure that you're not regularly underexposing or overexposing images once you have the fine-tuning adjustment in place. If so, just go back in and adjust the fine-tuning up or down, or turn it off.

**Timers/AE Lock**
Custom settings c1 to c4
(User's Manual pages 296–297)

### *Custom setting c1 –*
### *Shutter–release button AE-L*
(User's Manual page 296)
*Figure 19* shows the screens used to configure *Custom setting c1*.

There are only two selections in *Custom setting c1*:
- *On*
- *Off* (default)

This feature is designed to allow you to lock your D700's exposure when you press the shutter-release button down halfway. Normally that type of exposure lock only happens when you press and hold the *AE-L / AF-L* button.

However, when you have it set to *On*, your D700 will act like you have pressed the *AE-L / AF-L* button every time you start autofocus and take a picture.

This function allows you to meter from one area of the scene and then recompose to another area without losing the meter reading from the first area. For sunset shooters who like to include the sun in their image, this is a nice function. I don't think I'd leave it turned on all the time, since I might be holding the shutter-release button halfway down to track a moving subject through light and dark areas. I only use this feature when I really

Figure 19 – *Custom setting c1* screens

Figure 20 – *Custom setting c2* screens

need it, then turn it off. The rest of the time, I just use the *AE-L / AF-L* button to lock my exposure.

### Custom setting c2 – Auto meter-off display

(User's Manual page 296)
In *figure 20* we see the screens use to configure *custom setting c2.*

The default amount of time that your D700's light meter stays on after you press the shutter-release button halfway is 6 seconds. If you would like your light meter to stay on longer for whatever reason, such as multiple exposures, you can adjust it to the following settings:

- *4s* – 4 seconds
- *6s* – 6 seconds (default)
- *8s* – 8 seconds
- *16s* – 16 seconds
- *30s* – 30 seconds
- *1m* – 1 minute
- *5m* – 5 minutes
- *10m* – 10 minutes
- *30m* – 30 minutes
- ∞ – No limit (Meter stays on until camera is turned off.)

There are times when you want the light meter to stay on longer, or shorter, than normal. When I'm shooting multiple exposures, I leave mine set to *No limit*, but when shooting normally it stays at *8 seconds*. You can adjust it from 4 seconds to no limit. Easy enough!

The longer the light meter stays on, the shorter the battery life, so extend the meter time only if you really need it.

### Custom setting c3 – Self-timer delay

(User's Manual page 297)
*Figure 21* shows the screens used to configure *Custom setting c3.*

When you set your self-timer for those groups shots or self-portraits, do you find yourself running around wildly trying to get in position before the camera fires? Have you ever knocked anyone or anything down, or tripped and made a fool of yourself in the process? Come on now, admit it. I know I have!

Well, those problems are solved with the D700's adjustable self-timer delay. Whether you are shooting a group shot or just using the self-timer as a cheap cable release, it's good to

Figure 21 – *Custom setting c3* screens, shown with 10 sec delay

be able to adjust the time before release—up to 20 seconds, or down to two.

- *2s* – 2 seconds
- *5s* – 5 seconds
- *10s* – 10 seconds (default)
- *20s* – 20 seconds

Often, if I don't want to take the time to plug in a remote release cable, I'll just put my D700 on a tripod and set the self-timer to 2 or 5 seconds. This lets me make a hands-off exposure to keep from shaking the camera or tripod.

### Custom setting c4 – Monitor off delay

(User's Manual page 297)

In *figure 22* we are shown the screens used to configure *Custom setting c4*.

When I take a picture, I like to review it on the monitor. I admit I am a shameless "chimper" (slang for "checking image preview"). In the old film days, one could not tell whether the image was just right. Now that I have an opportunity, I love to look at each image. If it looks good, I then move on to another image opportunity. The Monitor LCD on the D700 is one of the best ever invented for a camera, with better than VGA resolution. It is like a small computer monitor. You can really zoom in and see how sharp a portion of the image is.

This setting allows a unique time to be specified for each of the four different types of information that can be displayed in the Monitor LCD: *Image review*, *Menus*, *Playback*, and *Shooting info display*, and each has its own default value.

- *4s* – 4 seconds (default for *Image review*)
- *10s* – 10 seconds (default for *Playback* and *Shooting info display*)
- *20s* – 20 seconds (default for *Menus*)
- *1m* – 1 minute
- *5m* – 5 minutes
- *10m* – 10 minutes

I set my *Image review* option to *1 minute*, since I often want to show the image to someone. If you want to conserve battery power, change it to 20 seconds, or leave it at the default of 4 seconds. If you want, you can eliminate image reviewing after each shot for maximum battery life. Simply go the *Playback Menu*, which is the top menu on the D700, and select *Image review*. You can set the review on or off there.

The longer the monitor stays on, the shorter the battery life, so only extend the monitor time if you really need it (using the EH-5 or EH-5a AC adapter avoids the depletion of the battery and effectively sets the

### Mirror Up for Steadier Shots

This side point is not exactly related to the self-timer delay, but it's relevant. Many do not realize it, but you can also use the Mirror Up (*MUP*) function for even steadier releases. If you use a tripod, and start an exposure with the camera set to *MUP*, the camera will wait 30 seconds and then fire the shutter before moving the mirror. Macro shooters often use either this feature or the self-timer delay to get the sharpest possible images.

Figure 22 – *Custom setting c4* screens

*Monitor off delay* value to 10 minutes for all the options). Like a small notebook computer screen, that big luxurious 3-inch Monitor LCD pulls a lot of power. This screen and the Control Panel backlight are probably the biggest power drains in the entire camera.

## Shooting/Display
Custom settings d1 to d11
(User's Manual pages 298–304)

### Custom setting d1 – Beep
(User's Manual page 298)
*Figure 23* shows the screens used to configure *Custom setting d1*.

I don't like my camera beeping at me, but you might love it. Either way, we can each have our wish. You can set the camera to beep at you with a high-pitched or low-pitched beeping sound. The low-pitched sound is not very loud, while the high-pitched sound is quite audible. In fact, it sets up a harmonic resonance with the bones in my skull and causes my eyeballs to vibrate.

The D700's self-timer *Beep* function is to let you know when the self-timer is about to fire. It counts down the seconds with a beep or two per second, then at the last moment it doubles the beeping frantically to say, "Hurry up!" The options are
- *High* (default)
- *Low*
- *Off*

If *Beep* is enabled, the D700 will let you know when you have focused successfully in *Single-servo Autofocus* (AF-S) by beeping once. It does not beep in *Continuous-servo Autofocus* (AF-C), since it would be beeping constantly as the focus adjusts to the subject. If you have *Custom setting a2* configured to *Release priority*, the beep will not sound for autofocus in AF-S.

The fact that the D700 is set to beep as a default belies the professional level of the camera. If I am using my camera in a quiet area, why would I want it beeping at me, disturbing those around me? I can just imagine zooming in on that big grizzly bear, pressing the shutter release, and listening to the grizzly roar his displeasure at my camera's beep. I want to live, so I turn off *Beep*.

When *Beep* is active, you'll see a little musical note displayed in the top-right quarter of your Control Panel LCD.

### Custom setting d2 – Viewfinder grid display
(User's Manual page 298)
In *figure 24* we see the screens used to configure *Custom setting d2*.

A few years ago, the 35mm film Nikon F80 was released with a viewfinder grid display, and I was hooked. Later, as I bought more professional cameras, I was chagrined to find that they did not have the "on-demand" grid lines that I had grown to love.

Figure 23 – *Custom setting d1* screens

Figure 24 – *Custom setting d2* screens

With the D700, you have not only view-finder grid lines, but also *Live View* (LV) grid lines. The best of both worlds! There are only two selections in *Custom setting d2*:

- *On* – On-demand grid lines are displayed in viewfinder and LV mode.
- *Off* – No grid lines are displayed.

I use these grid lines to line up things I shoot so that I won't have weird tilted horizons and such. If you turn these things on, I doubt you'll turn them back off. The nice thing is that you can turn them on and off at will. You don't have to buy an expensive viewfinder replacement screen for those times you need grid lines. Good stuff, Nikon!

### Custom setting d3 – Screen tips

(User's Manual page 298)
*Figure 25* shows the screens used to configure *Custom setting d3*.

With this setting, you can elect to see screen tips for items in the shooting info display.

- *On* – Tips will be shown.
- *Off* – Tips will not be shown.

### Custom setting d4 – CL mode shooting speed

(User's Manual page 299)
In *figure 26* we see the screens used to configure *Custom setting d4*.

The CL mode is for those of us who would like a conservative frame-advance rate. With the proper power, the D700 can record seven frames per second. However, unless you are shooting 200 mph race cars and have large memory cards, you may not want 43 frames of the same subject a few milliseconds apart.

As the last screen in *figure 26* shows, you can adjust *Custom setting d4* so that your D700 shoots at any frame rate from 1 to 7

Figure 25 – *Custom setting d3* screens

Figure 26 – *Custom setting d4 screens*

frames per second. The default is three frames per second. Remember, you always have CH mode for when you want to blast off images like there's no end to your memory card or when you want to impress bystanders with that extra cool Nikon shutter clicking sound.

Just the other day, I was over at a superstore parking lot, waiting in the car for my wife to spend all our money. For whatever reason, there were about a dozen seagulls flying around the parking lot. I got bored, pulled out my camera, and in just a few minutes had 450 images of gulls in every possible flying position. *Figure 26A* shows one of my favorites.

See how my camera blended just the right amount of cool wing motion blur, with a nice

sharp eye, and somehow even positioned my gull shot using the rule of thirds.

Use your favorite CL shooting speed and grab a few, or many, frames with each press of the shutter-release button.

### *Custom setting d5 –*
### *Max. continuous release*
(User's Manual page 299)
*Figure 27* shows the screens used to configure *Custom setting d5*.

This custom setting is a bit misleading. It sets the maximum number of images you can shoot in a single burst. It sounds like you can just start blasting away with your D700, shooting in a single burst until you have reached the number

Figure 26A – Gull flying

Figure 27 – *Custom setting d5* screens

specified in screen two of *figure 27*, which is up to 100.

While it is possible that you could reach 100 images in a single burst, it is improbable. As shown on pages 423 to 425 of the D700 User's Manual, your camera is limited by the size of its buffer, the selected image area, and the type of image you are shooting. Here is a list of what your D700's buffer will allow.

- NEF Raw Files – 17 to 26 images in FX mode, or 31 to 95 images in DX mode (according to whether you are shooting in 12- or 14-bit color depth and whether you are using compression or not.
- TIFF Files – 17 to 28 images in FX mode, or 23 to 59 images in DX mode, according to whether you are shooting L, M, or S size.
- JPEG files – 16 to 100 images, regardless of image area, according to whether you are shooting in L, M, or S size, in *Fine*, *Normal*, or *Basic*, and finally, whether you

have selected *Optimal quality* or *Size priority* compression.

So—unless you are shooting *Basic* JPEG files—with the *Size priority* option selected, you'll fill up your camera buffer long before you reach the maximum of 100 shots specified by *Max. continuous release*.

If you have a need to limit your camera to a maximum number of images in each shooting burst, simply change this number from its default of 100 images to whatever you feel works best for you.

### Custom setting d6 –
### File number sequence
(User's Manual page 300)
*Figure 28* shows the screens used to configure *Custom setting d6*.

This setting allows your camera to keep count of the image numbers in a running sequence from 0001 to 9999. After 9999, it

Figure 28 – *Custom setting d6* screens

rolls back over to 0001. Or, you can cause it to reset the image number to 0001 when you format or insert a new memory card. Here are the settings and explanations of how they work:

- **On** (default) – Image file numbers start at 0001 and continue running in a series until you exceed 9999, at which time the image numbers roll over to 0001 again. This process is used when a new folder is created, a new CF card is inserted, or the current CF card is formatted. If the file number exceeds 9999 during a shoot, the D700 will create a brand-new folder on the same memory card and start writing the new images in numbering order from 0001 into the new folder. Similarly, if you accumulate 999 images in the current folder, the next image capture will result in the D700 creating a new folder, but the file numbering will not be reset unless that 999th image had a file number of 9999.
- **Off** – Whenever you format a CF card or insert a new CF card, the number sequence starts over at 0001. If you exceed 999 images in a single folder, the D700 creates a new folder and starts counting images at 0001 again.
- **Reset** – This works in a way that is similar to the *On* setting. However, it is not a true solution to the "running total to 9999" problem, since the image number is dependent on the folder in use. The D700 simply takes the last number it finds in the current folder and adds 1 to it, up to 9999. If you switch to an empty folder, the numbering starts over at 0001.

I guess it figures that you have taken quite enough images in this session! The only way you will get your D700 to feel better and agree to take more pictures is to set *Custom setting d6* to *Reset* and format or insert a new memory card. What they mean by this weird sounding notice in the manual is clearly that you should

**Reaching Limits with the CH Setting**

Page 300 of the User's Manual describes an unusual situation that few of us will ever see. However, just in case you leave your frame rate set to CH and never let up on the shutter-release button, you might want to read this paragraph carefully. Each time you exceed 999 images in a folder, the D700 will create a new folder. If your current folder is #999 and has either 999 images or an image is numbered 9999, your D700 will stop responding to shutter-release button presses.

never number a folder up as high as 999 and then shoot over 999 images or let the D700's running total of images exceed 9999 in a folder numbered 999. Next time you manually create a folder, or set up active folder numbering (*Shooting Menu – Active folder* setting), keep your folder numbers less than 999 if you are going to shoot more than 999 images that day or if your number sequence in that folder is about to exceed 9999. Read this paragraph over 999 times and you'll understand just what I'm talking about.

### Custom setting d7 – Shooting info display
(User's Manual page 301)
*Figure 29* shows the screens used to configure *Custom setting d7*.

This next feature is a primary reason why I say that the Nikon D700 is one of the coolest cameras I have ever used.

Look on the back of your D700 for the *info* button, just below the *AF-area Mode Selector* switch (*figure 29A*). This button brings up a helpful info screen on the Monitor LCD (*figure 29B*).

The extremely cool thing about this shooting info display is that it can adjust its color and brightness according to the ambient light the D700 senses through its lens. Try this:

Figure 29 – *Custom setting d7* screens

With your lens cap off, camera turned on, and nothing showing on the rear screen, press the *info* button. If you have even dim ambient light present where you are, you'll see a light-blue info screen with black letters. Now, go into a dark area, or put your lens cap on, and cover the eyepiece with your hand. You'll see that anytime there is a dark ambient light condition, the D700 changes the info screen to light-gray characters on a black background. This keeps from blinding you when you display info in a dark area.

This may not impress you much, but I am easily entertained. Here are the selections in *Custom setting d7*.

- *Auto* – The D700 decides through its capless lens or uncovered eyepiece how much ambient light there is and changes the color and contrast of the info screen accordingly.

- *Manual* – This manual setting allows you to select the light or dark versions of the info screen manually. The two screens are *B*, dark on light, and *W*, light on dark.

If you want to impress your friends and make your enemies envious, just show them how cool your D700 is when it is smart enough to adjust its screen to current light conditions. I warned you that I'm easily entertained, didn't I?

***Custom setting d8 – LCD illumination***
(User's Manual page 302)
In *figure 30* we see the screens used to configure *Custom setting d8*.
This is a simple little setting that allows you to set how the illumination of the Control Panel LCD works.
Here are the two choices.
- *On*
- *Off* (default)

Figure 29A – The *info* button

Figure 29B – The *info* screen

Figure 30 – *Custom setting d8* screen

**On** – This setting makes the Control Panel LCD illumination come on anytime the light meter is active. If you are shooting in the dark and need to refer often to your Control Panel LCD, then switch this setting to *On*.

This setting will affect battery life since backlights pull a lot of power, so I wouldn't suggest using the *On* setting unless you really need it.

**Off** – If you leave *LCD illumination* set to *Off*, the Control Panel LCD will not turn on its backlight unless you tell it to with the "light on" setting on the ring surrounding the shutter-release button. If you use your shutter finger to pull the lever to the right, the Control Panel LCD will light up (*figure 30A*).

Figure 30A – Lever to turn on the Control Panel LCD backlight

**Custom setting d9 – Exposure delay mode**
(User's Manual page 302)
Shown in *figure 31* are the screens used to configure *Custom setting d9*.

This setting is *very* important to me. As a nature shooter, I use it frequently. When I am shooting handheld, or on a tripod, and want a really sharp image, I use this mode to prevent mirror movement from adding to any motion blur I might introduce. Here are the settings.

• *On*
• *Off* (default)

**On** – The D700 first raises the mirror and then waits about one second before firing the shutter. This allows the vibrations from the mirror to dissipate before the shutter fires. Of course, this won't be useful at all for shooting moving subjects or for taking any type of action shots. But for slow shooters of static scenes, this is great and keeps you from having to use Mirror up (*MUP*), which requires two shutter release presses to take a picture. It has the same effect as *MUP* but only requires one shutter release press.

**Off** – Shutter has no delay when this setting is turned off.

If you handhold your camera, shoot static subjects, and want sharp pictures, this will help. On a tripod, this is a time-saver compared to *MUP* mode.

Figure 31 – *Custom setting d9* screens

### Custom setting d10 – MB-D10 battery type

(User's Manual pages 302 – 303)

*Figure 32* shows the screens used to configure *Custom setting d10*.

If you do not have an MB-D10 attachment for your D700, this does not apply to you. It also applies only when you choose to use AA-sized batteries of various types in your MB-D10, not when you are using normal Nikon EN-EL3e, EN-EL4, or EN-EL4a Li-ION batteries, since they are intelligent and communicate with the camera.

If you do have an MB-D10 and plan on using cheaper AA batteries, then you'll need to tell the D700 what type of AA batteries you are using for this session. It certainly is not a good idea to mix AA battery types.

Here are the types the D700 will accept.

- *LR6* – AA alkaline batteries
- *HR6* – AA Ni-MH rechargeable batteries
- *FR6* – AA lithium batteries
- *ZR6* – AA Ni-Mn rechargeable batteries

Nikon allows (but does not recommend using) AA batteries, especially alkaline and Ni-Mn (nickel-manganese). Its primary objection to these two types (LR6 and ZR6) is that they do not work well at lower temperatures. In fact, once you go below 68 degrees F (20 degrees C), an alkaline battery starts losing the ability to deliver power and will die rather quickly. You may not get as many shots out of a set of AA batteries, so your cost of shooting may rise.

However, AA batteries are readily available, and relatively cheap, so many people like to use them. If you do choose to use AA batteries, why not stick with lithium types

Figure 32 – *Custom setting d10* screens

Figure 33 – *Custom setting d11* screens

(FR6) since that is the same type of cell used in the normal Nikon EN-EL batteries and is not affected as much by a low ambient temperature.

### Custom setting d11 – Battery order
(User's Manual page 304)
In *figure 33* we see the screens used to config-ure *Custom setting d11*.

If you use an MB-D10 attachment, you will need to choose in what order you want the batteries to be used: camera first, or MB-D10 first. Here are your choices.

- *MB-D10* – Use MB-D10 batteries first (default).
- *D700* – Use camera battery first.

Which battery do you want to draw down first? Personally, I like to use the MB-D10 batteries first and have my camera's internal battery available as a backup. That way, if I

remove the MB-D10, my camera won't sud-denly go dead due to a depleted battery. It also ensures that I have access to the fastest frame rates the camera can provide. Nikon thinks the same way I do, evidently, since the D700 defaults to MB-D10 – *Use MB-D10 batteries first*.

### Bracketing/Flash
Custom settings e1 to e7
(User's Manual pages 305–317)
### Custom setting e1 – Flash sync speed
(User's Manual pages 305–307)
*Figure 34* shows the screens used to configure *Custom setting e1*.

The D700 has a more flexible flash sync speed than many cameras. You can select a basic sync speed from ⅟60 of a second (s) to ⅟250 s. Or, if you prefer, you can use the two *Auto FP* modes of your D700 (*1/250 s Auto*

Figure 34 – *Custom setting e1* screens

FP or *1/320 s Auto FP*). These *Auto FP* modes are only available with certain external Speedlights, and *not* with the built-in popup Speedlight. As this book was being written, the following four Nikon Speedlights were compatible with the D700 in *Auto FP* high-speed sync mode:

- SB-900
- SB-800
- SB-600
- SB-R200

*Auto FP* high-speed sync enables the use of fill-flash even in bright daylight with wide aperture settings. It allows you to set your camera to the highest shutter speed available, up to $1/8000$ s, and still use the external flash unit to fill in shadows. Here are your choices:

- *1/320 s (Auto FP)*
- *1/125 s*
- *1/250 s (Auto FP)*
- *1/100 s*
- *1/250 s*
- *1/80 s*
- *1/200 s*
- *1/60 s*
- *1/160 s*

When you are using *Auto FP* mode, the guide number of your flash is reduced by about one stop. This poses two questions.

Why? Plus, how does the D700 allow me to shoot at any shutter speed I want, while firing my flash, without cutting off part of the frame like in the old days?

## Auto FP High-Speed Sync Review

The answers are simple. In a normal flash situation, with shutter speeds of $1/250$ of a second and slower, the entire shutter is fully open and the flash can fire a single burst of light to expose the subject. It works like this: There are two shutter curtains in your D700. The first shutter curtain opens, exposing the sensor to your subject; the flash fires, providing correct exposure; and then the second shutter curtain closes. For a very brief period, the entire sensor is uncovered. The flash fires during the time that the sensor is fully uncovered.

However, when your camera's shutter speed goes above $1/250$ of a second, the shutter curtains are never fully open for the flash to expose the entire subject in one burst of light. The reason is that, at higher shutter speeds, the first shutter curtain starts opening, and then the second shutter curtain immediately follows it. In effect, a slit of light is scanning across the surface of your sensor, exposing the subject. If the flash fired normally, the width of that slit between the shutter curtains would get a flash of light, but the rest of the sensor would be blocked by the curtains. So you would have a band of correctly exposed images, and everything else would be underexposed.

What happens to your external Speedlight to allow it to follow that slit of light moving across the sensor? It changes into a strobe unit instead of a normal flash unit. Have you ever danced under a strobe light? A strobe works by firing a high-speed series of pulses of light. When your camera's shutter speed is so high that the Speedlight cannot fire a single burst of light for correct exposure, it uses its FP mode and fires a series of light bursts over and over as the shutter curtain slit travels across the sensor. The speedlight can fire thousands of bursts per second, but to a photographer or subject it still looks like one big flash of light, even though, in reality, it is hundreds or thousands of bursts of light firing off consecutively.

When you are in *Auto FP* mode, you'll see something like this on your Speedlight's LCD monitor: *TTL FP* or *TTL BL FP*.

This tells you that the D700 and Speedlight are ready for you to use any shutter speed you'd like and still get a good exposure. Even with wide open apertures!

You can safely leave your camera set to *1/320 s Auto FP* or *1/250 s Auto FP* all the time, since the high-speed sync mode does not kick in until you crank the shutter speed above the maximum setting (½₅₀ or ⅓₂₀). Below those shutter speeds, the flash works in normal mode and does not waste any power by pulsing the output. This pulsing of light reduces the maximum output of your flash by about one stop but allows you to use any shutter speed you'd like while still firing your external Speedlight. Now you can use wide apertures to isolate your subject in direct sunlight, which requires high shutter speeds. The flash will adjust and provide great fill light if you are using *Auto FP* high-speed sync mode.

If you are only using the built-in pop-up Speedlight, your D700's maximum flash shutter speed is limited to ⅓₂₀ s. If you use the external Speedlights SB-900, SB-800, SB-600, or SB-R200, you can use any shutter speed and the flash will adjust.

### Custom setting e2 – Flash shutter speed
(User's Manual pages 308 and 188)
In *figure 35* we see the screens used to configure *Custom setting e2.*

This particular custom setting controls the minimum shutter speed your camera can use in various flash modes. Let's consider each of the modes and the minimum shutter speed for it:

Front-curtain sync (default), Rear-curtain sync, or Red-eye reduction – In *P-Program* mode or *A-Aperture Priority* mode, the

slowest shutter speed can be selected from the range of ¹⁄₆₀ second to 30 seconds (*figure 35*). *S-Shutter Priority* mode and *M-Manual* mode cause the camera to ignore *Custom setting e2,* and the slowest shutter speed is 30 seconds.

Slow sync, Red-eye reduction with slow sync, or Slow rear-curtain sync – These three modes ignore *Custom setting e2,* and the slowest shutter speed is 30 seconds.

The User's Manual is a bit confusing on this feature, but my explanation is a result of my study and testing. Additionally, *Custom setting e2* is only partially used by the flash modes, since the default is preset to 30 seconds in *Shutter Priority* and *Manual* modes, as listed earlier.

### Custom setting e3 – Flash cntrl for built-in flash
(User's Manual page 309)
*Figure 36* shows the screens used to configure *Custom setting e3.*

The D700 has four distinct ways to control flash output. chapter 9, "Nikon Creative Lighting System", is devoted to using Nikon's Creative Lighting System (CLS) and covers each of the modes in much greater detail than the summary found here. Let's briefly consider each of these modes.

- *TTL* – Also known as iTTL, this mode is the standard way to use the D700 for

Figure 35 – *Custom setting e2* screens

Figure 36 – *Custom setting e3* screens

flash pictures. TTL stands for Through
The Lens, and allows very accurate and
balanced flash output using a pre-flash
method to determine correct exposure
before the main flash burst fires. This is
a completely automatic mode and will
adjust to distances, along with the various
shutter speeds and apertures your camera
is using.

- *Manual (figure 36A)* – This mode allows
  you to manually control the output of your
  flash. The range of settings can go from
  *Full* power to $^1/_{128}$ power and a range of settings in between.
- *Repeating flash* – This setting turns your
  D700 into a strobe unit, allowing you to get
  creative with stroboscopic multiple flashes.
  There are three settings, as shown in *figure
  36B*:

◊ *Output* – You can vary the output of the
flash from $^1/_4$ to $^1/_{128}$ of full power. The
more power the flash uses, the more it
will cut down on the number of times
the flash can fire. Here is a table of how
many times the built-in pop-up flash can
fire using the different *Output* levels:
*1/4:* 2 times
*1/8:* 2–5 times
*1/16:* 2–10 times
*1/32:* 2–10 or 15 times
*1/64:* 2–10, 15, 20, 25 times
*1/128:* 2–10, 15, 20, 25, 30, 35 times
◊ *Times* – Refer to the table above to set
the number of times the flash can fire.
Increasing the power output—going
toward ¼—will lower the number of
times, while decreasing the power—
going toward $^1/_{128}$—will increase the

Figure 36A – *Manual* flash mode screens

Figure 36B – *Repeating flash* mode screens

number of times the flash can fire like a strobe.

◊ *Frequency* – This setting controls the number of times the flash will strobe per second, between one and 10, then by 10 to 50. If you have *Output* set to $^1/_{128}$, *Times* set to 5, and *Frequency* set to 50, that means the the D700 will fire its built-in pop-up Speedlight at $^1/_{128}$ of full power, five times, with each flash burst divided up into (50 * shutter speed) pulses. Therefore, the flash will pulse a total of 250 times at $^1/_{128}$ power for a one-second exposure, or four times for a $^1/_{60}$ second exposure.

• *Commander mode* (User's Manual pages 311–314) – This mode allows your camera to become a Commander, or controller, of up to two banks of an unlimited number of external CLS-compatible

Speedlight flash units. The range of the farthest external flash unit is about 33 feet (10 meters) from the camera (see *figure 36C*). Refer to chapter 9, "Nikon Creative Lighting System", for details on how to use the built-in Commander mode to control external Nikon Speedlights.

**Custom setting e4 – Modeling flash**
(User's Manual page 315)
*Figure 37* shows the screens used to configure *Custom setting e4.*
• *On* (default)
• *Off*

*On* – This setting allows you to see (somewhat) how your flash will light the subject. If you have this setting turned *On* and *Custom setting f6* is set to *Preview*, the depth of field preview button strobes the pop-up flash, or any attached/controlled external SB

Figure 36C – *Commander mode* screens

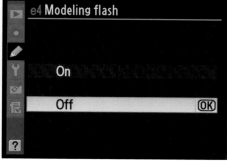

Figure 37 – *Custom setting e4* screens

Speedlight unit, in a series of rapid pulses. These pulses are continuous and simulate the lighting that the primary flash burst will give your subject. The modeling flash can only be used for a few seconds at a time, to keep from overheating the flash unit, so look quickly.

*Off* – This means that no modeling flash will fire when you press the depth of field preview button.

I often forget that I have this turned on and want to check my actual depth of field while using the flash on a product shot. Instead of depth of field, I get the modeling light. I don't find this feature to be particularly useful, and it often startles me. One of these days, I'll get around to turning it off. You might like it if you do a lot of flash photography. Give it a try, but just be prepared.

### Custom setting e5 – Auto bracketing set

(User's Manual page 315)

In *figure 38* we see the screens used to configure *Custom setting e5*.

This setting allows you to control how auto bracketing exposures are made.

You have four choices.

- *AE & flash*
- *AE only*
- *Flash only*
- *WB bracketing*

*AE & flash* – When you set up a session for bracketing, the camera will cause any type of shot you take to be bracketed, whether standard exposures or using flash. See the following section.

*AE only* – Your bracketing settings will affect only the exposure system and not the flash.

Figure 38 – *Custom setting e5* screens

Figure 38A – *Fn* button; *Main command* dial; Control Panel LCD with bracket marks

**Flash only** – Your bracketing settings will affect only the flash system and not the exposure.

**WB bracketing** – White balance bracketing is described in detail in chapter 4, "White Balance". As described in the next section, it works the same for exposure and flash bracketing, except it is designed for bracketing color in "mired" values instead of light in EV step values.

## How to Use the Auto Bracketing System

The following assumes that you have *Custom setting f5 – Assign FUNC. Button*'s setting called *FUNC. Button + dials* set to *BKT - Auto bracketing*. If you have changed this basic way to use auto bracketing, you'll need to use your preferred method to turn bracketing on instead. The *FUNC.* button is also known as the *Fn* button.

As shown in *figure 38A*, choose the number of shots in the bracket by pressing and holding the function (*Fn*) button on the right front of the D700. Turn the *Main command* dial to select the number of shots in the bracket.

Look for the *BKT* symbol to appear on the Control Panel LCD, along with lines below the +/- scale to show the number of shots you've selected, up to nine shots total. The number of lines hanging below the +/- scale equal the number of shots in the bracket and will

be equal to the number displayed preceding the *F* at the top of the Control Panel LCD. If you hold the *Fn* button and rotate the *Main command* dial to select five lines below the scale, that means the D700 will take a total of five exposures in the bracket: if *Custom setting e7* is set to its default value, there will be two underexposed, one exactly as the meter requires, and two overexposed.

You can use *Custom setting e7* to set the order of the exposures. We'll discuss that in the section on *Custom setting e7* later. The default order is *normal > underexposed > overexposed*. You can change it to *underexposed > normal > overexposed* if you'd like.

While holding the *Fn* button, you can rotate the *Sub-command* dial to change the EV value of each image in the bracket, in steps of ⅓, ½, or 1 EV. The EV step value is set in *Custom setting b2 – EV steps for exposure control*.

Therefore:

- *Fn* button plus *Main command* dial = number of exposures
- *Fn* button plus *Sub-command* dial = EV step value of bracketed exposures (⅓, ½, or 1 EV step)

*Figures 38B* through *38D* are a series of pictures of the Control Panel LCD set to various bracketing values.

*Figure 38B* shows a total of five exposures (5F) with 1.0 EV between each exposure.

*Figure 38C* shows a total of nine exposures (9F) with 0.7 EV between each exposure.

*Figure 38D* shows a total of three exposures (3F) with 0.3 EV between each exposure.

I normally bracket with a 1 EV step value (1 stop) so that I can get a good spread of light values in High Dynamic Range (HDR) images. In most cases, I will do a three-image bracket, with one image overexposed and one image underexposed by one stop. If the image is really important to me, I'll do a five-exposure bracket with one stop between each exposure.

This type of bracketing allows detail in the highlight and dark areas to be combined later in-computer, for the HDR exposures everyone is experimenting with these days.

### Custom setting e6 –
### Auto bracketing  (Mode M)
(User's Manual page 316)
In *figure 39* we are shown the screens used to configure *Custom setting e6.*
- *Flash/speed* (default)
- *Flash/speed/aperture*
- *Flash/aperture*
- *Flash only*

*Flash/speed* – This setting allows those who want to control the aperture for best depth of field while still doing bracketing. The camera will control the shutter speed. If *Custom setting e5* is set to *AE & flash*, the D700 will vary the shutter speed and flash level to expose the bracketed images. If *e5* is set to *AE only*, then the camera will only vary the shutter speed to get the exposures.

*Flash/speed/aperture* – This setting allows those who want to control the shutter speed and aperture while still doing bracketing. If *Custom setting e5* is set to *AE & flash*, the D700 will vary the shutter speed, aperture, and flash level to expose the bracketed images. If *e5* is set to *AE only*, then the camera will vary the shutter speed and aperture to get the exposures.

Figure 38B – Bracketing set for five exposures at 1.0 EV

Figure 38C – Bracketing set for nine exposures at 0.7 EV

Figure 38D – Bracketing set for three exposures at 0.3 EV

*Flash/aperture* – This setting allows those who want to control the shutter speed for best action shots while still doing bracketing. The camera will control the aperture. If *Custom setting e5* is set to *AE & flash*, the D700 will vary the aperture and flash level to expose the bracketed images. If *e5* is set to *AE only*, then the camera will only vary the aperture to get the exposures.

Figure 39 – *Custom settings e6 screens*

**Flash only** – This setting allows those who want to control only the flash while doing bracketing. The camera will only vary the flash level to get the bracketed exposures. *AE only* obviously does not apply with this setting.

Since I am mostly a nature shooter, I leave my D700 set to *Flash/speed* so that the camera will vary the shutter speed but not the aperture. That way I can control how much depth of field I allow in my images.

If I were shooting important outdoor action shots and wanted to bracket, I'd be shooting in *Flash/aperture* so that the camera will control the aperture and I can control the shutter speed.

If I let my flash control the exposure, as with indoor shots, I might use *Flash only*.

Finally, if I wanted to let the camera decide how to get the best exposure I might use *Flash/speed/aperture* so that all I have to do is shoot and let the camera do the rest.

### Custom setting e7 – Bracketing order
(User's Manual pages 132, 136, and 317)
*Figure 40* shows the screens used to configure *Custom setting e7*.

There are two bracketing orders available in the D700. These allow you to control which images are taken first, second, and third in the bracketing series.

- MTR = Metered value
- Under = Underexposed
- Over = Overexposed
- *MTR > under > over* (default)
- *Under > MTR > over*

**MTR > under > over** – With this setting, the normal exposure (MTR) is taken first, followed by the underexposed image, then the overexposed image. If you are taking a group

Figure 40 – *Custom setting e7 screens*

of five images in your bracket (see *Custom setting e5*), the camera will take the images like this:

- Normal exposure > most underexposed > least underexposed > least overexposed > most overexposed

*Under > MTR > over* – Using this order for bracketing means that the bracket will be exposed in the following manner:

- Most underexposed > least underexposed > normal exposure > least overexposed > most overexposed

I leave mine set to the default so that when the images are displayed in series by the camera, I can see the normal exposure first, then watch how it varies as I scroll through the bracketed images.

## Controls

Custom settings f1 to f12
(User's Manual pages 318–330)

### Custom setting f1 – Switch
(User's Manual page 318)

*Figure 41* show the screens that are used to select backlighting when the power switch is rotated to the light bulb icon, as shown in *figure 41A*.

The *LCD backlight* option will turn on only the Control Panel LCD's backlight when the power switch is fully rotated.

The *Both* option will turn on the Control Panel LCD's backlight and will display the Shooting information screen in the Monitor LCD.

### Custom setting f2 –
### Multi selector center button
(User's Manual pages 318 and 319)
*Custom setting f2* concerns how the Multi Selector's center button works. This setting comes in two parts, according to what mode the D700 is currently using. The two modes are as follows:

- *Shooting mode*
- *Playback mode*

*Shooting mode* is when you are actually using the camera to take pictures.

Figure 41A – Using the power switch to turn on Control Panel LCD backlighting

Figure 41 – *Custom setting f1 screens – Switch* modes

*Playback mode* is when you are examining pictures on the Monitor LCD.

First, let's examine how pressing the Multi Selector's center button works in *Shooting mode*. *Figure 42* shows the screens used to configure *Custom setting f2* in *Shooting mode*.

There are three selections in *Shooting mode*.

- *Select center focus point* (default)
- *Highlight active focus point*
- *Not used*

**Select center focus point** – Often when shooting, you'll be using your thumb to move the selected focus point (AF sensor bracket) around the viewfinder. You'll be using the spot meter or AF sensor to focus on the most appropriate area of your subject. When you are done, you have to scroll the AF sensor back to the center. Not anymore! If *Select center focus point* is selected, the focus point pops back to the center point of the viewfinder when you press the Multi Selector's center button. This is the default action of the button.

**Highlight active focus point** – Sometimes, when viewing certain subjects, it may be a little hard to see the small black AF sensor bracket in the viewfinder. When *Highlight active focus point* is selected and you press the Multi Selector's center button, the AF sensor lights up in red for easy viewing of its current location. Careful, though, because the Multi Selector button is sensitive

to sideways movement and it is easy to move the sensor while trying to find it.

**Not used** – This does what it says, and nothing happens when you press the Multi Selector button. When I first saw this setting, I thought it was a reserved setting for some future use. Finally, I realized that it means that the Multi Selector's center button is disabled when *Not used* is selected.

Now, let's look over how the Multi Selector's center button can be used in *Playback mode*. *Figure 42A* shows the screens used to configure *Custom setting f2* in *Playback mode*.

- *Thumbnail on/off*
- *View histograms*
- *Zoom on/off*
- *Choose folder*

**Thumbnail on/off** – This feature allows you to switch from viewing one image on your camera's Monitor LCD to viewing multiple thumbnails instead. It's a toggle, so you can press the Multi Selector's center button to turn thumbnail view on and off.

**View histograms** – I discovered this really cool feature while I was writing this book and immediately switched to it as my default setting. I love this! It shows a yellow "luminance" histogram, which seems to most closely represent the green channel of the RGB. When *f2* is set to *View histograms*, I can have an image open on my monitor, then press and hold the Multi Selector's center button to view the histogram. This saves a lot of scrolling around through the data, RGB

Figure 42 – *Custom setting f2 screens – Shooting mode*

Figure 42A – *Custom setting f2 screens – Playback mode*

histograms, and information screens. It's a quick histogram view that disappears when the Multi Selector's center button is released. Great feature!

*Zoom on/off* – If you regularly want to zoom into your image on the monitor without using the normal zoom in and out buttons, this is a good feature for you. If you have a monitor image showing and *Zoom on/off* is selected, when you press the Multi Selector's center button the image zoom jumps immediately to one of three levels of zoom, skipping the middle steps. Here are the three levels shown in *figure 42B*:

- *Low magnification*
- *Medium magnification*
- *High magnification*

*Low magnification* seems to be the same as viewing the image at 100% pixel-peeping level. *Medium magnification* is two levels deeper magnification, past 100%. And, finally, *High magnification* is as far in as the zoom

will go, the highest point of magnification, which is way past 100%. The zoom display centers on the focus point used to take the image.

If you are using thumbnail view, you can select from a series of images on the monitor. When you have one of the images selected, even though it is not full size, you can press the Multi Selector's center button and the image first goes to full size, then zooms to whichever of the three zoom magnification levels you selected previously. When you press the button again, it switches back to thumbnail view.

*Choose folder* – Some photographers like to use the multi-folder capability of the D700. (See chapter 5 in the section "Active folder" for more information.) If you have images in multiple folders on the current CF memory card in your D700, have the *All* option selected for *Playback Folder* in the *Playback Menu*, and have *Choose folder* selected in

Figure 42B – *Custom setting f2 screens – Playback mode* – magnification levels

Figure 42C – *Custom setting f2 screens – Playback mode – Choose folder – actual folder choice*

*Custom setting f2*, then when the Multi Selector's center button is pressed in *Playback* mode, the camera will present you with a menu of folders (those in addition to the current folder) to choose from (*figure 42C*).

If your current CF card has only one folder, or all other folders on the CF card are empty, this setting will have no effect; pressing the Multi Selector's center button will appear to be ignored.

There's quite a flexible series of functions all imbedded in the Multi Selector's center button, as controlled by *Custom setting f2*.

### Custom setting f3 – Multi selector
(User's Manual page 319)
The screens used to configure *Custom setting f3* are shown in *figure 43*.
- *Reset meter-off delay*
- *Do nothing* (default)

*Reset meter-off delay* – This setting is a handy way to turn the exposure meter on without pressing the shutter-release button halfway down. Maybe you'd like to meter the subject but not cause autofocus to start, so instead of using the shutter release to turn the meter on, you can use the Multi Selector instead.

I find this to be a useful function for another reason. I'll often want to move the AF sensor's focus point around the viewfinder, but the light meter has gone off, so it won't move. I have to press the shutter release halfway to activate the meter, then scroll the AF point around the viewfinder. When *Reset meter-off delay* is selected, any usage of the Multi Selector causes the light meter to come on. *Custom setting c2* controls how long it stays on; the default is 6 seconds.

Figure 43 – *Custom setting f3 screens*

Figure 44 – *Custom setting f4* screens

**Do nothing** – If the light meter is off, and you press the Multi Selector button, it stays off.

*Custom setting f4 – Photo info/playback*
(User's Manual page 320)
*Figure 44* shows the screens used to configure *Custom setting f4*.
- Info (left-right) / Playback (up-down) (default)
- Info (up-down) / Playback (left-right)

*Info (left-right) / Playback (up-down)*
This is the default value for *Custom setting f4*. When you are viewing a series of pictures, you can press the Multi Selector button left/right to scroll through your images or up/down to view each data screen and its histogram on a single screen.

*Info (up-down) / Playback (left-right)*
If you prefer scrolling through your memory card's images by pressing the Multi Selector button up/down, this is the setting to use. Left/right takes you through each data screen and its histogram on a single screen.

Nikon seems to want to make the D700 very flexible so that it can meet the needs of a wide range of user preferences.

Figure 45 – *Custom setting f5* screens

| f Controls | |
|---|---|
| f1 ☀️:switch | ☀️ |
| f2 Multi selector center button | 🖥 |
| f3 Multi selector | OFF |
| f4 Photo info/playback | OFF |
| f5 Assign FUNC. button | 🖥 |
| **f6 Assign preview button** | 🖥 |
| f7 Assign AE-L/AF-L button | 🖥 |
| f8 Shutter spd & aperture lock | 🖥 |

f6 Assign preview button

Preview button press     ⊗ ▶

| f6 Assign preview button | |
|---|---|
| Preview button press | |
| ⊞ Preview | OK |
| 🔒L FV lock | |
| 🔒 AE/AF lock | |
| 🔒 AE lock only | |
| 🔒⊗ AE lock (Reset on release) | |
| 🔒⊗ AE lock (Hold) | |
| 🔒 AF lock only | |

| f Controls | |
|---|---|
| f1 ☀️:switch | ☀️ |
| f2 Multi selector center button | 🖥 |
| f3 Multi selector | OFF |
| f4 Photo info/playback | OFF |
| f5 Assign FUNC. button | 🖥 |
| **f6 Assign preview button** | 🖥 |
| f7 Assign AE-L/AF-L button | 🖥 |
| f8 Shutter spd & aperture lock | 🖥 |

f6 Assign preview button

Preview button press     ⊗
Preview + command dials   OFF ▶

| f6 Assign preview button | |
|---|---|
| Preview + command dials | |
| ⊞ Choose image area | |
| ⊕⊗L Shutter spd & aperture lock | |
| ⊕⊗ 1 step spd/aperture | |
| Non CPU Choose non-CPU lens number | |
| BKT Auto bracketing | |
| [⊹] Dynamic AF area | |
| None | OK |

Figure 46 – *Custom setting f6* screens

*Custom setting f5 – Assign FUNC button*
*Custom setting f6 –*
*Assign preview button*
*Custom setting f7 –*
*Assign AE-L / AF-L button*
(User's Manual pages 320–325)
These three separate custom settings are discussed in this one section. All three work essentially the same, so instead of repeating the same instructions three times, I chose to explain them together. When I speak of the *Selected* button, I am talking about the FUNC. (*Fn*) button, the *Preview* button, or the AE-L / AF-L button.

*Figure 45* shows the screens used to configure *Custom setting f5* (User's Manual page 320).

*Figure 46* shows the screens used to configure *Custom setting f6* (User's Manual page 324).

*Figure 47* shows the screens used to configure *Custom setting f7* (User's Manual page 325).

*Custom setting f7* is designed to let you customize the usage of the *Selected* button alone, or the *Selected* and command

dials combination. There are many different functions to select from.

Carefully review the following list, paying close attention to the functions marked with a double asterisk (**). Setting those functions will disable functionality in another part of the D700.

*Custom settings f5, f6, and f7:*
- *f5 – FUNC button press*
- *f6 – Preview button press*
- *f7 – AE-L / AF-L button press*
  - ◊ *Preview*** – Normally, the depth of field function is controlled by the *Depth of field preview* button. Some users may not like the location of the *Depth of field preview* button, and since it is configurable too, they may decide to switch the *Fn* button with the *Depth of field preview* button. When *Preview* is selected in one of these custom settings, the *Selected* button will activate depth of field preview. Setting this function disables other functionality in the D700 (*see note at end of this list*). *Preview* is the default for *Custom setting F6*

Figure 47 – *Custom setting f7* screens

◊ **FV lock**\*\* – If you set *f5*, *f6*, or *f7* to *FV lock*, the **Selected** button will cause the built-in Speedlight, or the external Speedlight, to emit a monitor pre-flash and then lock the flash output to the level determined by the pre-flash until you press the **Selected** button a second time. (See page 192 in the D700 User's Manual for more information on *FV lock*.) Setting this function disables other functionality in the D700. (*See note at end of this list.*)

◊ **AE / AF lock** – Enabling this function causes AE (exposure) and AF (focus) to lock on the last meter and AF system reading while the **Selected** button is held down. *AE / AF lock* is the default for *Custom setting F7*.

◊ **AE lock only** – This allows you to lock AE (exposure) on the last meter reading when you hold down the **Selected** button.

◊ **AE lock (Reset on release)**\*\* – Enabling this function causes AE (exposure) to lock on the last meter reading when the **Selected** button is pressed once. It stays locked until the shutter is released, the exposure meters turn off,

or you press the **Selected** button again. In other words, the **Selected** button can be used to toggle AE lock. Setting this function disables other functionality in the D700. (*See note at end of this list.*)

◊ **AE lock (Hold)**\*\* – This function is identical to *AE lock (Reset on release)* except the lock is not released when the shutter is released. Setting this function disables other functionality in the D700. (*See note at end of this list.*)

◊ **AF lock only** – When set, this function locks the AF system (focus) on the last autofocus reading while you hold down the **Selected** button.

◊ **Flash off** – This is a temporary way to disable the flash for when you want to leave your flash turned on and still be able to take a non-flash picture. When you hold down the **Selected** button, the flash is disabled.

◊ **Bracketing burst** – Normally during a bracketing sequence with the shutter release set to *Single Frame Release Mode* (the *S* next to *CH* and *CL* on the *Release mode* dial), you have to press the shutter release once for each of the images in the bracket; the only way to shoot all the images in the bracketed series without letting up on the shutter release is to set the *Release mode* dial to *CL* or *CH*. If you set *Bracketing burst* in *Custom setting f5, f6,* or *f7,* then you can hold down the **Selected** button while holding down the shutter release and the camera will take all the images in the bracket without letup. This seems a bit redundant to me. I think I'd rather just set my *Release mode* to *CL* or *CH* and not fool with this additional complexity. This applies to both exposure and white balance bracketing.

◊  *Matrix metering* – If you do not use matrix metering as your primary metering system but want to use it occasionally, this setting allows you to turn matrix metering on while you hold down the **Selected** button. When you release the **Selected** button, the camera returns to your normally selected metering type, such as spot or center-weighted.

◊  *Center-weighted* – If you normally use matrix metering or even spot metering as your primary metering system, you can temporarily use center-weighted metering by setting *f5, f6,* or *f7* to *Center-weighted,* then holding down the **Selected** button. When you release the button, the camera returns to your customary meter type, such as spot or matrix.

◊  *Spot metering* – I personally use *Matrix metering* as my normal light meter. However, I often want to use the spot meter to meter more difficult subjects. I assigned my *Fn* button to *Spot metering* here in setting *f5*. Now I shoot normally, and whenever I want my spot meter, I just hold down the *Fn* button. Easy and fast! You can, of course, use

any of the **Selected** buttons instead of the *Fn* button, if you wish.

◊  ***Access top item in My Menu*** \*\* – If you frequently access your *My Menu* screen, this can be a real time-saver. . Once this option is assigned, you need only to press the **Selected** button and the *My Menu* screen is immediately displayed in the Monitor LCD, with the first item selected and ready for you to navigate to other *My Menu* options if necessary.

◊  ***Live view*** \*\* – This is a quick and easy way to grab that infrequent *Live View* shot. With this option assigned to a **Selected** button, pressing that **Selected** button turns Live View on, so long as the *Release mode* dial is not set to *LV* or *MUP*; pressing that button again turns Live View off.

◊  ***+NEF (RAW)*** \*\* – When you have *Image quality* set to *JPEG Fine, JPEG Normal,* or *JPEG Basic,* but you wish to record an NEF (RAW) image as well, then press the **Selected** button before pressing the shutter-release button; both the JPEG version and the NEF (RAW) version of the image will be stored.

◊  ***Virtual horizon*** \*\* – With this option enabled, you can press the **Selected** button to display an analog chart to assist in establishing a level horizon, a difficult task when the real horizon is not level! As shown in *figure 48,* the Control Panel LCD and the viewfinder will both indicate the camera's state; arrows point in the direction the camera body should be rotated to bring the camera to level. Always there; no need to fish for that bubble level. The D700 also provides an aircraft-style *Virtual horizon* facility, accessible from the

| Control Panel | | | |
|---|---|---|---|
| Viewfinder | | | |

Figure 48 – *Virtual horizon* views

*Setup Menu*; see chapter 8 for further information .

◊ **None** – When this setting is enabled, the **Selected** button does nothing. *None* is the default for *Custom setting F5*.

**Custom settings f5, f6, and f7:**
    **f5 – FUNC button + dials**
    **f6 – Preview + command dials**
    **f7 – AE-L / AF-L + command dials**

* *Choose image area*
* *Shutter spd & aperture lock*
* *1 step spd/aperture* (does not apply to *f7*)
* *Choose non-CPU lens number* (default)
* *Auto bracketing*
* *Dynamic AF area*
* *None*

**Choose image area** – When this option is assigned to a **Selected** button, you can press the **Selected** button, then rotate either command dial to choose between the FX *Image area* and the DX *Image area*.
**Shutter spd & aperture lock** – By assigning this option to a **Selected** button, you can press that button and rotate the *Sub-command* dial to lock/unlock the aperture, or rotate the *Main command* dial to lock/unlock the shutter speed. Once locked, the aperture and/or shutter speed settings

are locked until unlocked by repeating the procedure.

    **1 step spd/aperture** – If you have *Custom setting b2* set to ⅓ EV steps like most photographers, you can change your D700's shutter speed and/or aperture in ⅓ EV steps while in *A-Aperture priority*, *S-Shutter priority*, and *M-Manual*. However, you may want to use larger EV steps occasionally. By setting *1 step spd/aperture* in *f5* or *f6* (it cannot be set in *f7*), you can hold down the **Selected** button and the camera will then allow you to change the shutter speed or aperture in one-stop increments (1 EV step) instead of the normal ⅓ EV steps. Example shutter speeds in ⅓ EV steps are ¹⁄₁₀₀, ¹⁄₁₂₅, ¹⁄₁₆₀, ¹⁄₂₀₀. Example shutter speeds in 1 EV step are ¹⁄₁₀₀, ¹⁄₂₀₀, ¹⁄₄₀₀, ¹⁄₈₀₀.

    **Choose non-CPU lens number** – If you have configured non-CPU lenses under the D700's *Setup Menu – Non-CPU lens data*, then you'll be able to hold down the **Selected** button while rotating the *Sub-command* dial to scroll through a list of up to nine non-CPU lenses.

    **Auto bracketing** – This is the default action of *Custom setting f5 – FUNC. button + dials*. This works quite well for me, since I can hold the *Fn* button down with a finger while rotating the *Main command* dial to set

## ** Warning! Setting Some Functions May Disable Others

If you decide to use this particular function, please realize that it will disable the *Selected* button + command dials feature of the D700. It will set *Selected* button + command dials to None as soon as you select this feature. You'll see a warning on the screen when you set it, but by then it will have turned the *Selected*

button + command dials to None. If you then go back and try to set a value under *Selected* button + command dials, the D700 will give you a warning and set the *Selected* button function to None. Both settings cannot be used at the same time.

the number of shots, then rotating the *Sub-command* dial to set the bracketing EV value. Nikon was wise to provide this functionality after removing the *BKT* button from the D700. I use bracketing quite often for High Dynamic Range (HDR) images. This is not quite as good as a *BKT* button, but works well enough. If you choose to, you can use any of the *Selected* buttons to do auto bracketing instead.

   **Dynamic AF area** – This function only works under specific circumstances:

- *Continuous-servo AF* must be on. (*Focus mode selector* is on C.)
- *Dynamic-area AF* is selected. (*AF area mode selector* is in middle position.)

If you have chosen to use the *Dynamic-area AF* and you set *Custom setting f5, f6,* or *f7* (*Selected* button + dials), you can rotate either of the command dials on the camera's front or back and it will change the number of AF points to one of these four available settings:

- 9 points
- 21 points
- 51 points
- 51 points (3D-tracking)

(*See chapter 3, "Multi-CAM 3500FX Auto-focus", for details on these point selections.*)

   **None** – Nothing happens when you hold down the *Selected* button and rotate the command dials.

### Custom setting f8 –
### Shutter speed and aperture lock
(User's Manual page 326)

*Figure 49* shows the screens used to configure *Custom setting f8*. For frequent, short-term locking of shutter speed and/or aperture, using *Custom setting f5, f6,* or *f7* may prove the better choice. But for studio work in which you want to ensure that a particular shutter speed and/or aperture is consistently used and cannot be readily—

Figure 49 – *Custom setting f8 screens*

Figure 50 – *Custom setting f9* screens

or accidentally—changed, *Custom setting f8* is the tool to use.

### *Custom setting f9 – Customize command dials*

(User's Manual page 326)

*Figure 50* shows the screens used to configure *Custom setting f9*.

There are four settings under *Custom setting f9*, as follows.

- *Reverse rotation*
- *Change main/sub*
- *Aperture setting*
- *Menus and playback*

**Reverse rotation** – This setting allows you to change the functionality of the rotation direction of the command dials. There are two selections:

- **Yes** – The command dials are reversed. Here's an example: Normally when the D700 is set to *A – Aperture Priority mode* and you rotate the *Sub-command* dial to the right (clockwise), it changes the aperture in a smaller direction, like f/5.6 to f/6.3 to f/7.1, etc. If you set *Yes*, then

the direction of aperture changes will be reversed when you turn the *Sub-command* dial to the right, like this: f/5.6 to f/5 to f4.5, etc. Instead of getting smaller, the aperture gets larger. It is reversed.

- **No** – The direction of the command dials is set to the factory default.

**Change main/sub** – This setting allows you to swap the functionality of the two command dials. The *Main command* dial will take on the functions of the *Sub-command* dial and vice versa. There are two settings:

- **On** – When this is set to *Off*, the *Main command* dial controls shutter speed while the *Sub-command* dial controls aperture. By selecting *On*, you reverse the functionality so that the *Sub-command* dial controls shutter speed while the *Main command* dial controls aperture.
- **Off** – The functionality of the command dials is set to the factory default.

**Aperture setting** – *Figure 50A* shows the two selections that allow you to modify how the D700 treats CPU lenses that have aperture rings on the lens (non-G lenses):

  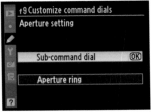

Figure 50A – *Custom setting f9* screens: *Aperture setting*

Figure 50B – *Custom setting f9 screens: Menus and playback*

- *Sub-command dial* – This is the factory default setting. The aperture is set using the *Sub-command* dial.
- *Aperture ring* – This setting allows photographers with older non-G type lenses with a CPU to use the lenses' aperture ring to adjust the aperture instead of using the *Sub-command* dial. The EV increments will only display in 1EV steps when this is active.

**Menus and playback** –As shown in screen three of *figure 50B*, there are two selections for how the menus and image playback works when you would rather not use the Multi Selector:

- *On* – While viewing images during playback, turning the *Main command* dial to the left or right scrolls through the displayed images. Turning the *Sub-command* dial left or right scrolls through the data and histogram screens for each image.

**Non-CPU Lenses and Aperture Setting**

When a non-CPU lens is used, the aperture ring instead of the *Sub-command* dial must always be used to set the aperture. If you are using a G-type lens with no aperture ring, you clearly can't set the aperture with a non-existent aperture ring, so the camera ignores this setting. Live View is not available when you change *Aperture setting* to *Aperture ring*!

While viewing menus, turning the *Main command* dial left or right scrolls up or down in the screens. Turning the *Sub-command* dial left or right scrolls left or right in the menus. The Multi Selector button works normally, even when this is set to *On*. This setting simply allows you to have two ways to view your images and menus.

- *Off* – This is the default action. The Multi Selector button is used to scroll through images and menus, as normal.

When using either of these settings, you can press *OK* or press the Multi Selector's center button to make a selection.

*Custom setting f10 –*
*Release button to use dial*
(User's Manual page 328)
*Figure 51* shows the screens used to configure *Custom setting f10*.

This custom setting allows those who hate holding down buttons and turning command dials at the same time to change to a toggling method.

- *Yes* – This setting changes a two-step operation into a three-step operation. Normally, you will press and hold down a button while rotating a command dial. When you select *Yes*, the D700 allows you to press and release a button, rotate the command dials, then press and release the button again. The normal (*No*) action is (1) press and hold a button, turn a command dial. The *Yes* actions are (1) press and release

Figure 51 – *Custom setting f10* screens

button, (2) turn dial, (3) press and release button. The initial button press locks the button, so that you do not have to hold your finger on it while turning the command dial. Once you have changed whatever you are adjusting, you must press the button a second time to unlock it.

- **No** – This is the default setting. You must press and hold down a button while rotating the command dials in order to change camera functionality.

If the exposure meter turns off while the *Yes* operation is active, you must press it again to lock the action.

### Custom setting f11 – No memory card?

(User's Manual page 329)
*Figure 52* shows the screens used to configure *Custom setting f11*.

This setting defaults to enabling the release of the shutter when you try to take an image without a CF memory card inserted in the camera. By enabling it, you can take pictures without a memory card. Here are the two settings.

**LOCK – Release locked** – When you choose this setting, your camera will refuse to release the shutter when there is no memory card present.

**OK – Enable release** – Use this setting if you simply want to preview a set of shots on the Monitor LCD without recording any images to the memory card. Note that a small red box containing the word *Demo* will appear in the upper-left corner of the displayed image.

Figure 52 – *Custom setting f11* screens

### Experimenting with Custom setting f11

I tried using the *OK* setting for other purposes, as an experiment. Without a memory card present, I set *f11* to *OK – Enable release* and went around the house taking pictures. Using *RAW – lossless compression*, I was able to take about 40 pictures before I ran out of internal camera buffer memory. The Monitor LCD displayed *Demo* on each image I took while the card was out of the camera, and I could scroll around in the pictures normally. Around picture 41 or 42, the camera dumped all the images and went back to number 1. So, once it reaches the end of buffer memory, the buffer is cleared. Okay, well, maybe I can just shoot some images,

turn the camera off, and then insert a memory card to write the buffer out to the CF card? Nope! As soon as I turned off the camera, it flushed the buffer and no images were left. Hmm, maybe I can just shoot some images and, without turning off the camera, insert a memory card? No, again! Even though I had several images waiting around in buffer memory, as soon as I inserted the card, the camera switched to the inserted card and dumped the buffer again, deleting my lovely buffer images in the process. I can find no way to write any of the images in the buffer out to a memory card. If you are the curious type, I hope this saves you some time.

*Custom setting f12 – Reverse indicators* (User's Manual page 330)
In *figure 53* we see the screens used to configure *Custom setting f12*.

   Normally, anytime you see the exposure indicators in your D700's Control Panel LCD, viewfinder, or the Monitor LCD's info display, the "+" is on the left, and the "–" is on the right. See *figure 53A* where I show the *info* screen and the exposure indicator.

   If you want, you can reverse this indicator so that the "–" is on the left and the "+" is on the right. Notice how the second screen of *figure 53A* has the exposure indicator reversed. Here are the two settings.

   **+o–** : This is the normal polarity (+/–) of the exposure indicator.

   **–o+** : This is the reversed polarity (–/+) of the exposure indicator.

   Select your favorite indicator direction for maximum camera comfort!

Figure 53 – *Custom setting f12 screens*

Figure 53A – Exposure indicator, as shown in the *info* screen: +/- on the left, and -/+ on the right

## My Conclusions – Using the Shooting Banks and Custom Banks Together

Now that you have set up and named each of the banks you are interested in using, you are ready to make your D700 act like a chameleon (or herd of chameleons). You know how each shooting bank and custom bank is configured. Now you can use them together.

Often, I will use a combination of shooting bank A and custom bank A, but nothing prevents you from using shooting bank B with custom bank D, or shooting bank C with custom bank A. Choose whatever combination you'd like to use.

That's where the D700's extreme flexibility comes in. Maybe you have shooting bank A set for fast, best-quality JPEGs and are shooting it with custom bank A, which is set for no focus-tracking. Suddenly, a flock of geese flies by

and you realize you must use focus-tracking to accurately capture the one big fat goose you like. You simply press the *MENU* button, scroll to custom bank B, and you are set. (You did configure custom bank B for focus-tracking, right?)

Or, maybe while you're using shooting bank A for good-quality JPEGs, an incredibly beautiful rainbow appears. You quickly switch to shooting bank B, where you've previously set uncompressed RAW mode for maximum quality.

Get the point? Your camera can change the way it shoots on the fly, in much less time than it takes to talk about it. Now that you've read this over, before you set up a few banks on your D700, give it some serious thought. Think of the ways you most often take pictures, and configure your D700 for each of those ways. Your camera will be customized to you!

# Playback Menu

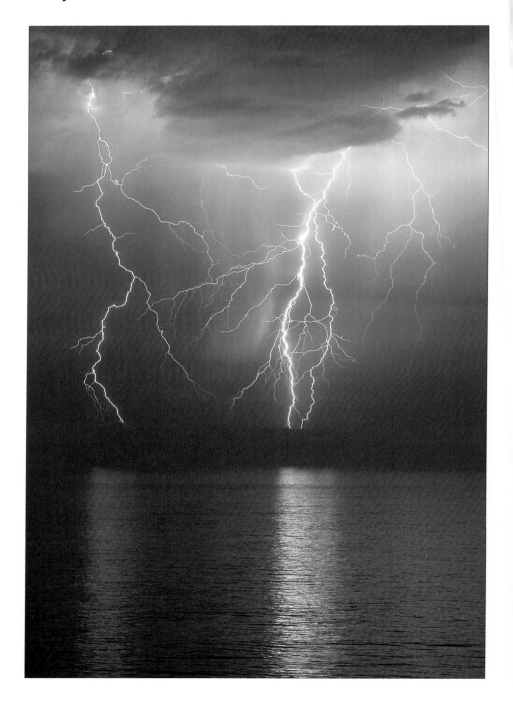

The D700 is one of the Nikon DSLRs with a monitor screen that has enough resolution, size, and viewing angle to really enjoy using it to preview images. Plus, the battery lasts long enough that it doesn't seriously impact shooting time to enjoy the results of your work immediately.

Everything you need to control your D700's image playback is concentrated in a series of menu selections. They're found under the first menu in the camera, the *Playback Menu,* and covered in the User's Manual starting on page 260.

We'll examine the nine selections of the *Playback Menu* in detail in the following sections.

## Delete Function

(User's Manual page 262)

The *Delete* function allows you to selectively delete individual images from a group of images in a single or in multiple folders. It also allows you to clear all folders of images without deleting the folders. This is sort of like a card format that only affects images. If you have protected or hidden images, this function will not delete them.

There are two parts to the *Delete* screen:
- *Selected*
- *All*

**Selected** – *Figure 1* shows the screens you'll use to control the *Delete* function for *Selected* images:

Notice in screen 3 that you have a list of images with their folder numbers and image numbers next to them. The numbers look like

Figure 1 – *Delete* screens for the *Selected* option

Figure 1A – *Delete* screens for the *All* option

"102-1," which stands for *folder number 102, image 1*. I only have one folder showing in screen 3, which is 100. There are more than six images in this folder.

To delete one or more images, you'll need to locate them with the Multi Selector and then press the center button to mark them for deletion. Once you've marked an image for deletion, a small garbage can symbol will appear in the top-right corner of the image. Select the images you want to throw away, and then press the *OK* button. A screen like the last screen in *figure 1* will appear asking you to validate the deletion of the number of images you have selected. To delete them, select *Yes* and press *OK*. To cancel, select *No* and *OK*, or just press the *Menu* button.

*All* – This is like a card format, except that it will not delete folders, only images. As mentioned previously, it will not delete protected or hidden images either. This is a quick way to "format" your card while maintaining a favorite folder structure (*see figure 1A*).

To delete all the images in all the folders, simply select *All*, then *Yes* from the next screen with the big red exclamation point and the urgent warning "*All pictures in all folders will be deleted. OK?*" (See the last two screens in *figure 1A*.)

When you select *Yes*, a final screen informing you that the dire deed has been accomplished, or has been "Done," will pop up briefly.

Being the paranoid type, I tested this well and found that the D700 really will not delete protected and hidden images. Plus, it will keep any folders you have created. However, if you are a worrier, maybe you should transfer the card data before deleting any images.

## Playback Folder

(User's Manual page 263)
If you regularly use your CF card in multiple cameras like I do and sometimes forget to transfer images, adjusting the *Playback folder* setting is a good idea.

I use a D700 and D2X on a fairly regular basis. Often, I'll grab an 8- or 16-gigabyte card out of one of the cameras and stick it in another for a few shots. If I'm not careful, later I'll transfer the images from one camera and forget that I have one or more folders on the CF card created by the other camera. It's usually only after I have pressed the format buttons that I remember the D2X images on my D700's memory card. The D700 can head off this kind of oversight with its *Playback folder* – *All* function.

Let's look at how the *Playback folder* function works by first looking at the screens in *figure 2*.

Here are the three selections you can choose from:
- *ND700* (default)
- *All*
- *Current*

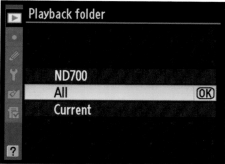

Figure 2 – *Playback folder* screens

*ND700* – Leaving your camera set to this default mode means that the image playback will show you images in all the folders that have been created by the D700 only. If there are other folders from other cameras on the memory card, it will ignore those images during playback.

*All* – This maximum flexibility setting has saved my buns several times, when I thought to check my camera for images *before* I formatted the card and found that I had other images on the card besides D700 images. During playback, the D700 will display images from other Nikons you've used with

Figure 3 – *Hide image* screens - *Select/set* option

the current memory card. Each camera creates its own unique folders. In this mode, the D700 intelligently displays its own images as well as any other Nikon images on the card. I leave my D700 set to this playback mode.

**Current** – This is the most limited playback mode available. Whatever folder your camera is using currently will be displayed during playback. No images from other folders will be displayed.

## Hide Image

(User's Manual page 263)
If you sometimes take images that would not be appropriate for others to view until you have a chance to transfer them to your computer, this setting is for you. You can hide one or many images, and once hidden, they cannot be viewed on the camera's monitor screen in the normal way. Once hidden, the only way the images can be viewed in-camera is by using the *Deselect all* option on the *Hide image* menu, as shown in *figure 3A*.

There are two selections in this menu item.
- *Select/set*
- *Deselect all?*

**Select/set** – This selection allows you to hide one or many images. You'll see them as shown in screen three of *figure 3*.

To hide an image:
1. Scroll to the image.
2. Press the Multi Selector's center button to select it.
3. Press the *OK* button.

You can select multiple images before pressing the *OK* button to hide more than one image at once. When an image is selected for

Figure 3A – *Hide image* screens – *Deselect all* option

**Losing Protection When You Unhide**

If you have images that are both hidden and protected and you unhide them, the protection is also removed at the same time. (For information on protecting images, see your D700 User's Manual page 235.)

hiding, it will show a little dotted rectangle with a slash.

The images that have been selected with the Multi Selector will be hidden when you press the *OK* button; the camera will briefly display "Done" on the Monitor LCD.

The number of images reported does not change when you hide images. If you have 50 images on the card and you hide 10, the camera still displays 50 as the number of images on the card. A clever person could probably figure out that there are hidden images if they are watching the number of images as they scroll through the viewable ones. If you hide all the images on the card and then try to view images, the D700 will tersely inform you, *All images are hidden*.

You can also use these menus to unhide one or many images, by reversing the process described earlier. As you scroll through the images, as shown in screen 3 of *figure 3*, you can reselect them with the Multi Selector, then press *OK* to unhide them.

*Deselect all?* – This is a much simpler way to unhide *all* the images on the card at

once. As shown in screen 3 of *figure 3A*, at the "Reveal all hidden images?" screen, select *Yes* and press the *OK* button. All hidden images on the card will be revealed and viewable. As the images are being unhidden, the camera's monitor will display *Marking removed from all images*.

## Display Mode

(User's Manual page 264)

This selection allows you to customize how the D700 displays all those histogram and data screens for each image. If you want to see a lot of information on each image, you can select it here. Or, if you would rather take a minimalist approach to image information, turn off some of the screens.

If you turn off certain screens, the camera still records the information for each image, such as lens used, shutter speed, and aperture. However, with no data screens selected you'll see only two screens. One is the main image view, and the other is a summary screen with a luminance histogram and basic shooting information. I have not found a way to turn this summary screen off. You get to the screens by using the Multi Selector to scroll vertically. I leave my camera set so that I can scroll through my images by pressing left or right on the Multi Selector. Then I can scroll through the data screens by scrolling up or down with the Multi Selector.

Figure 4 – *Display mode* menu screens

Here are the selections found in this menu item, and a description of what each does:

**Basic photo information**
- *Focus point*

**Detailed photo information**
- *Highlights*
- *RGB histogram*
- *Data*

When you make changes to these selections, be sure to scroll up to the word *Done* and press the *OK* button to save your setting. I keep forgetting to do this when I make changes. (*See figure 4.*)

**Basic photo information**
**Focus point** – If you are curious about which AF sensor(s) focused on your subject during the exposure, this mode makes it easy to see. As shown in *figure 4A*, if you are using *Single-point AF* or *Dynamic-area AF,* you'll see a single red AF indicator where the camera was focused when you took the picture. (If you are using *Single-servo* autofocus and *Auto-area AF,* you'll see each of the AF sensors that were providing autofocus in your image.)

This is a useful function for reviewing how the camera's AF system performs in different imaging situations.

Figure 4A – *Display mode* screens - *Focus point* option

Figure 4B – *Display mode* screens - *Highlights* option

Figure 4C – *Display mode* screens - *RGB histogram* option

### Detailed photo information

**Highlights** – If you put a check-mark next to the *Highlights* selection, as shown in *figure 4B*, you will turn on what I call the "blinky" mode of the camera.

You'll see the word *Highlights* protruding slightly into the bottom left of the image. When any part of the image is overexposed, that section will blink an alternating original-color and black. This is a warning that certain areas of the image are overexposed and have lost detail. You will need to use exposure compensation or manually control the camera to contain the exposure within the dynamic range of the camera's sensor.

Blinking indicates the areas of the image that have lost all detail, or have been "blown out". If you examine the histogram for the image, you'll see that it's cut off, or "clipped", on the right side. Current software usually cannot recover any data from the blown-out sections. The exposure has exceeded the range of the sensor and the image has become completely overexposed in the blinking area. In the third screen of *figure 4B*, I've attempted to capture the 'blinking' black indicators resulting from over exposing some portions of the petals, but this is apparent only after I selected the blue portion of the RGB spectrum! If you look down to the second screen of *figure 4C*, you'll see that the full-spectrum "luminance" histogram—the white histogram —does not seem to show any loss of highlights, but the blue histogram definitely shows loss at the right edge. Using the combination of the *Checkered thumbnail* button and the Multi Selector, I selected just the blue portion of the RGB spectrum, and the third screen in *figure 4C* shows the petals blinking

Blinky mode is an immediate way to allow your camera to warn you when you have surpassed what its sensor can capture and you are therefore losing image data.

**RGB histogram** – I like this feature, because it allows me to view, not just a basic luminance histogram (which is a combination of all three color channels) but all three color histograms and a luminance histogram in one screen (*figure 4C*).

Each color channel—red, green, and blue—is displayed with its own small histogram. This is quite useful, since it is possible to overexpose, or "blow out", only one color channel, as often happens with the red channel in my case.

You can view the three individual color histograms on the right and see the small combined luminance histogram on the bottom-left with a small version of the image on the top-left .

**Data** – Checking this setting will give you as many as four additional image data screens to scroll though. The data found on these screens is quite detailed and includes the following information:

**Image data,** *figure 4D* screen 2
- Light meter in use (matrix, spot, or averaging), shutter speed, and aperture
- Exposure mode (P,S,A,M) and ISO
- Exposure mode fine-tuning
- Lens focal length
- Lens overview (e.g, 18–70 mm f/3.5–4.5)
- AF/VR
- Flash mode and compensation

**Image data,** *figure 4D* screen 3
- White balance
- Color space (sRGB, Adobe RGB)
- Picture control detail (Base, Neutral, Standard, Vivid, Monochrome), sharpening, contrast, brightness, saturation, and hue

**Image data,** *figure 4D* screen 4
- Noise reduction
- Active D-Lighting (Off, Low, Normal, High)
- Vignette control
- Retouching
- Comment

Figure 4D – *Display mode* screens - Data option

**Image data,** *figure 4D* screen 5 (displayed only if *Copyright information* has been specified in *Setup Menu*).

- Artist
- Copyright

This large array of screens to scroll through provides a great deal of information on the image. Look how far we've come from the old film days of writing some date information on the lower right of the image, permanently marking it, or between the frames on the pro-level cameras.

Including the two standard display screens, there are seven screens just brimming with

data if you enable all the *Display modes* (eight, if you used a GPS). Or, you can get by with the main image display and one summary display. Complex control at your fingertips!

## Image Review

(User's Manual page 265)
The factory default for the D700 is to leave the Monitor LCD turned off during picture taking. This saves battery life. However, the D700's battery is long-lived since the camera does not use a lot of power. If you prefer to review or "chimp" each image after you take

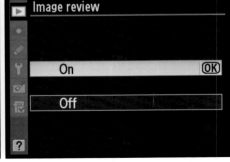

Figure 5 – *Image review* screens

it, then you'll need to turn this feature *On* (*figure 5*).

Image review settings:

1. *On* – Shows a picture on the Monitor LCD after each shutter release.
2. *Off* – The Monitor LCD stays off when you take pictures (default).

Most of us will turn this feature on right away, otherwise the only way to view an image after taking it is to press the *Playback* button.

## After Delete

(User's Manual page 265)
This is one of those weird functions that makes me scratch my head and wonder. Why is this needed?

If you delete an image during a playback session, after taking it and chimping, or after pressing the *Playback* button, one of your other images will display on the camera monitor. This function lets you select which image is displayed after you delete an image.

As shown in *figure 6*, the three selections are as follows:

- *Show next* (default)
- *Show previous*
- *Continue as before*

*Show next* – If you delete an image and it wasn't the last image on the memory card, the very next image will display in the monitor. If

you delete the last image on the card, the previously next to last image will display. *Show next* is the default setting of the D700.

*Show previous* – If you delete an image and it was the first image on the memory card, the next image will display. If you delete an image somewhere in the middle or at the end of the memory card, the previous image will display.

*Continue as before* – This weird little setting shows the flexibility of computer technology in all its glory. If you were scrolling to the right (order in which the images were taken) and decide to delete an image, the camera uses the *Show next* method listed earlier to display the next image. Since the computer in your D700 is aware which direction you are scrolling, if you happen to be scrolling to the left (reverse-order from which the images were taken) when you decide to delete a picture, the camera will use the *Show previous* method instead.

## Rotate Tall

(User's Manual page 265)
When you shoot an image as a vertical or portrait image (where you turn your camera sideways), the image is recorded to the card as a horizontal image lying on its side. You can look at the image later and the D700 will

Figure 6 – *After delete* screens

default to leaving it on its side so that you must turn the camera to view it comfortably.

If you would rather that the camera automatically rotate the image to normal viewing perspective, even though that causes a smaller upright vertical image, you'll need to set this option to *On* (*figure 6A*).

Here are the two available settings:

1. ***On*** – When you take a vertical image, the D700 will rotate it so that you don't have to turn your camera to view it. This downsizes the image so that a vertical image fits in the normal horizontal frame of the Monitor LCD. The image will be quite a bit smaller than normal to view.

2. ***Off*** – Vertical images are left in a horizontal direction so that you'll need to turn the camera to view an image as it was taken. This provides a larger view of the image.

I leave mine set to *On* since I can zoom in if I want more detail. That way I can view an occasional vertical image in its natural vertical orientation without turning my camera. However, if you've mounted your camera on a tripod for an extensive series of portraits, you will want to set this option to *Off*.

## Slide Show

(User's Manual page 266)

I used to do slide shows back in the old film days. I'd set up my screen, warm up my projector, load my slides, and watch everyone fall asleep by the 100th slide. For that reason, I hadn't been using the *slide show* functionality of my camera. However, all that changed recently.

One day I was up in the Great Smoky Mountains, shooting beautiful waterfalls and cascades. The day was about over, so I headed back into town with my lovely images and a desire for supper. I stopped in at the local buffet, got some food, set my camera up on one of those silver metal napkin boxes, and started watching my own little show while I ate. Before long, I was hearing ooohs and aaahs from people at the next table. Soon, there were several folks standing behind me watching the show. I became an instant celebrity.

It was so popular that I think I'll go back this spring and this time be prepared to charge admission! With the D700's giant 3-inch Monitor LCD and XGA resolution, it should be a satisfying experience for any tourist.

Here's how to set up a slide show with your D700.

As shown in *figure 7*, the easy way is to simply select the *Playback Menu*'s *Slide show*

Figure 6A – *Rotate tall* screens

Figure 7 – *Slide show* screens

setting, scroll right, and select *Start*. The slide show will commence immediately and have a default display time of two seconds per image.

If you want to allow a little more time for each image to display, you'll need to change the display time (the *Frame interval*) to a value of 3, 5, or 10 seconds. Shown in *figure 7A* are the menu screens to make the change.

You can select one of the following settings:
- **2s** – 2 seconds (default)
- **3s** – 3 seconds
- **5s** – 5 seconds
- **10s** – 10 seconds

To start the slide show, repeat the sequence shown in *figure 7*, except this time, the show will run at your slower speed setting.

There are several options that will affect how the images display during the slide show. These are as follows:

**Skip back/Skip ahead** – During the slide show, you can go back to the previous image for another viewing (duration is dependent on your *Frame interval* setting) by simply pressing left on the Multi Selector. You can also see the next image with no delay by pressing right on the Multi Selector. This is just a

Figure 7A – *Slide show* screens - *Frame Interval* option

Figure 7B – *Slide show* screens - *Pause* option

quick way to skip images or review previous images without stopping the slide show.

**View additional photo info** – While the slide show is running, you can press up or down on the Multi Selector to view the additional data screens. This is dependent on how you have your D700's *Display mode* configured (see the earlier section *Display mode*) for *Highlights*, *Focus point*, *RGB histogram*, and *Data*. If any of these screens are available, they can be used during the slide show.

**Pause slide show** – During the slide show you may need to pause, change the image display time, or even exit. When you press the *OK* button, the slide show pauses and you are presented with screen 1, as shown in *figure 7B*.

Using screen 1, you can select from the following:

- **Restart** – Pressing *OK*, or scrolling to the right on the Multi Selector continues the slide show from the image following the one last viewed.
- **Frame interval** – Scrolling to the right with the Multi Selector takes you to the screen that allows you to change the display time to one of four values. You can choose 2, 3, 5, or 10 seconds. After choosing the new *Frame interval* value, you'll have to select *Restart* to continue where you left off in the slide show.
- **Exit** – This does what it says, exits the slide show.

**Exit to the *Playback Menu*** – If you want to quickly exit the slide show, simply press the *Menu* button, and you'll jump directly back to the top of the *Playback Menu*, with no items selected.

**Exit to playback mode** – By pressing the *Playback mode* button (the right arrow icon, with a rectangle around it, on the top-left of the back of the D700), you'll stop the slide

show and change to normal full-frame or thumbnail image view of the last image seen in the show. This exits the show on the last image viewed.

**Exit to shooting mode** – Pressing the shutter button halfway down stops the slide show. The camera is now in shooting mode, meaning that it is ready to take pictures.

## Print Set (DPOF)

(User's Manual page 253)
This feature allows you to connect your camera directly to a PictBridge-compatible printer or any device that supports the Digital Print Order Format (DPOF). You will be creating a "print order" that allows a connected PictBridge-compatible printer, or service, to print only the images you have selected on your memory card via the PictBridge menu of the D700. This is not a difficult process to use but is quite complex to describe. In fact, it would take almost another entire chapter in this book to go over the nuances of PictBridge printing.

Since the D700 is aimed squarely at semi-pro and professional users, it is highly likely that few readers of this book will be interested in printing directly to PictBridge printers, preferring instead to use their computers to carefully postprocess each image. They are also likely to use a professional lab service to obtain optimum image quality for themselves and their clients. The D700 User's Manual on pages 243 to 254 gives a very detailed description of how to use PictBridge and DPOF for those who want to make use of this feature.

## My Conclusions

Wow! The D700 sure does have a lot of screens and menus. I remember the old days when to "play back" some images, you'd have to find the old shoebox full of pictures, or open an album and flip pages. Sometimes, I miss photo albums. You know what? I am going to run down to the superstore right now and buy several albums. Then, I'll have some actual images printed and put into those albums. Better yet, I think I'll go buy a PictBridge-compatible printer so I can print my own images for the albums and then I'll be able to write about it in my next book.

# Setup Menu, Retouch Menu, and My Menu

The three sections of this chapter cover the last three menu systems in the Nikon D700: the *Setup Menu*, *Retouch Menu*, and *My Menu*.

**Section 1**: The *Setup Menu* is quite extensive with 20 distinct features and settings that control various aspects of the camera. Also included in this section are references to optional computer software and external devices such as GPS units and cables.

**Section 2**: The *Retouch Menu* is composed of seven in-camera image adjustments which allow you to do things to the image that normally would only be done in a graphics program on your computer.

**Section 3**: *My Menu* is whatever collection of menu items you want it to be. If you use certain menus or settings in the camera on a regular basis, you can add them to *My Menu* and then use them without searching through other menus and screens.

In addition to this detailed information, this chapter provides many page references to the Nikon D700 User's Manual. Between this book and the User's Manual, you should be able to gain a very detailed knowledge of your camera's operation.

## Section 1: *Setup Menu*

(User's Manual page 331)
The *Setup Menu* on the Nikon D700 is a series of menu items for basic camera settings not generally related to taking pictures. They cover things like how bright you'd like the Monitor LCD, battery info, firmware version, the default language, image sensor cleaning, and many other basic settings.

These menu items are most likely the first you'll use when you prepare your new D700. You'll want to set your *World Time* and *Date* settings right away, then format a memory card and set your Monitor LCD brightness.

Figure 1 – *Setup Menu* screen

The *Setup Menu* is identified with a symbol that looks like a wrench. It is about midway down the menu tree, on the left. See *figure 1* for a look at the first page of the *Setup Menu* layout.

Let's examine each of the menu items in detail.

### Format memory card

(User's Manual page 332)
If you don't like using the external camera controls to format a memory card, the D700 allows you to do it with this screen instead. In *figure 2* are the screens involved in the process.

There are four screens you'll see when formatting a memory card. You'll make selections from only two of them. Here are the three steps to formatting a memory card:

1. Select *Format memory card* from the first screen.
2. Select *Yes* from the screen with the big red exclamation mark and the words *All pictures on memory card will be deleted. OK?*
3. Press the *OK* button.

While the actual formatting is happening, the first screen in *figure 3* will be shown. When the card has been successfully formatted, you'll see the last screen in *figure 3,* which says *Formatting complete.* Then the camera switches back to the *Setup Menu's* first screen. The card is now formatted.

Figure 2 – *Format memory card* screens, set one

Figure 3 – *Format memory card* screens, set two

### LCD brightness

(User's Manual page 332)

This setting is more important than many people realize. If you set the Monitor LCD brightness too low, you'll have trouble seeing your images in bright light. If you set it too high, you might allow some images to be underexposed because, in previewing, they look fine on the Monitor LCD. If the Monitor LCD is too bright, even a seriously underexposed image will look okay.

Figure 4 – *LCD brightness* settings

You can select from seven levels of brightness, from -3 to +3, as shown in *figure 4*. Here are the available values:

**-3, -2, -1, 0, +1, +2, +3**

Once you've selected *LCD brightness* from the *Setup Menu*, you'll see a screen like the second one in *figure 3*. Use the Multi Selector to scroll up or down through these values. Press the *OK* button once you've found the value you like best.

The camera defaults to 0 (zero), which is right in the middle yet is quite bright. I feel that 0 is a little too bright and makes my images look like they are exposed more brightly than when I see them later in the computer. Recently, I've been using -1 on my D700, as that seems bright enough for outdoor use but doesn't make my images appear overly bright.

Using the bars with varying levels of brightness, as shown on screen 2 of *figure 4*, adjust the brightness until you can barely make out a distinction between the last two dark bars on the left, which may be the best setting for your camera. Mine is best at -1 in normal outdoor light. Decide for yourself what looks best for you.

If you choose to set your camera to a level higher than about 0, just be sure that you check the histogram frequently to validate your exposures. Otherwise, you may find that you are allowing the camera to slightly underexpose your images. The D700 has one of the best exposure meters I've seen in a camera, yet it is not perfect and needs your help sometimes. Letting your Monitor LCD run too brightly might mask those times that it needs help. Use your histogram!

### Clean image sensor

(User's Manual page 332)

Dust is everywhere and eventually will appear to get on your camera's imaging sensor. Fortunately, the D700 provides sensor cleaning by vibrating the low-pass filter, which effectively shields the imaging sensor. These high-frequency vibrations will dislodge dust, making it fall off the filter, so that you won't see it as spots on your pictures. The low-pass filter is directly in front of the imaging sensor, so dust should never really get on the sensor itself.

If you go to the beach, where sand is blowing in the wind, and change your lenses a few times, you might develop a dust problem. *Figure 5* shows the screens used to clean the camera's sensor. (See User's Manual pages 392–394 for more details.)

Figure 5 – *Clean at startup/shutdown* screens

Figure 6 – *Clean now* screens

The cleaning options are as follows:

- *Clean now*
- *Clean at startup/shutdown*

**Clean now** – This option allows you to clean the sensor anytime you feel like it. If you detect a dust spot, or just get nervous because you are in a dusty environment with your D700, you can simply select *Clean now* and the camera will execute a cleaning cycle. To execute the cleaning function, select *Clean now* as shown in the second screen of *figure 6*, and then scroll to the right with the Multi Selector. While the cleaning is taking place, you can briefly hear small squeaking sounds if you hold your camera close to your ear. A screen will appear that says *Cleaning image sensor*. When the process is complete, another screen will appear that says *Done*. Then the camera switches back to the *Setup Menu*.

**Clean at startup/shutdown** – For preventative dust control, many users will set their cameras to clean the sensor at startup, shutdown, or both. There are four selections for startup/shutdown cleaning:

1. *Clean at startup*
2. *Clean at shutdown*
3. *Clean at startup & shutdown*
4. *Cleaning off* (default)

These settings are all self-explanatory and do what they say. I find it interesting that I do not detect any startup or shutdown delay when using the startup/shutdown cleaning modes. I can turn my camera on and immediately take

**Clean Now vs. At Startup/Shutdown**

When I am really concerned about cleaning the sensor, I use the *Clean now* method. That method seems to shake the low-pass filter for a longer period. I only suspect this due to testing how quickly I can shoot an image with *Clean at startup/shutdown* mode selected. However, even the seemingly brief shake of the filter on startup/shutdown should help prevent dust from staying on your filter.

a picture. The cleaning cycle seems to be very brief when using this mode.

Nikon suggests that you have the camera at the same angle as when you are taking pictures (camera in landscape orientation, with lens pointing to the horizon) when you use these modes to clean the sensor.

### Lock mirror up for cleaning
(User's Manual page 332)

If the high-frequency vibration method of cleaning your D700's sensor does not dislodge some stickier-than-normal dust, you may have to clean your sensor more aggressively.

In many cases, all that's needed is to use a dust blower to remove the dust with a puff of air. I remember having to do this with my Nikon D100 in 2002, and I was always afraid I might ruin the shutter if I did it incorrectly.

Figure 7 – *Lock mirror up for cleaning* screens

With the D100, I had to hold the shutter open in bulb mode with one hand while I blew off the sensor with the other.

The D700 helps out by providing this *Lock mirror up for cleaning* mode so that you can more safely blow a stubborn piece of dust off the low-pass filter. (See User's Manual pages 395 to 397 for more detail.) Using this function, it is much safer to blow off the low-pass filter.

Here are the three screens you'll use to select this mode for manual sensor cleaning:

As shown in *figure 7*, select *Lock the mirror up for cleaning* from the *Setup Menu* and scroll to the right. Next, select *Start* from the second screen, then press the *OK* button. When the camera is ready to lock the mirror and shutter in an open position and expose the low-pass filter in front of the sensor, you'll see the third screen that says, *When shutter button is pressed, the mirror lifts and shutter opens. To lower mirror, turn camera off.*

Make sure you have a fresh battery in the camera, since that's what holds the shutter open for cleaning. It must be above a 60% charge or the camera will refuse to allow you to start the process.

You'll need a good professional sensor-cleaning blower such as my favorite, the Giottos Rocket-Air blower with its long red tip for easy insertion. I bought mine from the Nikonians' Pro Shop (**PhotoProShop.com**).

At this point, remove the lens and press the shutter. You'll see that the mirror moves up out of the way and the shutter opens. When you look inside the front of the camera, you'll see the bluish looking low-pass filter in front of the sensor.

Carefully insert the tip of a blower, without touching the sensor, to blow the dust away with a few puffs of air. Turn the camera off to lower the mirror and close the shutter.

## Wet Cleaning Your Sensor? Be Careful!

If an air blower fails to remove stubborn dust or pollen, you will have to either have your sensor professionally cleaned or do it yourself. Nikon states that you will void your warranty if you touch the low-pass filter. However, many people still wet or brush clean their D700's sensor. I've done it myself, although I'll never admit it! It is critical that you are aware of the following information if you choose to wet clean your sensor.

The Nikon D700 has a special tin-oxide coating on the low-pass filter that is designed to make it harder for dust to stick to its surface. Unfortunately, this coating is adversely affected by the normal cleaning fluids that have been used for several years to clean sensors. You must purchase the correct cleaning fluid to wet clean the low-pass filter. It is called Eclipse E2, and it's safe for cleaning the filter without damaging the tin-oxide coating.

If all of this makes you nervous, then send your camera off to Nikon for approved cleaning, or use a professional service. Fortunately, a few puffs of air will often remove dust too stubborn for the high-frequency vibration method to remove. It helps to have the proper tools, such as the Giottos Rocket-Air blower from the Nikonians' PhotoProShop.com.

## *Video mode*
(User's Manual page 333)

If you plan on connecting your D700 to a video device, you'll need to be sure to use the correct video mode for communication with the device.

Figure 8 – *Video mode* screens

There are two video modes available in the D700:

- *NTSC*
- *PAL*

*Figure 8* shows the screens used to select the video mode.

You'll need to refer to the manual of your television, VCR, or other device to determine what video input it uses. The *Video Out* port is under the rubber flap on the side of the D700. Use screen 2 of *figure 8* as a reference for selecting the modes.

### High-Definition Multimedia Interface (HDMI)

(User's Manual page 333)
If you would like to display your images on a high-definition monitor or television, your

D700 has the modes and connector you need. You'll need an HDMI Type C (mini-pin) cable, which is not included with the camera but is available from many electronic stores.

*Before* you connect the camera to your HDMI display, you'll need to set one of these HDMI formats (*figure 9*):

1. *Auto* (default) – This allows the camera to select the most appropriate format for displaying on the currently connected device.
2. *480p (progressive)* – 640 × 480 progressive format.
3. *576p (progressive)* – 720 × 576 progressive format.
4. *720p (progressive)* – 1280 × 720 progressive format.
5. *1080i (interlaced)* – 1920 × 1080 interlaced format.

Figure 9 – *HDMI* screens

Figure 10 – *Time zone* screens

Figure 11 – *Date and time* screens

Clearly, the D700 can interface with both progressive and interlaced devices. The HDMI display will take the place of the Monitor LCD on the back of your D700. The Monitor LCD will turn off as soon as you connect an HDMI device.

### World time

(User's Manual page 334)

There are several functions to set under the *World Time* section of the *Setup Menus*:

1. *Time zone*
2. *Date and time*
3. *Date format*
4. *Daylight saving time*

**Time zone** – *Figure 10* shows the *Time zone* configuration screens. The screen used to set the zone uses a familiar world map interface to select the area of the world in which you are using the camera. To set the time zone, simply navigate to the last screen in *figure 10* and then use the Multi Selector to scroll left or right until your time zone is under the yellow vertical bar in the center. Once you have your time zone selected, press the *OK* button to save the setting.

**Date and time** – *Figure 11* shows the three *Date and time* configuration screens. The final screen in the series allows you to select the year, month, and day (Y, M, D), and the hour, minute, and second (H, M, S). Using the Multi

Figure 12 – *Date format* screens

**24-Hour Time Equivalents**

*A.M. Settings*
12:00 a.m. = 00:00 (Midnight)
01:00 a.m. = 01:00
02:00 a.m. = 02:00
03:00 a.m. = 03:00
04:00 a.m. = 04:00
05:00 a.m. = 05:00
06:00 a.m. = 06:00
07:00 a.m. = 07:00
08:00 a.m. = 08:00
09:00 a.m. = 09:00
10:00 a.m. = 10:00
11:00 a.m. = 11:00

*P.M. Settings:*
12:00 p.m. = 12:00 (noon)
01:00 p.m. = 13:00
02:00 p.m. = 14:00
03:00 p.m. = 15:00
04:00 p.m. = 16:00
05:00 p.m. = 17:00
06:00 p.m. = 18:00
07:00 p.m. = 19:00
08:00 p.m. = 20:00
09:00 p.m. = 21:00
10:00 p.m. = 22:00
11:00 p.m. = 23:00

Interestingly, there is no 24:00 time (midnight). After 23:59 comes 00:00 instead.

Selector, scroll left or right until you have selected the value you want to change. Then scroll up or down to actually change the value. When you have set the correct date and time, press the *OK* button to save the settings. Please note that the time setting uses the 24-hour military-style clock. To set 3 p.m., you would set the H and M settings to 15:00. For your convenience, here is a listing of the 24 hour time equivalents:

*Date format* – The D700 gives you three different ways to format the date, including the following (see *figure 12*):

- *Y/M/D* = Year/month/day (2009/12/31)
- *M/D/Y* = Month/day/year (12/31/2009)
- *D/M/Y* = Day/month/year (31/12/2009)

United States D700 owners will probably use the second setting, which matches the MM/DD/YYYY format so familiar to Americans. Other areas of the world can select their favorite date format.

*Daylight saving time* – Many areas of the USA use daylight saving time to "spring forward or fall back". In the spring many American residents set their time forward by

one hour on a specified day each year. Then in the fall they set it back, leading to the clever adage quoted above. You have two choices for *Daylight saving time*, namely, *On* or *Off*. If you live in an area that implements daylight saving time, select *On* and press *OK* to save the setting. Your camera will now automatically "spring forward and fall back," adjusting your time forward by one hour in the spring and back one hour in the fall of the year, in accordance with the dates established in 2008. (If these dates change, watch the Nikon Web site for a firmware update.)

*Language*
(User's Manual page 334)
Nikon is a company that sells cameras and lenses around the world. For that reason, your D700 can speak up to 15 languages. In *figure 13* are the screens used to select your choice of language. Screens 2 and 3 of *figure 13* are continuations of a single menu item that, of course, won't fit on a single D700 Monitor LCD screen.

Figure 13 – *Language* screens

The following languages are included with the D700 using firmware version 1.00:

- German
- English
- Spanish
- Finnish
- French
- Italian
- Dutch
- Polish
- Portuguese
- Russian
- Swedish
- Traditional Chinese
- Simplified Chinese
- Japanese
- Korean

The D700 should default to the language of the area in which you purchased the camera.

### Image comment

(User's Manual page 335)

This is a useful setting that you can use to attach a comment to each image you shoot. I might add "Nikonians D700 Project" for the photos for this book or place a short note and my phone number to assist someone if I were to lose my camera.

The three screens shown in *figure 14* are used to add a comment to each subsequent image.

From the second screen shown in *figure 14*, you'll select the *Input comment* line and scroll to the right with the Multi Selector. In the third screen, you'll see a series of symbols, numbers, and letters on top with a line of dashes at the bottom. The dashes are where you will put your text to attach a comment. In the upper-left corner of the characters area is a blank spot which represents a blank for insertion in the line of text. This is good for separating words. If you scroll down past the uppercase letters, you'll find some lowercase letters too.

Following is a series of steps to use while creating the image comment. You'll use the external camera controls shown in *figure 15* while creating and saving an image comment.

Figure 14 – *Image comment* initial screens

Figure 15 – Camera controls for adding an
*Image comment*

Steps to input new characters:

1. Use the Multi Selector to scroll through the
   numbers and letters to find the characters
   you want to use. Scroll down for lowercase
   letters.
2. Press the Multi Selector's center button to
   select a character. Keep selecting new characters until you have the entire *Image comment* in place. The comment can be as long
   as 36 characters, and blanks are counted as
   characters.
3. If you make a mistake, hold down the
   *Checkered Thumbnail* button while using
   the Multi Selector to move to the position
   of the error. Push the garbage can *Delete*
   button on the top left of the D700. The
   unwanted character will disappear.
4. Press the *OK* button to save the *Image comment*.

5. The camera will switch back to the second
   screen (as seen in *figure 14*). You'll need
   to select the *Attach comment* check box so
   that the comment will attach itself to each
   subsequent image. Scroll to the *Attach
   comment* line and press the *OK* button.
   You'll see a check mark appear in the little
   box.
6. Scroll up to *Done*, then press *OK* again.
   That completes the process.

Any comment you create here will be added
internally to the metadata of the image. It
*will not* show on the image itself, but it is displayed on the third page of the photo's *info*
display.

### Auto image rotation

(User's Manual pages 336 and 265)
The D700 has a direction-sensing device so
that it knows how a picture is oriented. This
setting allows you to record that information
with the image.

Portrait-mode pictures can be taken with
the handgrip either at the top of the camera or
at the bottom. Of course, the two image directions are 180 degrees apart and are upside
down from each other, but that is resolved
when the image is displayed.

With *Auto image rotation* set, subse-
quently-recorded vertical images will display as upright portrait images when viewed
in compatible software such as ViewNX or

Figure 16 – Menu screens for *Auto image rotation*

## CL or CH Mode and Image Orientation

If you are shooting in continuous frame-advance mode (*CL* or *CH*), the way you are holding your camera for the first shot sets the direction the images are displayed, even if you change direction while shooting.

Capture NX 2. Also, once *Auto image rotation* data is recorded with the image, the image can be rotated in playback mode, if *Rotate tall* has been turned on in *Playback Menu* (see User's Manual page 265).

In *figure 16* are the two screens used to set the *Auto image rotation* function.

You have two selections:

- *On* (default)
- *Off*

*On* – With *Auto image rotation* turned *On*, the D700 will automatically save the orientation information with the image.

*Off* – If it is turned *Off*, then the camera does not record orientation information with the image.

The User's Manual states that you might want to choose *Off* if you are pointing the lens up or down. However, I have tested it well, and the D700 seems quite good at determining when you have the camera held horizontally or vertically, even when you do have the lens pointed up or down. Test this for yourself and determine which you would prefer. I leave mine set to *On*, and I've had no problems.

### Dust off ref photo

(User's Manual page 337–339)
Often, you may go out and do an expensive shoot only to return and find that some dust spots have appeared in the worst possible place in your images. If you then create a *Dust Off* reference photo, you can use it to remove the dust spots from your images and afterward clean the sensor for the next shooting session. Here's how it works.

When you use the instructions in the next sections to create the *Dust Off* reference photo, you will be shooting a blank unfocused picture of a pure white or gray background. The dust spots in the image will then be readily apparent to Nikon Capture NX 2 software. When you load the image to be cleaned into Capture NX 2, along with the dust-off image, it will use that image to remove the spots in your production image.

The position and amount of dust on the low-pass filter may change, especially if you are using one of the *Clean image sensor* settings other than *Off*. It is recommended that you take reference images regularly and use a reference image that was taken within one day of the photograph you wish to clean up.

### Finding a Subject for the Dust Reference Photo

First, we need to select a "featureless" subject to photograph for the reference photo. The key here is to use a material that has no graininess, such as bright white, slick plastic, or a white card. I tried using plain white sheets of paper held up to a bright window, but the resulting reference photo was unsatisfactory to Capture NX 2. It gave me a message that my reference photo was "too dusty" when I tried to use it.

After some experimentation, I finally settled on three different subjects that seemed to work well:

- A slide-viewing light table with the light turned on
- A computer monitor screen with a blank white word-processor document displayed
- A plain white card in the same bright light in which your subject resides

All of these provided enough light and featurelessness to satisfy both my camera and Capture NX 2. The key is to photograph something fairly bright, but not too bright. You may need to experiment with different subjects if you have no light table or computer.

Now, let's prepare the camera for the actual reference photo.

### Menu and Screen Selections for Getting the Reference Photo

1. Press the *Menu* button on the back of your D700.
2. Select the *Setup Menu* and scroll down until you find the *Dust off ref photo* menu selection.
3. Once there, scroll to the right and you will find the *Start* selection. There is also a *Clean sensor and then start* selection. However, since I desire to remove dust on current pictures, I won't use this setting. It might remove the dust bunny that is imprinted on the last 500 images I just shot! I'll clean my sensor *after* I get a good *Dust Off* reference photo.
4. Scroll right on the *Start* selection and your camera is ready to take the reference image.

In *figure 17*, you'll find the sequence of screens to prepare your camera for taking the photo.

After you have selected *Start*, you will find the word *rEF* in the viewfinder and Control Panel. This simply means that you are ready to create the 'rEFerence' image.

### Creating the Reference Photo

Once you have the camera ready, hold the lens about 4 inches (10 cm) away from the blank subject. The camera will not try to autofocus during the process, which is good since you want the lens at infinity anyway. You are not trying to take a viewable picture, just creating an image that shows where the dust is on the sensor. Focus is not important, and neither is minor camera shake. If you try to take the picture and the subject is not bright enough or is too bright, you will see the screen shown in *figure 18*.

If you are having problems with too much brightness, use a gray surface instead of white. Most of the time this exposure-settings error is caused by insufficient light.

If you don't see the screen in *figure 18* and the shutter fires, you have successfully created a *Dust Off* reference photo. You will find the image shown in *figure 19* on your Monitor LCD. In either FX mode or DX mode, a

Figure 18 – *Exposure settings are not appropriate* screen

Figure 17 – *Dust off ref photo* screens

Figure 19 – *Dust off ref photo* checkered screen

2 megabyte file is created on your camera's image card with a file name extension of .ndf instead of the normal .nef, .tif, or .jpg (An example filename is DSC_1234.ndf.) This NDF file is basically a small database of the millions of clean pixels in your imaging sensor, and a few dirty ones.

The NDF file type is not intended for display on your computer. It will not open in any other graphics program that I tried.

**Where to Store the Reference Photo**
Copy the NDF file from your camera's memory card to the computer folder containing the images that have dust spots on them and for which you created this *Dust Off* reference photo.

Now we're ready to move into Nikon Capture NX 2 and use our new reference photo on its related images.

**Using the Dust Off Reference Photo in Nikon Capture NX 2**
Load Capture NX 2 and then open one of the dusty images from the folder containing the reference photo's NDF file. You must have an image open to proceed; otherwise, the menus

Figure 20 – Selecting *Image Dust Off* from Nikon Capture NX 2

will not display on the right side of Capture NX 2.

As seen in *figure 20*, the Capture NX 2 screen contains a toolbar on the right with a selection called *Develop*. Below that, select *Camera and Lens Corrections*. The Image *Dust Off* selection is a sub-category under *Camera and Lens Corrections*.

Click the *Change* button on the menu and a small window will pop up on your computer screen. It will look like the one shown in *figure 21*.

Capture NX 2 will automatically search the folder where you opened the test image and will display this window. It allows you to use the *Dust Off* reference photo stored with your images. To continue, click the *Yes* button.

Capture NX 2 will now present you with a window that lets you verify that the *Dust Off* reference photo it found is the one you want to use. If more than one *Dust Off* reference photo is found, you will be presented with an options dialog to select which image to use. It is recommended that you select the image that was taken as close to the time of the current image as possible. *Figure 22* shows the window that pops up when Capture NX 2

Figure 21 – Choosing the *Dust Off* photo, step 1

Figure 22 – Choosing the *Dust Off* photo, step 2

finds one good *Dust Off* reference photo in the folder with your images.

Notice in *figure 22* that a date and time appears in the field to the left of the *Change* button. This represents the date and time of the selected *Dust Off* reference photo. Click *OK* and the *Dust Off* process will complete.

Nothing pops up to tell you it is done, so allow a few seconds. It's very fast, since all that is happening is the re-interpolating of the few pixels that have dust on them. This re-interpolation process simply uses pixels surrounding the dust particle to decide how best to represent the few pixels under the dust. You will rarely see any visible change in your image, unless you have a big old hairy dust particle blocking half the sky.

I have found that in areas like blue skies, the *Dust Off* process works very well. In images with a lot of fine detail, like a forest scene, sometimes not all the dust particles are mapped out, and I have to manually adjust a few pixels.

Fortunately, you can't often see dust particles mixed in with fine image detail. I've had some large dust particles get on my sensor a time or two. One showed up even in the middle of a mountain's tree line. The *Dust Off* process got most of it, but I had to work a little in Photoshop to remove the rest. This has only happened a time or two, and it was a really big piece of something on the sensor. I can understand why Capture NX 2 might have problems in a background of confusing detail like tree leaves at a distance. How can it figure out how to re-interpolate something with no dependable pattern? I find that even I have trouble when I try to do it manually in Photoshop. I am surprised by how well the *Dust Off* process actually works.

This whole *Dust Off* technique can save you a lot of grief when you come back from an important shoot and find a big dust spot on all your images. It saves a lot of postprocessing work on individual images. Learn to use it and you'll not worry so much about dust (even though you still should).

Sometimes during the *Dust Off* process, one or more warning screens will appear. Let's look at each of them to see what they mean.

### Capture NX 2 Dust Off Warning Screens
*Warning Screen 1 Text* (*figure 23*):
"One or more Dust off ref photos were found, but none of them closely match the active image. Would you like to use the closest match?"

The warning screen in *figure 23* shows up more often than not, even with *Dust Off* reference photos I've created on site. I normally just click *Yes* and let the process complete. I've had no untoward results yet.

*Warning Screen 2 Text* (*figure 24*): "The selected Dust off ref photo contains too much dust and could cause image details to be lost. Do you want to use it anyway? Note: It is possible to receive this warning if the reference photo was not taken of a featureless surface. The reference photo should be taken of a plain surface, and should be taken fairly close to that surface. Press the 'Verify' button to see if the reference photo was captured correctly."

This warning screen is pretty self-explanatory, and I would pay attention to it carefully. Don't ignore this one! Image damage might result. Why?

It means that the surface you used to create your *Dust Off* reference photo was grainy or dirty, or you were not close enough to it when you clicked the shutter.

Remember, all your camera needs to create a *Dust Off* reference photo is a good bright look at the camera's sensor so that it can map the dirt spots into an NDF file (ref photo file). If you hold your camera too far away from the white surface you are photographing to create the ref photo, this warning will show up.

When your lens is a distance away from the surface, you might actually be photographing small dirt on the surface of your white subject. Those spots can mix in with the dust seen on the sensor and make an inaccurate *Dust Off* reference photo.

Later, when you use it to remove dust from an image, it removes the dust found on the sensor and all the other spots that were on the white surface. Those extra spots were not really on the image, so Capture NX 2 is removing spots it shouldn't remove. The image quality may go down from all the unnecessary re-interpolation.

If you get the warning shown in *figure 24*, go shoot another *Dust Off* reference photo with a nice bright and clean white surface. Put the lens very close to the surface, and make sure it is not in focus. You might even want to manually set the lens to infinity if you are having problems with this often.

Figure 23 – Barely matching *Dust Off* reference photo

Figure 24 – *Too much dust* in reference photo

Once you've found your favorite white or gray surface for *Dust Off* reference photos, keep it safe and use it consistently.

If you want to "verify" the *Dust Off* reference photo, you can do it here (*figure 24*). In fact, this is one of the only ways I've found to actually see a *Dust Off* reference photo. Click the *Verify* button and a little window will open with a view of the *Dust Off* reference photo. It's kind of small, so you won't see much, but it might satisfy your curiosity.

Figure 25A – Picture of EN-EL3e battery

### Battery info

(User's Manual pages 340–341)

The *Battery info* screens, seen in *figure 25*, will let you know how much battery charge remains (*Bat. meter*), how many images have been taken with this battery since the last charge (*Pic. meter*), and in what stage of *Charging life* the battery exists.

The D700 goes a step further than most cameras. Not only does it keep you informed as to the amount of "charge" left in your battery, but it also lets you know how much "life" is left. After some time, all batteries weaken and won't accept a full charge. By referring to the *Charging life* meter, you'll know when the battery needs to be replaced. It shows five stages of battery life, from New to ! (! = replace) or 0 to 4, so that you'll be

prepared for replacement before your battery gets too old to be of many-shot use.

In my opinion, it's important to use Nikon brand batteries in your D700 so that they work the best with the camera. Aftermarket batteries may not charge correctly in the D700 battery charger. In addition, they may not report correctly in the *Charging life* section of the battery screen. There may be an aftermarket brand that works correctly, but I've not found it personally. Instead, I choose to use the batteries designed by Nikon to work with this camera. I am a bit afraid to trust a camera that costs this much to a cheap aftermarket battery of unknown origin.

*Figure 25A* shows a picture of a genuine gray-colored Li-Ion Nikon EN-EL3e battery, for battery identification purposes. If you've upgraded from something like the Nikon

Figure 25 – *Battery info* screens

## Battery and Calibration Info

If you are using the MB-D10 Battery Pack with an EN-EL4a battery, or the EN-EL4 battery pack, your *Battery info* screen will also show *calibration* information. Calibration is optional but could be required after many charge/discharge cycles so that the *Battery info* screen will present accurate information. The battery charger for the Nikon D700 does not have a calibration feature, so many D700 users will have little knowledge of it. The battery charger for the EN-EL4a battery does. (If you also use a Nikon D2H/X/Xs you will be familiar with calibration). The *Battery info* screen will change the amount of information it displays to a significant degree, according to whether you have an MB-D10 Battery Pack mounted and what type of batteries are being used in the pack. There is a chart on page 341 of the User's Manual that shows the various informational items displayed according to the type of batteries.

D100 that uses the Nikon EN-EL3 battery, or the very similar EN-EL3a battery, you'll see that the dimensions are essentially identical; however, *DO NOT* use that battery in the D700.

This *Battery info* screen is just for information. There is nothing to set. When you have finished examining your *Battery info*, just press the *OK* button to exit.

### Wireless transmitter
(User's Manual pages 242 and 341)
This menu system is concerned with having the WT-4 Wireless Transmitter attached to the D700. Using the WT-4, you can send images wirelessly to a computer or printer.

You can also use Nikon's Camera Control 2.x software to control the D700 remotely.

Here are the four modes found in the D700 with a WT-4 attached:

- *Transfer mode* – Using this mode you can upload new or existing images to a computer or even to a File Transfer Protocol (FTP) server.
- *Thumbnail select mode* – This allows someone to preview images you are shooting on a remote computer. If they like the image(s), they can upload just the one(s) they like to the computer. Sports shooters love this!
- *PC mode* – This might have been called studio mode instead. It allows a studio artist to control their D700 from a computer using the Nikon Camera Control Pro 2.x software.
- *Print mode* – This allows someone shooting near a computer network to have the images printed on a printer connected to a network computer.

This book won't cover the use of the WT-4 transmitter in any more detail since it has its own comprehensive feature set and this book is limited to the Nikon D700. See page 242 in the User's Manual for more detail.

### Image authentication
(User's Manual page 342)
With film, one can easily detect whether a printed image has been modified from the original. All one must do is look at the original transparency or negative. However, with digital photography and programs like Photoshop, one can modify an image in amazing ways.

Many law enforcement agencies would like to use digital imaging to save money on film and processing costs but have been hampered by this ability to modify digital images so easily. Some courts have refused digital images as evidence for this reason.

Some major editorial houses, like those with large newspapers and magazines, have been embarrassed when one of their photographers modified a news image and was later caught.

Clearly there is a need to prove that a digital image has not been modified from its original form. Nikon has answered that need with the *Image authentication* feature of the Nikon D700 and other recent Nikon DSLR cameras. Working in conjunction with Nikon's Image Authentication Software, the D700 can stamp images with an electronic "seal" that allows an agency to prove that an image printed from the camera has not been modified in any way.

*Figure 26* shows one of Nikon's image information screens with the authentication stamp icon.

There are two settings in the *Image Authentication* function, as shown in *figure 27*.

These settings are as follows:

- *On*
- *Off* (Default)

*On* – *Image authentication* information, which can be used by Nikon's Image Authentication Software, is imbedded in the image. With this feature turned on, and with the

Figure 26 – Info screen with authentication stamp

authentication of the Nikon software, you can prove that a certain image has not been modified.

*Off* – No *Image authentication* embedding takes place. This is the default setting.

After a little thought, I decided to set my D700's *Image authentication* to *On* and leave it that way. I figure that one day I'll be sitting in the car waiting for my wife at the local superstore and a very important news event will occur right next to my car. I won't even have to get out of the car! In order to get my Pulitzer Prize, I'll want to be able to prove later that the images I took have not been modified in any way.

Figure 27 – *Image authentication* screens

Figure 28 – *Copyright information* screens

**Copyright information**
(User's Manual page 343)
Heretofore, the *Image comment* option has been used by some photographers to attach a copyright notice to images, but now there is a dedicated *Copyright* option as well as an *Artist* option to capture the photographer's name.

Any data recorded with these options is stored in the EXIF data associated with the image and can be viewed from ViewNX or Capture NX 2. If the *Data* option of *Display mode* is selected in the *Playback Menu*, then these two options and their data fields are displayed in the fourth shooting information screen.

*Figure 28* shows some of the screens involved in creating *Copyright* and *Artist*

data. The process of generating the actual data, shown in screen 4, is the same as we've covered earlier. Once the data fields have been created, ensure that you enable the display by selecting *Attach copyright information*, then navigate to the top of the menu and select *Done*. Now press *OK*.

Since creating the copyright information shown in screens 2 and 3, I've been advised that the data should actually be in the form of "Copyright 2009 J.W. Johnson"; you may want to follow that convention to maximize your opportunity to pursue any violation of your copyright. The *Artist* field can hold as many as 36 characters (blanks, periods, etc. do count as characters), and the *Copyright* field can hold as many as 54 characters.

Figure 29 – *Save/load settings* screens

**Save/load settings**
(User's Manual pages 344–345)
Do you have your D700 set up exactly the way you like it? Have you spent hours and hours with this book or the User's Manual, or simply exploring menus, and finally got all the settings in place? Are you worried that you might accidentally do a reset of your camera or that it could lose its settings in one way or another? Well, worry no more!

Once you have your camera configured to your liking, or at any time during the process, simply use this *Save/load settings* function to save the camera configuration out to your CF memory card. It creates a tiny 2K file named NCSETUP1.BIN in the root directory of your compact flash card. You can then save that file to your computer's hard drive and keep a backup of your camera settings.

Here are the two selections as shown in *figure 29*:

• *Save settings*
• *Load settings*

**Save settings** – Select this menu item and press the *OK* button. Your most important camera settings will be saved to your memory card.

**Load settings** – Insert a memory card with a previously saved NCSETUP1.BIN file on it, select *Load settings*, and press *OK*.

The settings you previously saved will be reloaded into the D700.

Here is a list of settings saved and loaded when you make use of these functions. It doesn't save or load every last setting in the D700, only the ones listed here.

*Playback Menu*
• Display mode
• Image review
• After delete
• Rotate tall

*Shooting Menu* – This saves the settings in all four banks (A, B, C, D).
• Shooting menu bank
• File naming
• Image quality
• Image size
• Image area
• JPEG compression
• NEF (RAW) recording
• White balance (includes your fine-tuning adjustments and presets d-0 to d-4)
• Set Picture Control
• Color space
• Active D-Lighting
• Vignette control
• Long exposure noise reduction (NR)
• High ISO noise reduction

- ISO sensitivity settings
- Live view settings

**Custom settings**
- All configurable custom settings are saved.

**Setup menu**
- Clean image sensor
- Video mode
- HDMI
- World time
- Language
- Image comment
- Auto image rotation
- Image authentication
- Copyright information
- GPS settings
- Non-CPU lens data

*My Menu*
- All items you've entered under the *My Menu* area.

If you change the name of the NCSETUP4.BIN file, the D700 will not be able to reload your settings from it. Also, if you save the settings when an existing NCSETUP4.BIN file exists on the CF card, it will be overwritten without prompting you for permission.

*GPS*
(User's Manual pages 213 and 346)
Nikon has wisely included the ability to GEO-tag your images with GPS location data. Now when you shoot a spectacular travel image, you can rest assured that you'll be able to find that exact spot next year. The D700 will record the following GPS information about your

Figure 30 – Picture of D700, GPS, and cables

location in the metadata of each image:

1. Latitude
2. Longitude
3. Altitude
4. Heading (North, South, etc., if your GPS device provides it)
5. UTC Time

The GPS unit you use must be compatible with the National Marine Electronics Association (NMEA0183) version 2.01 or 3.01 data format. I bought a Garmin eTrex Legend GPS unit to use with my D700, since the eTrex series is mentioned on page 213 of the User's Manual. I'll use it for my sample GPS in this section.

**What You'll Need to Use a GPS Unit with Your D700**

You'll need the following:

- A GPS unit that meets the NMEA0183 data format
- A data cable for that GPS unit that must have a D-sub 9-pin connector (not a USB)
- The Nikon MC-35 GPS adapter cable

The data cable for the GPS unit must have a D-sub 9-pin connector in order to plug into the Nikon MC-35 cable. The Nikon cable plugs into the larger of the connectors (10-pin remote connector) under the larger rubber flap on the right front of the D700. See *figure 30* for a look at the equipment.

There are several screens used in setting up the D700 for GPS use. First, a decision should be made about the exposure meter when a

GPS unit is plugged into the D700. While the GPS is plugged in, your exposure meter must be active to record the GPS data to the image. You'll have to do one of two things:

- Set the exposure meter to stay on for the entire time that a GPS is plugged in, which, of course, will increase battery drain.
- Press the shutter down halfway to activate the exposure meter before finishing the exposure. If you just push the shutter button down quickly and the meter was not active, you may not record GPS data to the image. The meter must be on before GPS data will be added.

*Figure 31* shows the screens to set the meter to stay on all the time the GPS is connected or to act normally and shut down after the *Auto meter-off delay* expires (see *Custom setting c2* – defaults to 6 seconds).

You can select one of the following:

- *Enable* (default)
- *Disable*

**Enable** (default) – The meter turns off at the end of the *Auto meter-off delay* time, as set in *Custom setting c2*. GPS data will only be recorded when the exposure meter is active, so take your time.

**Disable** – The exposure meter stays on all the time a GPS unit is connected. As long as you have good GPS signal, you will be able to record GPS data at any time.

There is also a *Position* setting, as shown in *figure 31*, screen 2. Notice that *Position* is grayed out in the image because a GPS is not

Figure 31 – *GPS* and *Auto meter off* screens

## Compatibility of GPS Units

Many of the newer handheld GPS units are not compatible with the D700 since they use a USB cable for interfacing, which is a good thing or a bad thing, according to how you look at it. The bad thing is that your brand-new USB-based GPS is useless for recording data to your images. The good thing is that you can buy older GPS units for very little money on eBay and even new (but out-of-production) stock from dealers. I bought my Garmin eTrex Legend mapping GPS on Amazon.com for just over $100. It came with a D-sub 9-pin data cable. I had to buy the Nikon MC-35 cable, and I was all set! Primarily, just be aware that the GPS unit must have a way to connect to the Nikon MC-35 cable in order to interface with the D700. Maybe a future firmware upgrade will give us the ability to use the built-in USB connector on our D700s with a USB-based GPS. Nikon, are you listening?

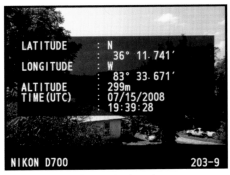

Figure 33 – *GPS* page in shooting information

1. *A* small GPS icon will be displayed in the Control Panel LCD (page 214 of the User's Manual).
2. *Position* information will be supplied by the GPS as shown in *figure 32*.
3. An additional shooting information page, as shown in *figure 33*, can be displayed when reviewing the captured images (page 229 of the User's Manual).

attached. Once a GPS is attached, selecting *Position* displays the actual GPS location data being detected by the D700.

When the D700 establishes communication with your GPS, it does three things:

If the GPS icon is flashing on the Control Panel LCD, it means that the GPS is searching for a signal. If you take a picture with the GPS icon flashing, no GPS data will be recorded. If the GPS icon is not flashing, it means that the D700 is receiving good GPS data and is ready to record data to a picture. If the D700 loses communication with the GPS unit for over two seconds, the GPS icon will disappear.

Figure 32 – *Position* information on the *GPS* screens

## Technology Continues to Evolve

As this book is being written, Nikon (and others) are announcing GPS units that plug directly into the 10-pin remote connector, eliminating the need for the MC-35 GPS adapter cable. They are designed to ride in the hotshoe but can also be clipped to the camera's carrying strap when the hotshoe is otherwise employed.

Make sure the icon is displayed before you take pictures!

Some GPS units also include a digital compass. If you want the GPS heading information to be accurate, keep your GPS unit pointing in the same direction as the lens. Point the GPS in the direction of your subject and give it enough time to stabilize before you take the picture or the *Heading* information will not be accurate.

Nikon also suggests that you keep the GPS at least 8 inches (20 cm) away from the Nikon D700. Maybe the D700 outputs enough electrical interference to throw off the digital compass!

### Virtual horizon
(User's Manual page 346)
*Figure 34* shows the *Virtual horizon* screens. This tool can be a great help in ensuring that the camera is parallel to the horizon, an essential when shooting multiple images for subsequent merging into a panoramic. When the camera is off-level, the Monitor LCD will display a picture similar to that in screen three of *figure 34*; notice the yellow line that horizontally bisects the camera silhouette. However, when the camera sensor determines that the camera is level, the yellow line becomes green, as shown in screen 2.

### Non-CPU lens data
(User's Manual pages 210 and 346)
Do you still have several older AI or AI-S Nikkor lenses? I do! The image quality from the older lenses is simply outstanding with the D700, even if they don't provide some of the features found on the newer lenses.

Since the D700 is positioned as a near-professional camera, it must have the necessary controls to use both autofocus (AF) and manual focus (MF) lenses. Many photographers on a budget use the older MF lenses to obtain professional-level image quality without having to break the bank on expensive lens purchases. One can acquire excellent AI/AI-S Nikkor lenses on eBay for $100 to $300 and have image quality that only the most expensive zoom lenses can produce.

Since lens manufacturers like Zeiss and Nikkor are still making MF lenses, and many of them do not have a CPU (electronic chip) that communicates with the camera, it is important to have a way to let the D700 know something about the lens in use. This *Non-CPU lens data* function allows you to do

Figure 34 – *Virtual horizon* screens

exactly that. You can store information on up to nine separate non-CPU lenses. Let's look at it how to do it.

There are four selections on the main *Non-CPU lens data* screen. Screen 2 of *figure 35* shows them. They are as follows:

* *Done*
* *Lens number*
* *Focal length (mm)*
* *Maximum aperture*

**Done** – When you have completed the setup of a particular lens, or several lenses, simply scroll to this selection and press the *OK* button. Your lens data will be saved within the D700. Later, you can put a non-CPU lens on your camera and select it from the list of nine lenses. You can use external camera controls, or the *Non-CPU lens data* menu item, to change to your current lens.

**Lens number** – Using the Multi Selector, you can scroll left or right to specify a numeric identifier for one of your lenses. There are a total of nine lens records available. When you select a lens number here, the focal length and maximum aperture of that lens will show up in the fields below the *Lens number* field. If you've not set lens parameters for a particular lens number, then you'll see double dashes -- in the *Focal length* and *Maximum aperture* fields.

**Focal length (mm)** – This field contains the actual focal length of the lens associated with this lens number. You can select focal lengths from 6 mm to 4000 mm. Hmm, I didn't know they even made a 4000 mm lens. I want one!

**Maximum aperture** – This field is for the maximum aperture of the lens. You can enter an F number from f/1.2 to f/22. Remember this is for the *maximum* aperture only (largest opening or f/stop). Once you've entered a maximum aperture, the camera will be able to determine the other apertures by your use of the aperture ring on the lens. (Remember those?)

Once you're done inputting your nine lenses, don't forget to use the *Done* selection to save your work! The *Done* selection serves double-duty by allowing you either to select a lens or save changes to one or all of your nine lenses.

When you have selected a lens for use, the *Setup Menu's Non-CPU lens data* selection will show the number of the lens you've selected. It will be in the format of No. 2, No. 5, No. 9, etc., which shows which of the nine lenses you have currently selected. Notice screen 1 of *figure 35* where you can see the lens selection (No. 3) at the end of the *Non-CPU lens data* line.

Figure 35 – *Non-CPU lens data* screens with lens No. 3 showing on both screens

### Selecting a Lens by Using the Non-CPU Lens Data Screen

When it's time to shoot pictures, you can select a non-CPU lens by doing the following:

- Open the *Non-CPU lens data* screen.
- Select a lens by scrolling left or right on the *Lens number* field.
- Scroll up to the *Done* selection and press the *OK* button.

### Selecting a Non-CPU Lens by Using External Camera Controls

The D700 allows you to customize many of its buttons to do things the way you want them to be done. You may have only a non-CPU lens or two, so it may be sufficient to just use the *Non-CPU lens data* screen to select a lens. However, if you are like me, with a good selection of AI lenses, you may wish Nikon gave us more than nine lens selections in the non-CPU lens array.

Since I use a lot of AI Nikkors, I have mapped my *AE-L/AF-L* button, in combination with the *Main command* dial, to select any of my nine lens selections from the Control Panel LCD. Some people use the *FUNC* (Fn) button along with a command dial to do the same. The D700 allows you to be creative in that respect. I use the *FUNC* button / *Main command* dial as my bracketing controls, since I can operate that combo

with one hand and shoot brackets quickly. This is why I use the *AE-L/AF-L* button, in combination with the *Main command* dial, to select my non-CPU lenses. It takes two hands to do the selection, but I've just changed lenses so I'm not ready to shoot anyway.

You can map any of several D700 buttons, in combination with a command dial, to select non-CPU lenses. Please see pages 320 to 328 of the Nikon User's Manual for information on mapping buttons. Also, see the "Controls" section of chapter 6 "Custom Setting Banks" for more detail on mapping buttons and dials.

### AF fine tune

(User's Manual pages 347–348)

One thing that really impresses me about the D700 is its ability to be fine-tuned in critical areas like metering and autofocus. Previous to the D700, if an AF lens had a back- or front-focus problem, you just had to tolerate it or send it off to be fixed by Nikon. Now, with the new *AF Fine Tune* system, you can adjust your camera so that the lens focuses where you want it to focus.

Nikon has made provision for keeping a table of up to 12 lenses that you've fine-tuned. Nikon does not recommend that you use the fine-tuning system unless you know what you are doing, and only when required. The idea behind fine-tuning is that you can push

Figure 36 – *AF fine tune* screens, set one

the focus a little bit forward or backward in small increments. You can do this up to 20 increments in a forward direction or 20 increments in a backward direction. When the little round green AF indicator comes on in your viewfinder, and *AF fine tune* is enabled for a lens you've already configured, the actual focus is moved from its default position forward or backward by the amount you've specified. If your lens had a back-focus problem, and you moved the focus a little forward, the problem is solved.

There are four selections on the *AF fine tune* screens:

- *AF fine tune (On/Off)* – factory default is off
- *Saved value*
- *Default*
- *List saved values*

*Figure 36* shows the first two screens in the *AF fine tune* series. Each of the selections listed above have their own screens for configuration. Let's look at each selection and discuss what it accomplishes.

**AF fine tune (On/Off)** – In *figure 37*, we see the *AF fine tune (On/Off)* screen and its configuration screen. There are two values you can select:

**On** – This setting turns the *AF fine tune* system on. Without this selection, the D700 focuses like a factory default D700.

**Off** – This default setting disables the *AF fine tune* system.

**Saved value** – With an AF lens mounted, this *Saved value* screen allows you to control the amount of front or back focus you'd like to allow for the lens currently listed. At the top left of the configuration screen (see screen 2 in *figure 38*) just under the words *Saved value*, you'll see the focal length of the lens mounted on your camera along with the maximum aperture and the numeric identifier you have assigned to the lens. If you are configuring a lens for the first time, you'll probably see *No. --*.

To the right of the lens information is a scale that runs from +20 on top to -20 on the bottom. The yellow pointer starts out at 0. You can move this yellow pointer up or down to change the amount of focus fine-tuning you want for this lens. Moving the pointer up on the scale pushes the focal point away from the camera, while moving it down pulls the focal point toward the camera. Once you are done, press the *OK* button.

**Default** – The *Default* configuration screen looks a lot like the *Saved value* screen, except there is no lens information listed. This *Default* value will be applied to all AF lenses you mount on your D700. If you are convinced that your particular camera always has a back- or front-focus problem, and you are not able or ready to ship it off to Nikon for repair,

Figure 37 – *AF fine tune* screens, set two

Figure 38 – *Saved value* screens

you can use the *Default* value to push the autofocus in one direction or the other until you are satisfied that your camera is focusing the way you'd like (*figure 39*).

To set a *Default AF fine tune* value, use the scale that runs from +20 on top to -20 on the bottom. The yellow pointer starts out at 0. You can move this yellow pointer up or down to change the amount of focus fine-tuning you want for whatever lens you currently have on the D700 if no value already exists in the *Saved values* for the lens. Moving the pointer up on the scale pushes the focal point away from the camera, while moving it down pulls the focal point toward the camera. Once you are done, press the *OK* button.

This allows you to use this *Default* value as a value for any of your AF lenses that do not

have a saved value. I tested this by setting a saved value of +1 for my AF-S Nikkor 18-70 mm. While the 18-70 was still mounted, I also set a value of -2 for the *Default* value. When I removed the 18-70 mm and mounted an AF Nikkor 60 mm Micro lens, the +1 in the *Saved value* field disappeared but the -2 in the *Default* field stayed put. So, it looks like you could use the *Default* field either for *all* AF lenses that have no saved value, or for a currently mounted AF lens that you want to adjust for this moment without saving a value.

**List saved values** – Notice in *figure 40* that there are several screens used to configure the list of saved values. This listing of lenses with saved values helps you remember which lenses you've fine-tuned the D700 to

Figure 39 – *Default* screens

Figure 40 – *List saved values* screens

use. It also allows you to set an identification number for a particular lens.

Many people use the last two digits of the lens serial number as the number for the *Saved value* of that lens. In the second screen of *figure 40*, you'll see a list of lenses that have saved values. As you'll see in the third screen, there is a little box in the middle after *No*. This little box is a scroll box that allows you to scroll the Multi Selector up or down to scroll from 00 to 99. That way, you can set whatever number you want to use for particular lenses. Note that you can configure a maximum of 12 lenses, regardless of the numeric values you assign.

### Firmware version

(User's Manual page 348)
This is a simple informational screen, like the *Battery info* screen. It informs you which version of the Nikon D700 firmware you are running. My D700 has the firmware included

with the D700 from the factory since a subsequent firmware update was not yet available at the time this book was published. In *figure 41* we see the two screens that display the firmware version numbers.

When a firmware update becomes available and you install it, this is the screen you'll use to validate that the firmware update was successful. Typically, the firmware update will be a two-part operation, including an update *A* and an update *B*.

## Section 2: *Retouch Menu*

(User's Manual page 349)
Retouching allows you to modify your images in-camera with no computer postprocessing. If you like to do digital photography but don't particularly like to work on a computer later, these functions are for you!

You can use the *Retouch Menu* directly and choose an image to work with, or you can

Figure 41 – *Firmware* screens

display an image in *Playback* mode and press the *OK* button to open the *Retouch Menu*. There are limitations imposed when you are working on an image that has already been retouched.

When you use the *Retouch Menu* items, the D700 does not overwrite your original file but always creates a JPEG file with the next available image number in the current folder on the memory card. Although the original image can be a RAW, JPEG, or TIFF image, the retouched image will always be saved as a JPEG. If you have images numbered DSC_0001 through DSC_0100 on your card and you are retouching image number DSC_0047, the resulting new JPEG image will have the number DSC_0101. The D700 looks to see how many images are in the current folder on the memory card, then adds the retouched image as a brand new exposure, assigning it the next available image number.

I am going to approach this section of the chapter with the idea that you are using the menus directly. Experiment with displaying an image and then pressing the *OK* button to open the *Retouch Menu* for that image. It works basically the same, except that the latter method leaves out the step of choosing the image since one is already on the screen.

### Retouching From the Playback Preview Screen

Just for fun, here are the steps to use if you want to work with an image you just took or are looking at on your D700's Monitor LCD. To use the *Retouch Menu* options, you'll do four basic steps (except with *Red-eye* and *Side-by-side* comparison):

1. Using *Playback Mode*, choose a picture by displaying it your D700's Monitor LCD.
2. Press the *OK* button to open the *Retouch Menu*.
3. Select one of the *Retouch Menu* functions.
4. Press *OK* to create the retouched copy.

Between steps 3 and 4, there can be extra steps if you want to modify the presented value. For instance, let's say you want to trim an image. You can press *OK* once you've selected *Trim* and the D700 will trim the image inside the crop frame it shows you. If you want, you can use the Multi Selector to move the crop frame around before you press *OK* to actually trim the image. Usually the default value is fine, so you can just press *OK* to complete the process.

Some of the retouch options are not available with this method, which is why I use the full menus for the rest of this chapter.

### Using the Retouch Menu Items Directly
Let's consider each section of the *Retouch Menu* in detail.

#### D-Lighting
(User's Manual page 354)
*D-Lighting* allows you to reduce the shadows and maybe even reign in the highlights a bit. It lowers the overall image contrast, so it should be used sparingly. The D700 is not aggressive with its D-Lighting so you can use it quickly if needed. Also, please remember it will create a copy of the image, so your original is safe.

The steps to D-Light an image are as follows:

1. Select *D-Lighting* from the *Retouch Menu*.
2. Select the image you want to modify (*figure 42*, screen 2).
3. Choose the amount of D-Lighting you want for the chosen image using the Multi Selector to scroll up or down. You'll choose from *Low*, *Medium*, or *High* (*figure 42*, screen 3).
4. When the image on the right looks the way you want it to look, press the *OK* button to save the new file. The D700 will display a brief "Image saved" notice, then switch to displaying the new file in full screen *Playback* mode.

Figure 42 – *D-Lighting* screens

### Red-eye correction

(User's Manual page 355)

If you have used flash to create a picture, the *Red-eye correction* function will work on the image if it can detect any red-eye. If it can't detect red-eye in the image, it will not open the red-eye system but will, instead, briefly display a screen informing you that the camera was "Unable to detect red eye in selected picture." If you try to run the red-eye routines on an image where flash was not used, the D700 will inform you, "Cannot select this file."

The steps to execute the *Red-eye correction* function on an image are as follows:

1. Select *Red-eye correction* from the *Retouch Menu*.

2. Select the image you want to modify (*figure 43*, screen 2).

3. Press the *OK* button and the *Red-eye correction* routines will execute. You'll see an hourglass on your screen for three to five seconds.

Figure 43 – *Red-eye correction* screens

4. After *Red-eye correction* is done you can use the normal zoom buttons to zoom in on the image to see how well it worked.

5. Press *OK* to save the file under a new file number (*figure 43*, screen 4), or you can press the *Playback* button to cancel.

### Trim

(User's Manual pages 356–357)

The *Trim* function allows you to crop an image in-camera, change its aspect ratio, and save the file out to a new image. Your original image is not modified.

Here are the steps to trim (crop) an image in the D700:

1. Select the *Trim* function from the *Retouch Menu*.

2. Select the image you want to modify (*figure 44*, screen 2).

3. You'll be presented with a screen that has a crop outline in yellow. Using the normal zoom buttons, you can zoom in for a deeper crop or zoom out for a lesser crop. You can use the Multi Selector to scroll the crop outline to the desired location on the image. Zoom and scroll until you find your best crop position.

4. Select the aspect ratio of the crop by rotating the *Main command* dial. Your choices are 3:2, 4:3, and 5:4.

5. Once you have the crop correctly located and sized, and the aspect ratio set, press the *OK* button to save the new image under a new file number.

### Monochrome

(User's Manual page 357)

The *Monochrome* functions in the D700 are fun to play with, and can make some nice images. You have the choice of three different types of monochrome:

- *Black-and-White*
- *Sepia*
- *Cyanotype*

If you select *Black-and-White*, the D700 provides only one level of lightness and darkness. However, for *Sepia* (golden toned) and *Cyanotype* (blue toned), you can fine-tune the tint from almost-not-there to pretty saturated.

Here are the steps to create a monochrome image from one of your color images on the memory card:

1. Select *Monochrome* from the *Retouch Menu*.

2. Select a *Monochrome* tone of *Black-and-White*, *Sepia*, or *Cyanotype* (*figure 45*, screen 2).

3. Select the image you want to modify (*figure 45*, screen 3).

4. For *Sepia* and *Cyanotype*, you can use the Multi Selector to saturate or desaturate the tone. Use the Multi Selector to scroll up or down, and watch the screen until the tint is just where you want it to be. You can cancel with the *Playback* button (*figure 45*, screen 4).

5. Press the *OK* button to save the new image under a new file number.

Figure 44 – *Trim* screens

Figure 45 – *Monochrome* screens

### Filter effects

(User's Manual page 358)

Many times when shooting images outdoors under an overcast sky, or under certain types of artificial lighting, the image can have a bluish cast or feel "cool". The *Filter effects* function can help with that.

The *Filter effects* selection is a simple way to apply two specific filter effects to an existing image as follows (*figure 46*):

1. *Skylight* – Provides an effect similar to a skylight filter, which removes some of the blue in an image.
2. *Warm filter* – Provides an even stronger warming effect by adding a reddish tint to the image. This is sort of like an 81A or Nikon A2 warming filter.

To execute the filter effect you'd like, follow these steps:

1. Select *Filter effects* from the *Retouch Menu*.
2. Select either *Skylight* or *Warm filter* (*figure 46*, screen 2).
3. Select the image you want to modify (*figure 46*, screen 3).
4. Press the *OK* button to save the new image under a new file number or the *Playback* button to cancel.

### Color balance

(User's Manual page 358)

This is a useful function for people who do not like to use computers. You can visually add a light or strong color cast to your images. You might just want to warm things up a bit by adding a touch of red or cool things down with a touch of blue. Or, you could get creative and simply add various color casts to

Figure 46 – *Filter effects* screens

the image for special effects. You'll see what I mean when you try it.

*Figure 47* shows the *Color balance* screens to use.

To modify the color balance of an image, follow these steps:

1. Select *Color balance* from the *Retouch Menu*.
2. Select the image you want to modify (*figure 47*, screen 2).
3. Use the Multi Selector to move the tiny black indicator square in the center of the

color box toward whatever colors make you happy. Watch the histograms as they display the changing color relationships between the red, green, and blue color channels. You can see the color changes as they are applied to the small version of your image in the upper-left corner of the screen (*figure 47*, screen 3).

4. Press the *OK* button to save the new image under a new file number or the *Playback* button to cancel.

Figure 47 – *Color balance* screens

## Image overlay

(User's Manual page 359)

The *Image overlay* function is a cool way to combine two RAW images as if they were taken as a multiple exposure. You can select a couple of images and combine them into a new image that is of higher quality than an image from graphic programs on a computer because they are combined using RAW image data. *Figure 48* shows the *Image overlay* screens.

To execute an image overlay and combine two images into one, do the following steps:

1. Select *Image overlay* from the *Retouch Menu*.

2. Select the first image in the *Image 1* box (outlined in yellow) by pressing the *OK* button and using the Multi Selector to select an image from the selection screen (*figure 48*, screen 3). Press *OK* again to

return to the combination screen (*figure 48*, screen 4).

3. Use the Multi Selector to move the yellow box to *Image 2*. Press *OK* to move to the image selection screen, scroll to the desired image, then press *OK* again to select that image and return to the combination screen (*figure 48*, screen 7). Anytime that *Image 1* or *Image 2* is selected, you can use the Multi Selector to scroll image gain either up or down, with the result being displayed in the *Preview* area.

4. Move the yellow box to the *Preview* area, and you'll see two selections below. The first is *Overlay*, and the second is *Save*. If you select *Overlay*, the D700 will present you with another screen that allows you to see the images more closely. You can press

Figure 48 – *Image overlay* screens

the *OK* button to save the new image under a new file number or press the *Checkered Thumbnail* button to return to the previous screen (*figure 48*, screen 7).

5. If you choose to press the *OK* button instead of the *Overlay* button, the D700 immediately combines the two images, saves the new image out to your memory card under a new file number, and displays that new image in the Monitor LCD (*figure 48*, screen 9).

**Side-by-side comparison**
(User's Manual pages 362–363)
After using the *Retouch Menu* to optimize a picture, you may want to compare the finished product with the original. To do so, use the Multi Selector to select the retouched image, then press *OK*. As shown in screen 2 of *figure 49*, scroll down to the *Side-by-side comparison* option and press OK. The D700 will locate the original and display both images, side-by-side, as shown in screen 3. Note that the *Retouch Menu* options used are displayed above the images in screen 3. To see either image in full-screen mode, use the Multi Selector to select the desired image, then press the *Zoom in* button.

## Section 3: *My Menu*

The D700 is quite a complex camera. There are key functions and settings that each of us might use frequently. For instance, I often

turn *Exposure delay mode* (*Custom Setting d9*) on and off. Instead of having to search through all those *Custom setting* screens and options, trying to remember which is *Exposure delay mode*, I simply added that custom setting to *My Menu*. Now, whenever I want to add a delay to my exposure so that mirror vibrations can settle down, I just go to *My Menu* and enable *Exposure delay mode*.

There are several other functions and settings I keep in *My Menu* along with *Exposure delay mode*. I'm sure you'll have a few you use often, too. Let's examine the screens to add and remove items from *My Menu*.

When you first open *My Menu*, you'll find only four menu choices, as shown in *figure 50*:

• *Add items*
• *Remove items*
• *Rank items*
• *Choose tab*

Let's examine each of these menu choices in detail.

**Add items**
To add an item to *My Menu*, you'll need to locate the item first. Search through the menus until you find the item you want to add and then make note of where it is located. You could do this from within the *Add items* screen, but I find that it is harder to find what I am looking for if I have not already confirmed in my mind where it lives. Is it under *Custom Setting Menu* or *Shooting Menu*, for instance?

Figure 49 – *Side-by-side comparison* screens

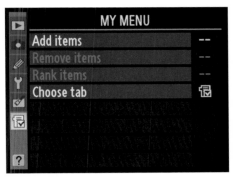

Figure 50 – *My Menu* screen

Figure 52 – *Add items* screen with *Playback menu* highlighted

Once I have found the item I want to add and made note of its location, I do the following:

1. Select *Add items* from the *My Menu* screen (*figure 51*).
2. I use the Multi Selector to scroll right and find a list of menus to choose from. These menus are all the menus available in the D700 except *My Menu* (*figure 52*).
3. I will add *Custom setting d9 – Exposure delay mode* to *My Menu* as an example. I have already looked and know that *Exposure delay mode* is under the *Custom Setting Menu*, so I'll scroll down to it. After selecting it I'll scroll to the right (*figure 53*).

4. Now I should see the *Custom settings a-f* (*figure 54*). I scroll down to *Custom setting d* and scroll to the right again so that I can select the actual *Custom setting* I want.

Figure 53 – *Add items* screen with *Custom setting menu* highlighted

Figure 51 – Customized *My Menu* screen with *Add items* highlighted

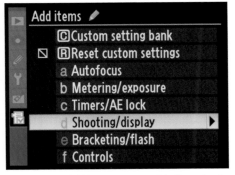

Figure 54 – *Add items* screen with *Shooting/display* highlighted

Figure 55 – *Add items* screen with *d9 Exposure delay mode* highlighted

Figure 56 – *Choose position* screen with *d9 Exposure delay mode* selected

5. Now that I have found *Custom setting d9*, all I have to do is highlight it and press the *OK* button (*figure 55*). Once I've done that, the D700 switches to the *Choose position* screen.

6. Since I already had a couple other items added to *My Menu*, I now have to decide in which order I want them to be presented. The new *d9 Exposure delay mode* is on top since it is the newest entry. I think I'll move it down one slot and let *Set Picture Control* move to the top position. To move the position of the selected item, I simply scroll down. *d9 Exposure delay mode* stays highlighted with a yellow box surrounding it. As I scroll down, a yellow underline moves to the next position (*figure 56*).

This yellow underline represents the place to which I will finally move *d9 Exposure delay mode*. Once I have decided on the position and have the yellow underline in place, I just press the *OK* button.

7. The screen pops back to the beginning *My Menu* screen as shown in screen 2 of *figure 57*, with everything arranged the way I desired.

**Remove items**

Now that I've showed you how to *Add items*, I want to examine how *Remove items* works. I've decided that one of my items, *Active D-Lighting*, is not used often enough to waste a spot on *My Menu*, so I'll remove it.

Figure 57 – *My Menu* screen, before and after adding and positioning an item

Figure 58 – *My Menu* with *Remove items* highlighted

Figure 59 – *Remove items* screen with *Active D-Lighting* checked

Here's how:

1. I select *Remove items* from *My Menu* (figure 58) and scroll to the right.

2. The *Remove items* screen presents a series of check boxes. However many of them I check will be deleted when I select *Done*. You can check the boxes by scrolling to highlight the line item and then press the *OK* button, or you can scroll right on each item you want to check. I like to use the *OK* button method since trying to uncheck a selection by scrolling left does not work but takes you back to the *My Menu* screen. Pressing the *OK* button acts like a toggle and will check or uncheck a line item (figure 59).

3. Once I have the items I want to delete checked, I'll simply scroll back up to the *Done* selection and press *OK* (figure 60). A small white box pops up and asks, "Delete selected item?" I press the *OK* button

again, and the item is removed from *My Menu*. A box pops up informing me that the item has been deleted, and then the D700 switches to *My Menu's* main screen.

### Rank items

*Rank items* works very similarly to positioning new additions in *My Menu*. All the *Rank items* selection does is move the item up or down in *My Menu*. You can switch your most used *My Menu* items to the top of the list. Here's how:

1. Select *Rank items* from *My Menu* (figure 61) and scroll to the right.

2. Now you are presented with the *Rank items* screen and all the current *My Menu* items. I have decided that I use the *d9 Exposure delay mode* more than *Set Picture Control*, so I'll move the former to the top. I scroll my yellow highlight down to

Figure 60 – *Remove items* screens with *Active D-Lighting* being deleted

Figure 61 – *My Menu* screen with *Rank items* highlighted

Figure 62 – *Rank items* screen with *Exposure delay mode* highlighted

*d9 Exposure delay mode* and press the *OK* button to select it (*figure 62*).

3. A yellow underline can now be scrolled around with the Multi Selector. In screen 1 of *figure 63*, I've moved the yellow underline up to the top to represent where I am finally going to position *d9 Exposure delay mode*. (*d9 Exposure delay mode* is still highlighted with a surrounding yellow box.) Once my

yellow underline is at the position I want, I press the *OK* button and *d9 Exposure delay mode* moves to the top, as shown in screen 2. If I like the current order, I can simply scroll left and I'm back at *My Menu's* main screen, but with my new menu order, as shown in screen 3.

Figure 63 – *Rank items* screens

Figure 64 – *Choose tab* and *Recent settings* screens

*Choose Tab and Recent*

The D700 remembers 20 of your most recent settings and can give you access to that list, with the most recent setting at the top of the list.

To access this list, scroll to *Choose tab* in *My Menu*, then press the right side of the Multi Selector. As shown in screen 2 of *figure 64*, there are two options: The *My Menu* option takes you back to the *My Menu* screen, and the *Recent settings* option will open a list of as many as 20 most-recent settings. As with *My Menu,* to apply any of these listed settings, scroll to the desired setting and press *OK*. To return to *My Menu*, scroll to the bottom of the list, select *Choose tab* and press the right side of the Multi Selector; from the *Choose tab* screen, select *My Menu* and press *OK*.

## My Conclusions

Whew! The D700 may seem like a complex little beast, but that's what you get when you cram professional-level functionality into a relatively small DSLR body. Complex as it is, though, I'm certainly delighted with it.

# Nikon Creative Lighting System

## What Is the Nikon Creative Lighting System (CLS)?

CLS is an advanced wireless lighting technology that allows you to use your imagination in designing "creative" lighting arrangements. No wires are used, and the CLS-compatible remote flash units are controlled by a "commander device", or what Nikon refers to as a "master flash unit". You can use the *Commander mode* built into the D700, or you can use a hotshoe-mounted commander device such as the SB-900 AF Speedlight, the SB-800 AF Speedlight, or the SU-800 Wireless Speedlight Commander unit. We'll look at these options in this chapter.

As I've yet to get my hands on the new SB-900 AF Speedlight, it is not covered in this chapter as a separate device. However, in reviewing the specifications, it appears to perform in the same manner as the SB-800.

You can easily experiment with setups and flash output by using the visual preview combined with the pulsed modeling capability within Nikon's Speedlights when you press the D700's *depth of field preview* button.

There is no need to figure complex lighting ratios when you can control your flash groups right from the camera and see the results immediately. CLS simplifies the use of multiple flash-unit setups for portraiture, interiors, nature, or any situation where several Speedlights need to work in unison.

You can simply position the flash units where you'd like them to be and let CLS automatically figure the "correct" exposure, or you can change the lighting ratios directly from the D700's *Custom setting e3* menu's *Commander mode* options or a hotshoe-mounted commander device.

Nikon's Creative Lighting System is world class in power and not too difficult to use. The Nikon D700 camera contains everything you need to control a simple or complex CLS setup. Let's learn how to use it!

## How Does the D700 Fit into the CLS Scheme?

In *Commander mode*, the Nikon D700 camera functions as a controller for multiple Nikon Speedlight flash units. While the professional-level Nikon D3 and D3X *requires* the separate purchase of a hotshoe-mounted commander device, the D700 body has full Nikon Creative Lighting System (CLS) technology built right into the camera.

You can use normal i-TTL flash technology with the D700's built-in flash (Nikon calls it a Speedlight) or use *Commander mode* and the built-in flash to control up to two groups of an unlimited number of external Nikon Speedlight flash units. Nikon makes the powerful SB-900 and SB-800 flash units, along with their slightly less-powerful SB-600 brother and several other smaller Speedlight units, such as the SB-400 or SB-R200. Many of us using the D700 will have an external flash unit, and it will usually be the SB-800 or SB-600, so we'll consider those in detail in this chapter. The Nikon D700 is happy to let you arrange professional lighting setups using these relatively inexpensive and very portable Speedlights.

Later in the chapter, we'll also consider how the D700 can use the SB-900 or SB-800 Speedlight's *Master mode* or the SU-800 Commander unit instead of the camera's built-in *Commander mode* since the external units provide maximum range and flexibility in large flash bank arrangements. The cool thing about the D700 is that it can *be* a CLS flash commander device or can *use* Nikon's other CLS flash commander devices at will. You have great control with this fine camera!

Figure 1 – *Commander mode* setup screen

## What Is Commander Mode and How Does it Work?

*Commander mode* is controlled from a screen on a menu of your D700. It looks like the screen in *figure 1*.

If you examine this *Commander mode* screen, you will see that you have controls for the built-in flash and two groups, or banks, for external flash units. You'll also see that you can set exposure compensation for either of these.

If you leave *Custom setting e4 – Modeling Flash* set to the factory default setting of *ON*, you can test fire your Speedlight's built-in

modeling light by pressing and holding the D700's *depth of field preview* button. Or, if you prefer, simply take a picture and look at it.

If the main light is too bright, you can either move it farther away or dial its power down by setting compensation (*Comp*) to underexpose a little. You can set *Comp* in ⅓ stop increments, so you have very fine control of each group's flash output. The point is that you have control to experiment until you get the image just the way you want it. Sure, you could do things the old way, use a flash meter, or get your calculator and figure out complex fill ratios. Or, you can simply use CLS to vary your settings visually until the image is just right.

Isn't it more fun to simply put some initial settings in your *Commander mode* screen and then take a test shot? If it doesn't look right, change the settings and do it again. Within two or three tries you'll probably get it right and will have learned something about the performance of your CLS system. In a short time you'll have a feel for how to set the camera and flash units and will use your flash/camera combo with authority (*figure 2*).

Figure 2 – This sample CLS photo by J. Ramon Palacios required one SU-800 as the commander device, coordinating with two SB-800 Speedlights.

## Using the Nikon D700 in Commander Mode

Gather up your Nikon D700, its User's Manual, and your external flash units with their manuals. Keep them close by since I will refer to the camera and flash unit menus and manuals for additional details.

Let's start by putting our Nikon D700 camera into *Commander mode*. We'll do that by changing *Custom setting e3* to *Commander mode*. Look at *figure 3* for the screen series to set this option.

Normally, *Custom setting e3* defaults to TTL, as shown in screen 2 of *figure 3*. TTL represents the single-flash i-TTL technology used by your built-in Speedlight or by any i-TTL compatible flash unit you put in your Nikon D700's hotshoe. Since this chapter is about controlling multiple flash units, we'll

User Manuals Reference Pages

• Look on pages 309–314 of your D700 User's Manual for detailed information on *Commander mode*.

• In the Nikon SB-800 manual, "wireless" information is found on pages 74–83. (For the SB-600, look on manual pages 52–65.)

• On page 311 of the D700 User's Manual, you will find a chart of settings that complement the *Commander mode* screen.

have to change that setting to *Commander mode* as shown in screen 3 of *figure 3*.

Figure 3 – *Commander mode* screens

### Monitor Pre-Flashes

What are "monitor pre-flashes"? Here is a short tutorial. When you press the shutter-release button with the flash open, the D700's built-in Speedlight fires several brief pre-flashes, then fires the main flash (unless the *Commander mode* screen has been set to put the built-in flash into "--" mode). These pre-flashes fire anytime the built-in flash is open and your camera is set to i-TTL mode, even if your D700 is controlling multiple flash units. The camera can determine a very accurate exposure by pre-flashing your subject, adjusting the exposure, and then firing the main flash burst.

Figure 4 – Selecting the *Mode* option in the *Commander mode* screen

Let's discuss the settings. First we'll look at *Commander mode* in *TTL* mode, which is the easiest to use, since it allows you to set exposure compensation for the built-in flash as well as for each of your flash groups. Next, we'll look at *M* mode, since that gives you fiddly control of your flash from full-power to ¹⁄₁₂₈ power. We'll briefly look at *AA* mode. Then finally, we'll consider the "--" mode, which prevents the D700 built-in flash from firing its main flash output, but does not stop the necessary monitor pre-flashes, nor the firing of the external flash units.

When your D700 is controlling external Speedlights, you must *always* raise the built-in flash on your D700. The D700 communicates with the external flash units during the monitor pre-flash cycle.

#### Nikon D700 Commander Mode Settings

Basically, the *Commander mode* screen's *Mode* fields will display the selections listed in the following sections. Use the Multi Selector to change the values, as shown in *figure 4*.

**Mode Settings:**
1. *TTL* or i-TTL mode
2. *AA* or Auto Aperture mode
3. *M* or Manual mode
4. "--" or double-dash mode (what else would one call it?)

*TTL* **mode** – The TTL setting represents using the full power of i-TTL technology. By leaving *Mode* set to *TTL* (as shown in *figure 4*) on each of the *Built-in flash* or *Group A* or *B* options, you derive maximum flexibility and accuracy from all your flash units. In this mode, the *Comp* setting (*figure 4*) will display exposure values from -3.0 EV to + 3.0 EV, a full 6-stop range of exposure compensation for each group of Speedlights. You can set the *Comp* in ⅓ EV steps for very fine control.

### Speedlight Tip

Position the sensor window on each of the external Speedlights where they will pick up the monitor pre-flashes from the built-in flash. Take particular care when not using a tripod.

9

### Effects of Pre-Flashes on Lighting

Since the built-in's monitor pre-flashes always fire, be careful that they do not influence the lighting of your image. Use a smaller aperture, or move the camera farther away from your subject if the pre-flashes add unwanted light.

Figure 5 – *Channel* selection screen in *Commander mode*

*A A* **mode** – I am only briefly touching on the *A A* mode since it is an older non-i-TTL technology included for those accustomed to using the older technology. With the SB-900 and SB-800, it is used primarily by cameras not compatible with the Creative Lighting System. It is not available for the built-in Speedlight on the D700, nor for the SB-600. You can safely ignore the *A A* mode unless you want to experiment with it. It may not provide as accurate a flash exposure as *TTL* mode though, since it is not based on the amazing i-TTL technology. Otherwise, it works pretty much the same as *TTL* mode.

*M* **mode** – This allows you to set different levels of flash output in ⅓ stops for the built-in flash or the Speedlights in groups A or B. The settings you can put in the *Comp* field are between ¹⁄₁ (full) and ¹⁄₁₂₈. The intermediate ⅓ stop settings are presented as decimals within the fractions. For example, ¹⁄₁.₃ or ¹⁄₁.₇ are ⅓ and ⅔ stops below ¹⁄₁ (full). Many people are used to working with flash units this way, so it seems more familiar. CLS is willing to oblige those experienced in working manually.

-- **mode (double-dash mode)** – The built-in Speedlight will not fire its main flash in this mode. It will fire the monitor pre-flashes since it uses them to determine exposure and communicate with the external flash groups. Be sure you always raise the D700's built-in flash in any of the *Commander mode* modes, otherwise the external flash groups

will not receive a signal and won't fire their flashes.

When setting the mode for *Group A* or *B* to *double-dash* mode, that entire group will not fire any flash output. You can use this mode to temporarily turn off one of the flash groups for testing purposes.

### Setting the Channel (CH) for Communication

Look at *figure 5*, or your D700's *Commander mode* screen, and you'll notice that just below *Group B* you'll see a *Channel 1 CH* selection. The number "1" (factory default) is the communication channel your D700 is expecting to use to talk to the external flash groups.

You can select any number from 1 to 4. There are four channels available, just in case you happen to be working in the vicinity of another Nikon user who is also using *Commander mode*. By using separate channels, you won't interfere with each other.

It is important that you realize that all your external flashes in all the groups must be on the same channel. This involves setting up your individual flash units to respond on a particular channel. They might be in separate groups, but they must be on the same channel.

We'll next examine how to do that for the SB-800 and SB-600 Speedlight units. We'll also look at using the SB-800 and SU-800 as commander devices.

This CLS reference section is quite long, so I have created a mini table of contents here. The sections that follow include:

**Using the Nikon SB-800 AF Speedlight as a slave unit:**
The SB-800 flash unit makes an excellent slave unit too, and we'll configure it.

**Nikon SB-600 AF Speedlight Slave configuration:**
The SB-600 is both affordable and a great CLS slave unit.

**Using the Nikon SB-800 Speedlight as a commander device:**
The SB-800 flash unit can work as a master flash.

**Examining the Nikon SU-800 Wireless Speedlight Commander unit:**
This helps with understanding and configuring the SU-800 Commander.

### Using the Nikon SB-800 AF Speedlight as a Slave Unit

Now we'll turn to the setup of the Speedlight units themselves. Most of us have either a Nikon SB-800 or SB-600 with our Nikon D700 camera. If you have both, that is even better.

Use the following information to configure each flash unit you have, and try to become familiar with the wireless slave mode entry and exit procedures. Once you learn how to get in and out, you can usually figure the rest out by scrolling through menus on the flash units.

The Nikon SB-800 Speedlight has built-in commander-device functionality, as we dis-

cussed earlier. Setting the Nikon SB-800 as a slave to be used in a group is quite easy.

The difference is in setting the SB-800 to *Remote* mode. When you are in *Remote* mode, the flash is ready to respond to input from an external controller. Here are the steps and LCD Panel views to prepare the SB-800 to be a slave controlled by a commander device.

### Setting Remote Mode on the SB-800

**Overview of Settings:**
1. Turn the flash on with the *ON/OFF* button.
2. Press and hold the *SEL* button in the middle of the Multi Selector for about two seconds (SB-800 manual page 68).
3. Once you enter the next screen, press *SEL* once again and the current mode selection will become highlighted. Use the **Down–** button to scroll down to *Remote* and press *SEL* again to select it.
4. Hold *SEL* down for another two-second period and the LCD Panel will switch to the *Remote* settings screen
5. Press *SEL* once and CH will be highlighted. Now use the **Up+** or **Down–** button to select the channel.
6. Press *SEL* once and *GROUP* will be highlighted. Now use the **Up+** or **Down–** button to select A or B. Don't use C, since the D700 cannot control that group.

**Detail of Settings:**
In *figure 6*, you'll find a picture of the SB-800's controls. You'll use the *SEL* button and the **Up+** and **Down–** buttons to configure remote mode.

Turn the SB-800 on, then press and hold the *SEL* button until the screen shown in *figure 7* appears.

Now we'll set the SB-800 into *Remote* mode using the instructions that follow.

Press the *SEL* button once more and the

Figure 6 – SB-800 Speedlight controls

Figure 7 – The SB-800 start-up screen

Figure 8 – Selecting he *Remote* option

Figure 9 – The *Remote* screen

current mode will be highlighted. Scroll down until *Remote* is highlighted (as shown in *figure 8*), and press *SEL* to select it. When *Remote* is selected, the highlight will go away and an arrowhead will appear to the left of the word *Remote*.

*Figure 9* shows the *Remote* screen, which we'll select by holding down the *SEL* button for about two seconds.

You can move around this screen by pressing the *SEL* button. As shown in *figure 10*, move to the *CH* setting on the top left, and select a channel with the **Up+** or **Down–** buttons. Then use *SEL* to move down to the *GROUP* setting on the bottom right. Use the **Up+** or **Down–** buttons to select a group.

You are now ready to shoot pictures with the SB-800 as a remote wireless slave flash. Do a test shot to see if your D700 and the commander device will fire the SB-800 remotely. If not, check to make sure *Channel* and *Group* on the SB-800 are set to the same settings as your camera's *Commander mode* channel and group.

### How to Exit the Remote Mode on the SB-800 Flash

This drove me nuts for a while, since the manual never really tells you how to exit once you've set your SB-800 to *Remote* mode. Oh, it does tell you that you hold down the *SEL* button for two seconds or press *ON/OFF* to return to the normal setting mode. However, what it does not tell you is that until you get the SB-800 out of *Remote* mode, it will never

Figure 10  – The *Channel* and *Group* selection screens

go back to being a normal flash. Here's how to do it:

1. While in the *Remote* screen listing the channels and groups, hold down the *SEL* button for two seconds and it will switch back to the screen that allows you to select *Master*, *Remote*, or in this case, the all-important *OFF* selection.
2. Press *SEL* again, and scroll up to *OFF*, then press *SEL* again to select *OFF*.
3. Hold down the *SEL* button for two seconds again and it will then switch back to being a normal i-TTL stand-alone flash.

### Nikon SB-600 Speedlight Slave Configuration

The Nikon SB-600 Speedlight is designed to be a stand-alone i-TTL flash or a remote wireless slave flash for the CLS system. It does not have a *Master mode* like the SB-800 does.

It is a simple but powerful Speedlight flash and does a great job as a slave for your D700 or a commander device to control. While referring to *figure 11*, let's look at the configuration method for the SB-600. It is quite different from the SB-800.

#### Setting Remote Mode on the SB-600
##### Overview of Settings:

1. Turn the SB-600 on with the *ON/OFF* button on back.
2. Hold down the *ZOOM* and **Down–** buttons for about two seconds.

Figure 11 – SB-600 Speedlight controls

3. Use the *MODE* button to turn *Remote* mode on.
4. Hold down the *ZOOM* and **Down–** buttons for about two seconds again, and the flash will switch to the *Remote* screen.
5. You can move around this screen by pressing the *MODE* button.
6. Move to the *CH* setting and select the channel with the **Up+** or **Down–** buttons.
7. Press *MODE* again to move to the *GROUP* setting and select the group with the **Up+** or **Down–** buttons.
8. Press the *MODE* button again to finish.

#### Detailed Settings with LCD Panel images:

Use the controls, as shown in *figure 11*, to set the flash to *Remote* slave mode so that your commander device can control it.

Turn the SB-600 on, then press and hold down the *ZOOM* and **Down–** buttons at the same time for about two seconds. It will switch to the screen as seen in *figure 12*.

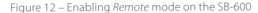

Figure 12 – Enabling *Remote* mode on the SB-600

Figure 13 – SB-600 *Remote* mode setup screen

Now press the *MODE* button to change *Off* to *On* as shown on the right in *figure 12*. This has enabled the *Remote* wireless slave functionality of the SB-600, but we need to validate the channels and groups settings to be sure they match our commander device's settings.

Hold down the *ZOOM* and **Down–** buttons again, for a couple of seconds, and the SB-600 will switch to the screen that allows you to set the channel (*CH*) and group (*figure 13*).

Notice how proper use of CLS can take out the harsh highlights and shadows produced by conventional direct flash.

Use the *MODE* button to move around this screen (*figure 13*). Move between the *CH* and *GROUP* settings while making sure they match your commander device's settings.

Press the *MODE* button until you see the channel (*CH*) number flashing. Now use the **Up+** or **Down–** button to change the channel number.

Press the *MODE* button again until you see the *GROUP* letter flashing. Now use the **Up+** or **Down–** button to change the *GROUP* letter to match that used by the commander device.

Press *MODE* again to finish and you are ready to take some pictures.

Do a test shot to see if your D700 will fire the SB-600 remotely. If not, check to make sure the channel and group on the SB-600 are set to the same settings as set in your commander device (D700 in *Commander Mode*, SU-800, SB-900, or SB-800).

### How to Exit the Remote Mode on the SB-600 Flash

It is relatively simple to turn off *Remote* mode on the SB-600. Simply follow these steps and the SB-600 will return to a normal iTTL stand-alone condition:

1. Hold down the *ZOOM* and **Down–** buttons for about two seconds. The screen will change to the remote *On/Off* screen.
2. Push the *MODE* button once to change *On* to *Off*.

Hold down the *ZOOM* and **Down–** buttons for about two seconds again and the SB-600 is now back to iTTL stand-alone mode.

### Using the Nikon SB-800 Speedlight as a Commander Device

To use the SB-800 in *Commander* mode, the SB-800 must be placed in the camera's hotshoe. Nikon refers to *Commander* mode on the SB-800 Speedlight flash unit as the

Commander Function or Master Flash. We'll use the term *Master mode* for clarity.

When using the SB-800 Speedlight as a commander device controlling one or more other Speedlights, it is important not to allow the SB-800 to fire its main flash, unless you really want to use this flash on the camera as one of the units that light the subject. We'll discuss how to disable the SB-800's main flash as we proceed, if you want to do that.

Another concern is the monitor pre-flash from the SB-800 in *Master mode*. Even though the SB-800's main flash is turned off, the pre-flash puts out quite a bit of light. If the subject is too close, the pre-flash could make a bright spot or even influence the exposure in an undesireable way.

The SB-800 Instruction Manual says this is not a problem unless the ISO is set to a high sensitivity or the subject is very close. The solution offered is to tilt the flash unit up into bounce mode and/or move the subject farther away from the main flash. (Use a longer lens.)

With this fact in mind, let's look at how to configure the SB-800 as a commander device so that we can use it to control multiple groups of other Speedlight flash units.

### Configuring the SB-800 as a Commander Device

To start our configuration process, we'll need to get out of normal flash mode and into *Master mode*.

### Setting Master Mode on the SB-800

Let's look at a brief overview of the configuration steps, and then we'll go into more detail. Please get your SB-800 flash unit so that you can apply what we cover directly to the flash. It's a lot easier to remember this information if applied immediately.

**Overview of Settings:**

1. Turn the flash on with the *ON/OFF* button.
2. Press and hold the *SEL* button in the middle of the Multi Selector for about two seconds until the LCD Panel switches screens.
3. Once you enter the next screen, press *SEL* once again and the currently active mode will become highlighted. Use the **Down–** button to scroll down to *Master* and press *SEL* again to select it.
4. Hold *SEL* down for another two-second period, and the LCD Panel will switch to the *Master* settings screen.
5. Press *SEL* again and *M TTL 0.0* will be highlighted. This is where we turn off the SB-800's main flash.
6. Press *MODE* three times, or until *M ---* is displayed. This actually disables the main flash to prevent a direct flash look on your subject.
7. Press *SEL* again to scroll down one place to *A TTL 0.0* to configure the first group of flash units (group A).
8. Press the *MODE* button numerous times to scroll through the various flash modes. Stop at the mode you want (*TTL, AA, M, ---*).
9. Press the **Up+** button or **Down–** button to select the flash output value, which determines exposure compensation.
10. Press the *SEL* button to select group B, which defaults to *B ---* unless configured previously.
11. Press the *MODE* button to select a flash mode and then the **Up+** or **Down–** buttons to set the flash output value. Repeat steps 10 and 11 for group C, if needed. (You only need to configure as many groups as you'll need.)
12. Press the *SEL* button multiple times until *CH 1* (or some other number) is selected. Use the **Up+** or **Down–** buttons to select a communications channel (1 to 4).
13. Configure the slave units, and take your pictures.

Figure 14 – SB-800 Speedlight controls

**Detail of Settings:**

To work on any of the following settings, you'll have to take these four basic steps first. This switches the SB-800 Speedlight out of its normal flash mode and into *Master mode*. *Figure 14* shows the controls you'll use to set your SB-800 to *Master mode*.

**Enter the Master Mode**

1. Turn the flash on with the *ON/OFF* button.
2. Press and hold the *SEL* button in the middle of the Multi Selector for about two seconds until the LCD Panel switches screens. *Figure 15* shows what you'll now see.
3. Once you enter the next screen, press *SEL* once again and the currently active mode will become highlighted (*figure 15*). Use the **Down–** button to scroll down to *Master* and press *SEL* again to select it.
4. Hold *SEL* down for another two-second period, and the LCD Panel will switch to the *Master* settings screen (*figure 16*).

Figure 15

Figure 16

Figure 17

Figure 18

Figure 19

Figure 20

Now we'll need to configure the following modes for the Master Flash (*M*) and all three slave groups A, B, and C.

**Flash Modes:** The selections you'll find under the flash modes are as follows:

1. *TTL* **mode:** The image in *figure 17* shows group A in TTL mode. In *Master mode*, this is the normal i-TTL automatic mode of the SB-800 and causes the slave units to use i-TTL in measuring the flash output. You can adjust the flash output level of each of the groups of slave Speedlights directly on the SB-800 LCD panel. See the "Flash Output Level" section below.

2. *AA* **mode:** The image in *figure 18* shows group A in *AA* mode. This "Auto Aperture" mode is only available if you have a CPU lens mounted on your D700. If a non-CPU lens is mounted, the slave units switch to non-TTL auto flash instead. *AA* mode works similarly to *TTL* mode.

3. *M* **mode:** The image in *figure 19* shows group A in *M* mode. This is "Manual" mode, which means you can control the group in fractions of full-power light values. This mode is for those who are used to controlling flash power levels by setting different levels of power, like ½ or ¼ power. Notice how the image shows ¼ power has been set. Look just after the *M* at the small 1 and large 4. It may look weird, but it is functional.

4. --- **mode:** This is a simple mode. It means the group is disabled and will not fire any slave units in that group. In *figure 20*, you'll see that I have set all the groups, including group A, to --- mode. This setup is not very useful since *no* flash unit will fire, but it does illustrate the idea.

Let's see how to configure the flash mode on one of our groups and disable the SB-800's main flash output. Any information learned in these steps can be applied to any of the groups A, B, C, or even M for the master flash on

Figure 21

Figure 22

Figure 23

Figure 24

the *M* selection in the top left of the screen. You may only have to press *SEL* once, if you've never been in the Master screen before.

Once *M* is selected you will need to change it from *M TTL 0.0* to *M ---* , as shown in *figure 22*. Press the *MODE* button numerous times until *M ---* appears. This disables the *M* or master flash from firing its main flash burst, but not its monitor pre-flash. Remember, the master flash is the one mounted on your camera.

Now we'll configure one of the main groups, such as group A. Repeat these steps for groups B and C, if needed.

Since we are already in the Master screen, just press the *SEL* button until you've high-lighted the A group. Press the *MODE* button until the Flash Mode you desire (as described earlier) is showing (*TTL, AA, M,* or ---). Notice in *figure 23* that I have group A set to *TTL* with 0.0 or no flash output compensa-tion. Group B is also set to *TTL*, but it has -1.0 EV or -1.0 stops of compensation. Group A is main light, and group B is fill light. We'll talk more about adjusting the compensation or flash output level in the next section.

Repeat the steps in the last paragraph until all three groups are set to your desired modes. If you do not need to use any groups besides group A (one group of flash units) simply set B and C to --- using the *SEL* and *MODE* but-tons. Notice in *figure 24* how I only have group A active, and all the other groups are in --- mode, or disabled.

Often a group might only have one flash unit, and another group might have a dif-ferent single unit. If you want to control the flash groups individually, so that one group has less or more power output for main or fill purposes, you'll need to configure at least two groups. That allows you to control them on an individual basis.

**Flash Output Level**: Now we'll configure the flash power output levels for each group.

camera. (M is normally not used, and left at --- mode, but it can be used if you need direct flash in addition to your slave units.)

First use the steps in the section "Enter the Master Mode". See *figure 14* for the controls.

Once you are in *Master mode*, you will see the screen shown in *figure 21*.

First, we'll normally disable the *M* group on top (if it's not already disabled). Press the *SEL* button on your SB-800 until you scroll to

Let's say you want to set group A as the main flash and group B as the fill flash. We'll configure groups A and B in that manner as a learning exercise. Later you can experiment with various power levels and group combinations.

You have already set your flash mode (*TTL, AA, M,* or ---) in the previous section, so now you will set the flash output level for this group. Really, you could have set the flash output level just after setting the flash mode, but we separated the events for learning purposes.

To set the flash output level on our main flash group A, press the *SEL* button until you have highlighted the group you want to modify. Now, press the **Up+** button to add EV(more light) or the **Down−** button to remove EV(less light).

If you are using *TTL* or *AA* mode, you will see that you have the following stop values available in a plus or minus direction:

**0.0, 0.3, 0.7, 1.0, 1.3, 1.7, 2.0, 2.3, 2.7, 3.0**

If you are using *M* mode instead, you will find that the following fractional power setting range is available:

$\frac{1}{1}, \frac{1}{2}, \frac{1}{4}, \frac{1}{8}, \frac{1}{16}, \frac{1}{32}, \frac{1}{64}, \frac{1}{128}$

Since group A is our main light source we should leave it set to flash output level 0.0 in *TTL* or *AA* modes and $\frac{1}{1}$ in *M* mode, which means use normal power for the main group.

To configure our fill light source, we will set the power output on group B to a somewhat lower value, such as -0.7 in *TTL* or *AA* modes, or -½ in *M* mode. Notice in *figure 25*

that I have group A set to *TTL* with 0.0 or no flash output compensation. Group B is also set to *TTL*, but it has -1.0 EV or -1.0 stops of compensation. This is a good example of using main and fill lights. Group A is the main light with normal power, and group B is a fill, with 1-stop less light output.

You can simply play with the values, shooting test exposures and examining them on the camera's Monitor LCD, or break out a handheld light meter and do it the old-fashioned way. The powerful thing about using Nikon CLS, though, is to control the slave units from your commander device and adjust the exposures on the fly, using the histogram in your camera to judge proper exposure and using your camera's Monitor LCD to zoom in and view light and shadow. Why go to all the trouble of figuring out complex lighting ratios when the camera and flash units will do it for you? Of course, you may be the type of person that enjoys doing it yourself. Nikon CLS gives you that choice!

**Channel Number**: This is a critical setting since it describes to your commander device what channel to use for communicating with the groups of slave flash units.

Once you've set this value, you'll need to set the slave units to the same channel or they will just stand there grinning at you and whispering silently among themselves about the nut fiddling with his camera.

I normally leave my channel set to 1, but that's just my preference. Yours may be different. The point is to get your commander

Figure 25

Figure 26

device and all slaves on the same channel. *Figure 26* shows how to set the channel number.

Referring to *figure 26*, press the *SEL* button until the cursor moves to the top right of the Master screen, where the number *1* stands between the *CH* and that squiggly looking S-shaped arrow. That digit is the channel number. Once you have the cursor there, simply press the **Up+** or **Down–** button to select your favorite channel number. You can select any number from 1 to 4.

Your SB-800 is now fully configured and ready to control all those pesky little SBs sitting out there on their stands, waiting patiently. Be sure your slave units are segregated by group and all are assigned the correct channel number. Now go experiment and enjoy your powerful CLS system!

To exit *Master mode* and return your SB-800 to regular flash unit functionality, simply follow these steps:

1. While in the Master screen with the channels and groups, hold down the *SEL* button for two seconds and it will switch back to the screen that allows you to select *Master*, *Remote*, or in this case the all-important *OFF* selection.
2. Press *SEL* again, and scroll up to *OFF*, then press *SEL* again to select *OFF*.
3. Hold down the *SEL* button for two seconds again, and it will then switch back to being a normal i-TTL stand-alone flash.

## Examining the Nikon SU-800 Wireless Speedlight Commander Unit

In case you choose to use the more powerful SU-800 Commander unit, instead of the built-in D700 *Commander mode*, I've included some information on it here. *Figure 27* shows a front/back picture of the SU-800 Wireless Speedlight Commander unit.

Figure 27 – SU-800 Wireless Speedlight Commander unit

This small unit is less costly than buying an SB-800 Speedlight. It is considerably lighter and smaller, and has twice the commander-to-slave range: 66 feet compared to 33 feet (20 m versus 10 m).

Most professionals will purchase this unit if they are interested in doing professional flash output since the SU-800 does not use pre-flash to control the flash units in its groups. It uses infrared instead. This doubles the range and does not output an unnecessary flash burst that wastes battery power.

The SU-800 uses a small CR-123 type photo lithium battery that lasts a long time. This saves considerable weight compared to using alkaline batteries.

### What Is the Scope of This Section?

Our primary concern in this section is using Commander units to control groups of Speedlights to light up large and small areas. For that reason, we will focus our discussion on *Commander mode* shooting. I will briefly discuss a couple of other modes that are available with the SU-800, in case you are interested.

The following is a brief discussion of two of the SU-800's modes—*Close-up* and *Repeating*—and a very detailed discussion of our main concern, *Commander mode*. I wish that we had room for considering the additional functionality; however, CLS is a very complex subject, and this chapter couldn't begin to cover it all.

*Close-up Mode Shooting:* If you are a heavy macro shooter. you can purchase one of two Nikon kits, which vary in what they contain. The R1C1 Close-up Speedlight Commander Kit and the R1 Close-up Speedlight Remote Kit (both of which include two SB-R200 Speedlights) give your D700 complete control of various macro shooting arrangements. The close-up mode is beyond the scope of this chapter, since macro shooting is a highly specialized and less-used functionality.

The R1C1 kit includes an SU-800 Wireless Speedlight Commander Unit, but the R1 kit does not. The R1 kit relies on the camera to provide one of the various commander devices.

9

Figure 28 – *Close-up* and *Commander mode* switch

When using the SU-800 for macro shooting with the kits and their SB-R200 Speedlights, you'll need to take your SU-800 out of *Commander mode* by flipping a small switch just inside the battery cover (see *figure 28*), which puts the SU-800 into *Close-up* or macro mode, allowing the SU-800 to continue to function as a commander device for the SB-R200 units.

*Repeating Mode Shooting:* There is another mode in your SU-800 that is enabled by turning the unit on, then holding down the *SEL* button for several seconds. This is called *RPT,* or repeating flash, mode. It allows you to cause your Speedlight flash units to pulse their flashes in various output levels and frequencies. You can set the SU-800 unit to cause the Speedlights to output anything between ⅛ power and $1/128$ power, flashing or pulsing from 1 to 100 times per second, resulting in repeating the flashes from 1 to 90 times for each image. The SB-800 Speedlight, in *M* mode, also provides this stroboscopic flash. I have no idea what this type of flash photography is used for, but if you need it, it's there. In any case, it is beyond the scope of this chapter.

*Commander Mode Shooting:* Since we're concerned with using the SU-800 as a camera-attached commander device, let's consider its configuration and use in detail.

The primary purpose of the SU-800 is to be used as a controller for groups of Speedlights, supporting up to three groups (A, B, C) and up to four communication channels (1, 2, 3, 4). You can set up "groups" of an unlimited number of Speedlights to light up large areas, like a factory, or just a few for product shots or portraits. The SU-800 is limited to firing Speedlights located up to 66 feet (20.1 meters) away.

When you plug an SU-800 unit into the hotshoe of your D700, you can rest assured that it becomes the Speedlight "boss".

The SU-800 is designed to let you control individual groups right from the back of the unit. You don't have to walk to each Speedlight and set light values or use a light meter. Instead, you simply take a picture, zoom in and look at it on the Monitor LCD of your camera, then adjust the power of individual groups from the SU-800 until you have just the light balance you want. Very convenient!

## Configuring the SU-800 Wireless Commander Unit

Turn your SU-800 unit on and verify that the LCD panel looks similar to the *Commander mode* image in screen 1 of *figure 29* and shows groups A, B, C. If not, your unit is probably in *Close-up* mode (screen 2) or repeating flash (*RPT*) mode (screen 3).

The reason I mention this is that my SU-800 came from the factory switched to *Close-up* mode, and I was quite confused trying to figure out why my screens didn't work like *Commander mode* on my SB-800 Speedlight and Nikon D700. Later, in the manual, I found out about the little hidden *Close-up/Commander* switch and set it to the correct mode.

If your SU-800 is in *Close-up* mode (as shown in screen 2 of *figure 29*), be sure to

Commander Mode

Close-up Mode

Repeating Flash Mode

Figure 29 – SU-800 configuration screens

open the battery compartment and flip the switch to *Commander* mode. See *figure 28* for the location of the switch.

Open the battery door on the front lower side of the SU-800, and find the switch on the left. Flip it toward the bottom of the Commander unit, away from the "Close-up" flower symbol. The symbol you want looks like a small SU-800 Commander unit blasting a wave of light.

To get out of repeating flash mode, simply hold down the *SEL* button until the screen looks like the *Commander mode* screen in *figure 29*.

Now that the unit is configured for *Commander mode*, let's configure it as if we had two groups of Speedlights. We'll use groups A and B, and channel 3. Get your SU-800 so that you can follow the instructions with an actual unit, which makes it much easier to understand and remember.

We'll need to consider setting the following items at least once before using the SU-800 as a controller.

### Overview of Settings:

1. **Flash Mode**
   - *TTL*
   - *AA* (with SB-800 slaves and CPU lenses only)
   - *M*
   - --- (means No Flash for this group; disables the group)
2. **Group Name**
   - *A, B, C*

3. **Flash Output Level**
   - Varies according to flash mode
4. **Channel Number**
   - *1, 2, 3, 4*

### Detail of Settings:

**Flash Mode:** We'll set the A group initially. Press the *SEL* button on the back of the SU-800 until the group's row starts blinking. Now press the *MODE* button repeatedly to scroll through the various flash modes. Once selected, wait a second or two until the group stops blinking, or immediately press the arrow buttons, < left or right >, to set the compensation value. If you wait too long, you'll have to press the *SEL* button again to use the arrow buttons. Press the *SEL* button to tab between the groups and repeat for groups B and C.

Look at the first screen in *figure 30*. See how the A group is now set to *AA* mode and the compensation is set to +1.3 Ev? Now look at the second screen in *figure 30*, and notice how the A group is now set to *M* mode, and ¼ of full power output. Groups B and C are still at the default of *TTL* with no compensation set, in both screens.

**Group Name:** This is where you'll set the number of groups you want to use in this session. Select the triple-dash --- mode for any groups you do not want to use. If there are any Speedlights on that group, they will no longer fire. See, in *figure 31*, how A and C have *TTL* mode selected and 0.0 EV compensation

Figure 30

Figure 31

Figure 32

Figure 33

values, while B is set to --- mode and is now disabled.

**Flash Output Level:** This varies according to which flash mode you have selected. Look at *figure 32* as we work through the various output levels.

*TTL* **Mode:** You can set the following compensation levels using the *SEL* and < arrow > buttons. These go in a +EV direction with the right > arrow button and a –EV direction with the left < arrow button. "+" means more light, "-" means less light. So +1.3 EV means you are adding one and a third stops of light to that group (1.3 stops). Here are the available EV steps <-/+>:

0.0, 0.3, 0.7, 1.0, 1.3, 1.7, 2.0, 2.3, 2.7, 3.0

Look at the screen in *figure 32*. See how the compensation (or flash output level) is set to

+0.0 EV on all three groups? This means that the flash will use whatever output it needs to make a proper exposure. There is no compensation applied, so a normal flash output level is being used. Notice there is no + or – sign between *TTL* and 0.0!

*AA* **Mode:** If you are using SB-800 Speedlights and CPU lenses, you can use this mode to set the following compensation levels using the *SEL* and < arrow > buttons. Like *TTL* earlier, these go in a +EV direction with the right > arrow button and a –EV direction with the left < arrow button:

0.0, 0.3, 0.7, 1.0, 1.3, 1.7, 2.0, 2.3, 2.7, 3.0

In *figure 33*, notice the plus "+" sign is between the *AA* and 1.3 Ev, which means this is a +EV operation and that 1.3 stops more light are being applied.

*M* **Mode:** This works similarly to *TTL* and *AA*. You'll use the *SEL* and < left- and > right-arrow buttons to select the group and set the compensation level. This is a manual mode, which means you can control the group in fractions of full-power light values. For instance, the default is ¹/₁, which means full power output, while ½ means one-half of full-power output for the whole group. If you use either the < left or right > arrow buttons you can scroll through the following power output values:

¹/₁, ½, ¼, ⅛, ¹/₁₆, ¹/₃₂, ¹/₆₄, ¹/₁₂₈

Notice in *figure 34* how the flash output level is set to ¼ of full-power output.

I think they left this mode in our CLS system since so many people have used this very method to control various flash units for so many years. It is second nature to some, especially those who like to use a handheld flash meter to critically control light values on the subject. The cool thing is that your Speedlights will obey you from the SU-800 unit without having to go to each flash unit and set up ½ or ¼ flash power.

Figure 34

--- (triple-dash): This is the simplest of all settings. It means "do nothing!" Any groups you set to this value do not fire their flash output at all. With this setting, you could use all three groups at once, then select any two, or just one. You can vary your flash output for testing or creative purposes. This acts like a light switch for an entire group of Speedlights: on or off!

**Channel Number:** This is pretty simple, since you only have four choices. Press the *SEL* button until the *CH* number starts blinking. Only the number will blink. Use the arrow buttons to scroll through the four available channels. Available selections are as follows:

*CH 1, CH 2, CH 3, CH 4*

Each of these numbers represents a communications channel. You can use only one communications channel per session. This is a very similar idea to the channels on the portable phones we carry around the house. I suppose one could use a different channel if there were several people using CLS in the same area. It certainly would be aggravating if every time your neighbor pressed his shutter release, all your groups of Speedlights fired too.

Notice in *figure 35* how I normally leave my SU-800 set to Channel 3 and have my flash units programmed to receive commands on that channel too. You choose your favorite channel, and make sure that your SU-800 and Speedlights are on the same one.

Invariably, if one of my Speedlights is not firing, I find that it is no longer on its assigned channel for some reason. Once you have found the channel number you want to use, you'll need to program that number into your external Speedlights.

**Using the SU-800 Commander Unit**

At this point, you should understand how to configure your SU-800. It is not all that hard, and all this instruction becomes unnecessary after you've done it a couple of times.

Just be sure that all your Speedlights are on the same communications channel. You can set your Speedlights to groups A, B, or C, according to how you have the SU-800 configured. You can vary the output of any of the groups by EV stop values in *TTL* and *AA* modes, or by fractions of full power in *M* mode. You can even turn a group off with --- mode.

Experiment with this as soon as you can and you'll have a better understanding of the configuration steps.

**My Conclusions**

Once you've mastered the settings, I suggest you get a good book on lighting techniques and study it well. You'll have to learn how to control shadows and reflections. Plus, you'll have to understand something about lighting ratios so that you can recognize a good image when you see one.

Figure 35

Buy a couple of light stands and some inexpensive white flash umbrellas and set up some portrait sessions of your family, or even some product shots. With the Nikon D700 and even one extra Speedlight, you can create some very impressive images with much less work than ever before.

The really nice thing is that the Nikon Creative Lighting System, executed by your Nikon D700's *Commander mode* or a hotshoe-mounted commander device with external Speedlights, will allow you to shoot without worrying so much about detailed exposure issues. Instead, you can concentrate on creating a great-looking image.

# Nikonians Gold Membership

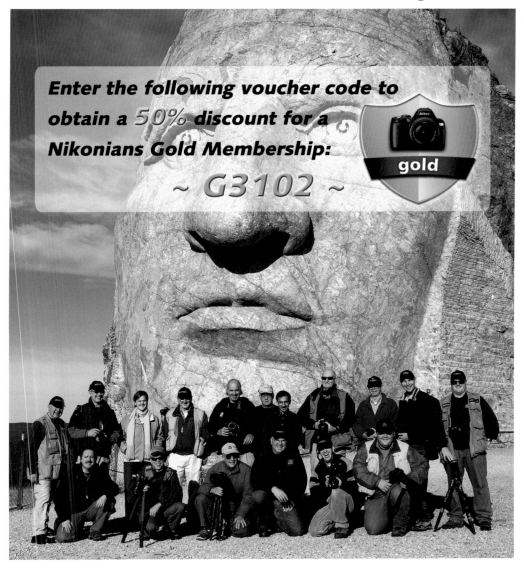

Enter the following voucher code to obtain a *50%* discount for a Nikonians Gold Membership:

~ *G3102* ~

gold

# Nikonians® - *Worldwide home for Nikon users*
nikonians.org

With over 170,000 members from over 160 nations, Nikonians.org is the largest Internet community for Nikon photographers worldwide.

member

# Credits for Chapter Opening Images

**Chapter 1**
Tom Trujillo (tjtrujillo)
Luck, California
Exposure Time: 1/125"
Aperture: ƒ/5.6
ISO: 400

**Chapter 2**
Sylvain Duford (Sduford)
Man and Cat, Panama
Exposure Time: 1/200"
Aperture: ƒ/7.1
ISO: 200

**Chapter 3**
Sylvain Duford (Sduford)
Large Garden Spider, Panama
Exposure Time: 1/60"
Aperture: ƒ/2.8
ISO: 250

**Chapter 4**
Michael Alan Bielat (MichaelAlan)
Letchworth Falls, New York
Exposure Time: 1/5"
Aperture: ƒ/22
ISO: 200

**Chapter 5**
Charles Penner (rolledmymazda)
Skateboarder, Canada
Exposure Time: 1/8000"
Aperture: ƒ/4.5
ISO: 1600

**Chapter 6**
Mark Rainer (mrainer)
Giant Honey Flower, Washington
Exposure Time: 1/160"
Aperture: ƒ/6.3
ISO: 200

**Chapter 7**
Josh Harris (DrRoebuck)
Lightning, California
Exposure Time: 30"
Aperture: ƒ/8.0
ISO: 200

**Chapter 8**
Tom Trujillo (tjtrujillo)
Two Hour Parking, Bodie Ghost Town, CA
Exposure Time: 1/250"
Aperture: ƒ/5.6
ISO: 200

**Chapter 9**
Michael Alan Bielat (MichaelAlan)
Crimson Bride, New York
Exposure Time: 1/500"
Aperture: ƒ/2.8
ISO: 200

**Back cover**
James Johnson (TechRead)
Goldfields in the Temblors, California
Exposure Time: 1/100"
Aperture: ƒ/14
ISO: 200

# Index

## Symbols

3D Color Matrix, 19, 120
3-inch monitor, 10
9 points, 108
11-point autofocus, 113
12-bit color depth, 13, 75
14-bit color depth, 13, 75
21 points, 108
51 AF sensors, 41
51-point autofocus, 12, 113
51 points, 108
51 points (3D-tracking), 108
81A warming filter, 203
1005-segment RGB sensor, 19
-- mode, 217
.ndf filename extension, 183

## A

AA mode, 217
AC adapter
  EH-5, 123
  EH-5a, 123
Active autofocus (AF) point, 22
Active D-Lighting, 12, 89, 163, 190
Active folder, 70, 128
Adobe RGB color space, 88, 163
  File naming, 71
AE / AF lock, 147
AE/AF lock (for MB-D10), 114
AE-L / AF-L + command dials, 149
AE lock (hold) (for MB-D10), 114
AE lock only (for MB-D10), 114
AE lock (Reset on release) (for MB-D10), 114
AF activation, 109
AF-Area modes, 41
  Auto-area, 41, 48
  Dynamic-area, 41, 46
  Single-point, 41, 45

AF-assist illuminator, 113
AF-C priority selection, 105, 106
AF fine tune, 196
AF lock only (for MB-D10), 114
AF-ON (for MB-D10), 114
AF-ON for MB-D10, 113
AF point illumination, 111
AF point selection, 112
AF-S priority selection, 105, 106
After delete, 165
Aperture, 27
Aperture priority, exposure mode, 23
Assign AE-L / AF-L button, 146
Assign FUNC button, 146
Assign preview button, 146
Auto-area AF, 41, 48
Auto bracketing, 138
Auto bracketing (Mode M), 139
Auto bracketing set, 137
Autofocus sub-menu
  Custom settings a1 to a10, 105
Auto FP high-speed sync, 133
Auto gain, 98
Auto image rotation, 180
Auto meter-off display, 122
Averaging meter, 22

## B

Banks
  Custom Setting Menu, 103
  Shooting Menu, 67
Battery
  CR-123, 228
  EN-EL3e, 8, 131, 186
  EN-EL4, 131, 187
  EN-EL4a, 131, 187
  FR6 - AA lithium, 131
  HR6 - AA Ni-MH, 131
  LR6 - AA alkaline, 131
  ZR6 - AA Ni-Mn, 131
Battery info, 186
Battery order, 132

Battery Pack
  MB-D10,  7, 8, 49, 113, 114, 187
Beep,  124
Bit depth,  75
Bracketing,  116
Bracketing burst,  147
Bracketing/flash sub-menu
  Custom settings e1 to e7,  132
Bracketing order,  140
Built-in AF-assist illuminator,  113

**C**

Camera
  Nikon D100,  3
  Nikon D200,  3
  Nikon D300,  4
  Nikon D700,  6
Capture NX 2,  73, 181, 183, 189
Center-weighted area,  118
Center-weighted meter,  21
Center-weighted metering,  148
Clean image sensor,  173
CL mode shooting speed,  125
CLS. *See* Creative Lighting System
CMOS sensor,  8
Color space,  88
  Adobe RGB,  88
  sRGB,  88
Color temperature,  55
Combined NEF and JPEG shooting,  78
Commander mode,  136, 213
Compact flash (CF) memory card,  8
Continuous-servo focus mode,  41
Controls sub-menu
  Custom settings f1 to f12,  141
Copyright information,  189
Creative Lighting System,  213
  Close-up mode shooting,  228
  R1C1 close-up Speedlight commander kit,
    228
  R1 close-up Speedlight remote kit,  228
  SB-600, exiting remote mode,  222

SB-600 slave configuration,  220
SB-800 as a commander device,  222
SB-800 as a slave unit,  218
SB-800, exiting remote mode,  219
SB-800, master mode,  222
Setting the channel,  217
Cross-type sensors,  42
Customize command dials,  151
Custom Setting Bank
  Renaming,  103
Custom Setting Menu,  103
  Banks,  103
  FUNC button + dials,  149
  Preview + command dials,  149
  Reset custom settings,  104

**D**

Delete (images),  157
DEMO,  154
Depth of field (DOF),  26
Depth of field preview button,  136, 146, 213, 214
Digital Print Order Format (DPOF),  168
Display mode,  161
D-Lighting,  200
DNG (Digital Negative),  81
DOF (depth of field),  26
DSLR,  3
Dust off ref photo,  181
DX-format,  83, 84, 90, 149
DX image sensor,  7
DX mode,  127, 182
Dynamic AF area,  108
Dynamic-area AF,  41

**E**

Easy exposure compensation,  117
EV steps for exposure cntrl,  115
EVs, the low-down,  114
Exp comp/fine tune,  116
EXPEED image processor,  7

Exposure compensation button, 117
Exposure delay mode, 14, 130
Exposure modes, 23
  A-aperture priority, 23
  M-manual, 23
  P-programmed auto, 23
  S-shutter priority, 23
Exposure or flash compensation, 117
Eyepiece shutter, 100

**F**

File naming, 71
File number, 71
File number sequence, 127
Fine tune optimal exposure, 120
Fine-tuning, 11
Firmware version, 199
Flash cntrl for built-in flash, 134
Flash compensation button, 116
Flash shutter speed, 134
Flash sync speed, 132
Flash: What is the Nikon Creative Lighting
        System, 213
Focus modes, 41
  Continuous-servo, 41, 44
  Manual, 41
  Single-servo, 41, 43
Focus point, 162
Focus point wrap-around, 111
Focus tracking with lock-on, 109
Format memory card, 171
Frames per second, 8
Front-curtain sync, 134
Fuji NPS, 11
Fuji Provia, 11
Fuji Velvia, 11
FV lock, 147
FX Autofocus Module, 41
FX-format, 149
FX image sensor, 7, 14
FX mode, 127, 182

**G**

Garmin eTrex Legend GPS, 192
Giottos Rocket-Air blower, 175
GPS, 191

**H**

HDMI, 176
HDMI device port, 15
Hide image, 160
High ISO noise reduction, 91
Highlights, 163
Histogram, 29, 30, 32, 142, 162, 163

**I**

Image area, 83
Image authentication, 187
Image comment, 179
Image data, 163
Image quality, 72
Image review, 164
Image size, 83
Interval timer shooting, 98
ISO-AUTO, 94
ISO number, 93
ISO sensitivity, 93
ISO sensitivity auto control, 94
ISO sensitivity step value, 115
iTTL, 135, 215

**J**

JPEG basic, 76
JPEG compression, 77
JPEG fine, 76
JPEG normal, 76

**K**

Kelvin temperature, 55
Kodak Portra, 11

**L**

Language,  178
LCD brightness,  172
LCD illumination,  129
Live view,  10, 96
Live View mode,  42
Lock mirror up for cleaning,  174
Long exposure noise reduction,  90


**M**

Manage Picture Control,  87
Manual exposure mode,  23
Manual focus mode,  41
Matrix metering,  19, 148
Max. continuous release,  126
MB-D10 battery type,  131
Metering/exposure sub-menu
   Custom settings b1 to b6,  114
Mirror up, for steadier shots,  123
Mirror Up mode (MUP),  14
M mode,  217
Mode button,  24
Modeling flash,  136
Monitor off delay,  123
Monitor pre-flashes,  216
Monochrome,  86
Multi-CAM 900 AF module,  41
Multi-CAM 1000 AF module,  41
Multi-CAM 3500FX Autofocus Module,  41
Multiple exposure,  97
Multi selector,  144
Multi selector center button,  141
My Menu,  14, 171, 206
   Add items,  206
   Choose tab,  211
   Rank items,  209
   Recent,  211
   Remove items,  208

**N**

NCSETUP1.BIN,  190
NEF (RAW)
   Bit depth,  75
   Compressed,  14, 74
   Lossless compressed,  13, 73
   Uncompressed,  14, 75
Nikon A2 warming filter,  203
Nikon MC-35 GPS adapter cable,  192
NMEA0183,  192
Noise control,  9
No memory card,  153
Non-CPU lens data,  194
NTSC,  176


**P**

PAL,  176
Photo info/playback,  145
PictBridge,  168
Picture control,  11
Playback folder,  158
Playback Menu,  157
   After delete,  165
   Delete,  157
   Display mode,  161
   Hide image,  160
   Image review,  164
   Playback folder,  158
   Print set (DPOF),  168
   Rotate tall,  165
   Slide show,  166
Predictive focus tracking,  44
Preview,  146
Print Set (DPOF),  168


**Q**

QUAL button,  72

# R

RAW. *See* NEF (RAW)
Rear-curtain sync,  134
Red-eye reduction,  134
Reference photo,  181
Release button to use dial,  152
Release mode,  42
  Continuous high speed,  49
  Continuous low speed,  49
  Live view,  49
  Mirror up,  49
  Self-timer,  49
  Single frame,  49
Release mode dial,  49
Release modes,  49
Repeating flash,  135
Reset shooting menu,  69
Retouch Menu,  14, 171, 199
  Color balance,  203
  D-Lighting,  200
  Filter effects,  203
  Image overlay,  205
  Monochrome,  202
  Red-eye correction,  201
  Side-by-side comparison,  206
  Trim (crop),  202
Reverse indicators,  154
RGB histogram,  163
Rotate tall,  165


# S

Same as FUNC button (for MB-D10),  114
Save/load settings,  190
SB-400,  213
SB-600 Speedlight,  213
SB-800 AF Speedlight,  213
SB-900 AF Speedlight,  213
SB-R200,  213
Screen tips,  125
Self-timer delay,  122
Sensor dust cleaning,  11

Set Picture Control,  85
  Monochrome,  86
  Neutral,  85
  Standard,  85
  Vivid,  85
Setup Menu,  171
  AF fine tune,  196
  Auto image rotation,  180
  Battery info,  186
  Clean image sensor,  173
  Copyright information,  189
  Dust off ref photo,  181
  Firmware version,  199
  Format memory card,  171
  GPS,  191
  HDMI,  176
  Image authentication,  187
  Image comment,  179
  Language,  178
  LCD brightness,  172
  Lock mirror up for cleaning,  174
  Non-CPU lens data,  194
  Save/load settings,  190
  Video mode,  175
  Virtual horizon,  194
  Wireless transmitter,  187
  World time,  177
Shooting/display sub-menu
  Custom settings d1 to d11,  124
Shooting info display,  128
Shooting Menu,  67
  Banks,  67
  Reset,  69
Shooting Menu Bank
  Renaming,  67
Shutter and Exposure,  116
Shutter priority, exposure mode,  23
Shutter–release button AE-L,  121
Shutter speed and aperture lock,  150
Single-point AF,  41
Single-servo focus mode,  41
Slide show,  166

Slow sync, 134
Spot meter, 22
Spot metering, 148
sRGB color space, 88
    File naming, 71
SU-800 Wireless Speedlight Commander,
        213
Switch, 141

**T**

TIFF format, 78
Timers/AE-Lock sub-menu
    Custom settings c1 to c4, 121
TTL, 135, 215
TTL mode, 216

**V**

VGA resolution, 10
Video mode, 175
Viewfinder
    95% viewfinder frame, 14
Viewfinder grid display, 124
ViewNX, 73
Vignette control, 89
Virtual horizon, 148

**W**

WB bracketing, 138
WB button, 56
Wet cleaning your sensor, 175
WhiBal pocket card, 57
White balance, 55, 85
    and RAW (NEF) mode, 63
    Auto, 63
    Based on a previously captured image, 60
    Bracketing, 62
    Customizing, 62
    Manually selected, 61
    PrE, 57
    Saving a reading to memory, 58
    Storing values for future use, 58
    Tips and tricks, 64
Wireless transmitter, 187
World time, 177
WT-4 Wireless Transmitter, 187